MCSE NT
Server 4.0
Ace It!

MCSE NT Server 4.0 Ace It!

Mark B. Cooper

IDG Books Worldwide, Inc.
An International Data Group Company
Foster City, CA • Chicago, IL • Indianapolis, IN • New York, NY

MCSE NT Server 4.0 Ace It!

Published by
IDG Books Worldwide, Inc.
An International Data Group Company
919 E. Hillsdale Blvd., Suite 400
Foster City, CA 94404
www.idgbooks.com (IDG Books Worldwide Web site)

Library of Congress Catalog Card Number: 98-71156

ISBN: 0-7645-3266-9

Printed in the United States of America

10 9 8 7 6 5 4 3 2 1

1P/RQ/RR/ZY/FC

Distributed in the United States by IDG Books Worldwide, Inc.

Distributed by Macmillan Canada for Canada; by Transworld Publishers Limited in the United Kingdom; by IDG Norge Books for Norway; by IDG Sweden Books for Sweden; by Woodslane Pty. Ltd. for Australia; by Woodslane (NZ) Ltd. for New Zealand; by Addison Wesley Longman Singapore Pte Ltd. for Singapore, Malaysia, Thailand, Indonesia, and Korea; by Norma Comunicaciones S.A. for Colombia; by Intersoft for South Africa; by International Thomson Publishing for Germany, Austria, and Switzerland; by Toppan Company Ltd. for Japan; by Distribuidora Cuspide for Argentina; by Livraria Cultura for Brazil; by Ediciencia S.A. for Ecuador; by Ediciones ZETA S.C.R. Ltda. for Peru; by WS Computer Publishing Corporation, Inc., for the Philippines; by Unalis Corporation for Taiwan; by Contemporanea de Ediciones for Venezuela; by Computer Book & Magazine Store for Puerto Rico; by Express Computer Distributors for the Caribbean and West Indies. Authorized Sales Agent: Anthony Rudkin Associates for the Middle East and North Africa.

For general information on IDG Books Worldwide's books in the U.S., please call our Consumer Customer Service department at 800-762-2974. For reseller information, including discounts and premium sales, please call our Reseller Customer Service department at 800-434-3422.

For information on where to purchase IDG Books Worldwide's books outside the U.S., please contact our International Sales department at 317-596-5530 or fax 317-596-5692.

For consumer information on foreign language translations, please contact our Customer Service department at 1-800-434-3422, fax 317-596-5692, or e-mail rights@idgbooks.com.

For information on licensing foreign or domestic rights, please phone +1-650-655-3109.

For sales inquiries and special prices for bulk quantities, please contact our Sales department at 650-655-3200 or write to the address above.

For information on using IDG Books Worldwide's books in the classroom or for ordering examination copies, please contact our Educational Sales department at 800-434-2086 or fax 317-596-5499.

For press review copies, author interviews, or other publicity information, please contact our Public Relations department at 650-655-3000 or fax 650-655-3299.

For authorization to photocopy items for corporate, personal, or educational use, please contact Copyright Clearance Center, 222 Rosewood Drive, Danvers, MA 01923, or fax 978-750-4470.

is a trademark under exclusive license to IDG Books Worldwide, Inc., from International Data Group, Inc.

ABOUT IDG BOOKS WORLDWIDE

Welcome to the world of IDG Books Worldwide.

IDG Books Worldwide, Inc., is a subsidiary of International Data Group, the world's largest publisher of computer-related information and the leading global provider of information services on information technology. IDG was founded more than 25 years ago and now employs more than 8,500 people worldwide. IDG publishes more than 275 computer publications in over 75 countries (see listing below). More than 90 million people read one or more IDG publications each month.

Launched in 1990, IDG Books Worldwide is today the #1 publisher of best-selling computer books in the United States. We are proud to have received eight awards from the Computer Press Association in recognition of editorial excellence and three from *Computer Currents'* First Annual Readers' Choice Awards. Our best-selling *...For Dummies*® series has more than 50 million copies in print with translations in 38 languages. IDG Books Worldwide, through a joint venture with IDG's Hi-Tech Beijing, became the first U.S. publisher to publish a computer book in the People's Republic of China. In record time, IDG Books Worldwide has become the first choice for millions of readers around the world who want to learn how to better manage their businesses.

Our mission is simple: Every one of our books is designed to bring extra value and skill-building instructions to the reader. Our books are written by experts who understand and care about our readers. The knowledge base of our editorial staff comes from years of experience in publishing, education, and journalism — experience we use to produce books for the '90s. In short, we care about books, so we attract the best people. We devote special attention to details such as audience, interior design, use of icons, and illustrations. And because we use an efficient process of authoring, editing, and desktop publishing our books electronically, we can spend more time ensuring superior content and spend less time on the technicalities of making books.

You can count on our commitment to deliver high-quality books at competitive prices on topics you want to read about. At IDG Books Worldwide, we continue in the IDG tradition of delivering quality for more than 25 years. You'll find no better book on a subject than one from IDG Books Worldwide.

John Kilcullen
CEO
IDG Books Worldwide, Inc.

Steven Berkowitz
President and Publisher
IDG Books Worldwide, Inc.

*Eighth Annual
Computer Press
Awards ≥1992*

WINNER
*Ninth Annual
Computer Press
Awards ≥1993*

WINNER
*Tenth Annual
Computer Press
Awards 1994*

*Eleventh Annual
Computer Press
Awards ≥1995*

Welcome to Ace It!

Looking to get certified? The *Ace It!* series is what you're looking for! The *Ace It!* series has been designed to meet your need for a quick, easy-to-use study tool that helps you save time, prioritize your study, and cram for the exam. *Ace It!* books serve as a supplement to other certification resources, such as our award-winning *Study Guides* and *MCSE...For Dummies* series. With these two series and *Ace It!*, IDG Books offers a full suite of study tools to meet your certification needs, from complete tutorial and reference materials to quick exam prep tools.

Ace It's exam-expert authors give you the ace in the hole: our unique insider's perspective on the exam itself — how it works, what topics are really important, and *how you really need to think* to ace the exam. Our features train your brain to understand not only the essential topics covered on the exam, but how to decipher the exam itself. By demystifying the exam, we give you that extra confidence to know that you're really prepared!

Ace It! books help you study with a wealth of truly valuable features in each chapter:

- **Official Word** lists the official certification exam objectives covered in the chapter.

- **Inside Scoop** immediately follows the Official Word and gives you the author's insight and expertise about the exam content covered in the chapter.

- **Are You Prepared?** is a chapter pretest that lets you check your knowledge beforehand: If you score well on the pretest, you may not need to review the chapter! This helps you focus your study. The questions are immediately followed by answers with cross-references to the information in the chapter, helping you further target your review.

- **Have You Mastered?** is a chapter post-test that includes five to ten multiple-choice questions with answers, analysis, and cross-references to the chapter discussion. The questions help you check your progress and pinpoint what you've learned and what you still need to study.

- **Practice Your Skills** consists of three to five exercises related to specific exam objectives. They provide an opportunity to relate exam concepts to real-world situations by presenting a hypothetical problem or guiding you through a task at the computer. These exercises enable you to take what you've learned for the exam and put it to work.

Within each chapter, icons call your attention to the following features:

 Test Tips give hints and strategies for passing the exam to help strengthen your test-taking skills.

 Test Traps warn you of pitfalls and loopholes you're likely to see in actual exam questions.

 Pop Quizzes offer instant testing of hot exam topics.

 Know This provides a quick summary of essential elements of topics you will see on the exam.

In the front and back of the book, you'll find even more features to give you that extra confidence and prepare you to get certified:

- **Ace Card:** Tear out this quick-review card for a distilled breakdown of essential exam-related terms and concepts to take with you and review before the exam.

- **Insider's Guide:** This helpful certification profile describes the certification process in general, and discusses the specific exam this book covers. It explains the exam development process, provides tips for preparing for and taking the exams, describes the testing process (how to register for an exam, what to expect at the testing center, how to obtain and evaluate test scores, and how to retake the exam if necessary), and tells you where to go for more information about the certification you're after.

- **Practice Exam:** A full-length multiple choice practice exam. Questions and answer selections mimic the certification exam in style, number of questions, and content to give you the closest experience to the real thing.

- **Exam Key** and **Exam Analysis:** These features tell you not only what the right answers are on the Practice Exam, but why they're right, and where to look in the book for the material you need to review.

- **Exam Revealed:** Here's your ace in the hole — the real deal on how the exam works. Our exam-expert authors deconstruct the questions on the Practice Exam, examining their structure, style, and wording to reveal subtleties, loopholes, and pitfalls that can entrap or mislead you when you take the real test. For each question, the author highlights part of the question or answer choices and then, in a sentence or two, identifies the possible problem and explains how to avoid it.

- **Glossary:** Not familiar with a word or concept? Just look it up! The Glossary covers all the essential terminology you need to know.

With this wealth of features and the exclusive insider's perspective provided by our authors, you can be sure that *Ace It!* completes your set of certification study tools. No matter what you've got, you still need an *Ace It!*

Credits

Acquisitions Editor
Tracy Thomsic

Development Editors
Jennifer Rowe
BC Crandall

Technical Editor
Tony Houston

Copy Editor
Brian MacDonald

Project Coordinator
Susan Parini

Cover Coordinator
Cyndra Robbins

Book Designer
Dan Zeigler

Graphics and Production Specialist
Stephanie Hollier

Graphics Technicians
Linda Marousek
Hector Mendosa

Quality Control Specialists
Mick Arellano
Mark Schumann

Illustrator
David Puckett

Proofreader
Arielle Carole Mennelle

Indexer
Richard Shrout

About the Author

Mark B. Cooper has been working with enterprise networking technologies for the last ten years. Since 1992, he has been working as a consulting engineer for the Fortune 500, providing consulting and solution designs for large, complex networking environments. He is also the director of publishing for the Enterprise Networking Association's *Enterprise Networking* magazine. Mark is an MCSE+I, MCT, CBE, Compaq ASE, Sun CSSA, and CNP. Mark enjoys hearing from readers, and can be contacted at `mcooper@teleport.com`.

To my family and friends who supported me through the years.
Especially to those still willing to lend me money!

Insider's Guide to MCP Certification

The Microsoft Certified Professional exams are *not* easy, and require a great deal of preparation. The exam questions measure real-world skills. Your ability to answer these questions correctly will be greatly enhanced by as much hands-on experience with the product as you can get.

About the Exams

An important aspect of passing the MCP Certification exams is understanding the big picture. This includes understanding how the exams are developed and scored.

Every job function requires different levels of cognitive skills, from memorization of facts and definitions to the comprehensive ability to analyze scenarios, design solutions, and evaluate options. To make the exams relevant in the real world, Microsoft Certified Professional exams test the specific cognitive skills needed for the job functions being tested. These exams go beyond testing rote knowledge — you need to *apply* your knowledge, analyze technical solutions, solve problems, and make decisions — just like you would on the job.

Exam Items and Scoring

Microsoft certification exams consist of four types of items: multiple-choice, multiple-rating, enhanced, and simulation. The way you indicate your answer and the number of points you receive differ depending on the type of item.

Multiple-choice item

A traditional multiple-choice item presents a problem and asks you to select either the best answer (single response) or the best set of answers (multiple response) to the given item from a list of possible answers.

For a multiple-choice item, your response is scored as either correct or incorrect. A correct answer receives a score of 1 point and an incorrect answer receives a score of 0 points.

In the case of a multiple-choice, multiple-response item (for which the correct response consists of more than one answer), the item is scored as being correct only if all the correct answers are selected. No partial credit is given for a response that does not include all the correct answers for the item.

For consistency purposes, the question in a multiple-choice, multiple-response item is always presented in singular form, regardless of how many answers are correct. Always follow the instructions displayed at the bottom of the window.

Multiple-rating item

A multiple-rating item presents a task similar to those presented in multiple-choice items. In a multiple-choice item, you are asked to select the best answer or answers from a selection of several potential answers. In contrast, a multiple-rating item presents a task, along with a proposed solution. Each time the task is presented, a different solution is proposed. In each multiple-rating item, you are asked to choose the answer that best describes the results produced by one proposed solution.

Enhanced item

An enhanced item is similar to a multiple-choice item because it asks you to select your response from a number of possible responses. However, unlike the traditional multiple-choice item that presents you with a list of possible answers from which to choose, an enhanced item may ask you to indicate your answer in one of the following three ways:

- Type the correct response, such as a command name.
- Review an exhibit (such as a screen shot, a network configuration drawing, or a code sample), and then use the mouse to select the area of the exhibit that represents the correct response.

- Review an exhibit, and then select the correct response from the list of possible responses.

As with a multiple-choice item, your response to an enhanced item is scored as either correct or incorrect. A correct answer receives full credit of 1 point, and an incorrect answer receives a score of 0 points.

Simulation item

A simulation imitates the functionality of product components or environments, complete with error messages and dialog boxes. You are given a scenario and one or more tasks to complete by using that simulation. A simulation item's goal is to determine if you know how to complete a given task. Just as with the other item types, the simulation is scored when you complete the exam. A simulation item may ask you to indicate your answer in one of the following ways:

- Review an exhibit (such as a screen shot, a network configuration drawing, or a code sample), and then use the GUI simulation to resolve, configure, or otherwise complete the assigned task.
- Based on information in the exam scenario, resolve, configure, or otherwise complete the assigned task.

As with the other item types, you receive credit for a correct answer only if all of the requested criteria are met by your actions in the scenario. There is no partial credit for an incomplete simulation item.

Exam Formats

Microsoft uses two different exam formats to determine how many questions are going to be presented on the exam. The majority of Microsoft exams have historically used fixed-length exams, with between 50 and 100 questions per exam. Each time you take the exam, you are presented with a different set of questions, but still comprising an equal number of questions. Recently, Microsoft has attempted to increase the reliability of its testing procedures, and has implemented new strategies to that end. The newest format is called computer adaptive testing. A computer adaptive test (CAT) is tailored to the individual exam taker. You start with an easy-to-moderate question; if you answer the question correctly, you get a more difficult follow-up question. If that question is answered correctly, the difficulty of subsequent questions likewise increases. Conversely, if the second question is answered incorrectly, the following questions will be easier. This process continues only until the CAT determines your ability. As a result, you may have an exam that is only 15 questions, but contains extremely difficult questions. Alternately, you may have an exam that contains 50 moderately difficult questions.

Preparing for a Microsoft Certified Professional Exam

The best way to prepare for an exam is to study, learn, and master the job function on which you'll be tested. For any certification exam, you should follow these important preparation steps:

1. Identify the objectives on which you'll be tested.
2. Assess your current mastery of those objectives.
3. Practice tasks and study the areas you haven't mastered.

This section describes tools and techniques that may be helpful as you perform these steps to prepare for the exam.

Exam Preparation Guides

For each certification exam, an Exam Preparation Guide provides important, specific information about what you'll be tested on and how best to prepare. These guides are essential tools for preparing to take certification exams. You'll find the following types of valuable information in the exam preparation guides:

- **Tasks you should master:** Outlines the overall job function tasks you should master
- **Exam objectives:** Lists the specific skills and abilities on which you should expect to be measured

- **Product resources:** Tells you the products and technologies with which you should be experienced
- **Suggested reading:** Points you to specific reference materials and other publications that discuss one or more of the exam objectives
- **Suggested curriculum:** Provides a specific list of instructor-led and self-paced courses relating to the job function tasks and topics in the exam

You'll also find pointers to additional information that may help you prepare for the exams, such as *Microsoft TechNet*, *Microsoft Developer Network* (MSDN), online forums, and other sources.

By paying attention to the verbs used in the "Exam Objectives" section of the Exam Preparation Guide, you will get an idea of the level at which you'll be tested on that objective.

To view the most recent version of the Exam Preparation Guides, which include the exam's objectives, check out Microsoft's Training and Certification Web site at `www.microsoft.com/train_cert/`.

Assessment Exams

When preparing for the exams, take lots of assessment exams. Assessment exams are self-paced exams that you take at your own computer. When you complete an assessment exam, you receive instant score feedback so you can determine areas in which additional study may be helpful before you take the certification exam. Although your score on an assessment exam doesn't necessarily indicate what your score will be on the certification exam, assessment exams give you the opportunity to answer items that are similar to those on the certification exams. The assessment exams also use the same computer-based testing tool as the certification exams, so you don't have to learn the tool on exam day.

An assessment exam exists for almost every certification exam.

Taking a Microsoft Certified Professional Exam

This section contains information about registering for and taking an MCP exam, including what to expect when you arrive at the testing center to take the exam.

How to Register for an Exam

Candidates may take exams at any of more than 700 Sylvan Prometric testing centers around the world. For the location of a Sylvan Prometric testing center near you, call (800) 755-EXAM (755-3926). Outside the United States and Canada, contact your local Sylvan Prometric Registration Center.

You can also take exams at any of the over 160 different Virtual University Enterprises testing centers around the world. To register for an exam at VUE at a testing center in your area, call (888) 837-8616. Outside the United States and Canada, contact your local Virtual University Enterprises Registration Center.

Sylvan Prometric offers online registration for Microsoft exams at its Microsoft registration Web site — `https://www.slspro.com/msreg/microsof.asp`. You can also register for an exam at a VUE testing center by visiting `http://www.vue.com/ms`.

To register for an MCP exam:

1. Determine which exam you want to take and note the exam number.

2. Call the Sylvan Prometric or VUE Registration Center nearest to you. If you haven't registered with them before, you will be asked to provide information to the Registration Center.

3. You can then schedule your exam at your choice of locations. Once the exam is scheduled, you will be asked to provide payment for the exam. Both types of testing centers accept major credit cards and offer prepayment options for purchasing exam certificates for future or corporate use.

When you schedule the exam, you'll be provided instructions regarding the appointment, cancellation procedures, and ID requirements, as well as information about the testing center location.

Exams must be taken within one year of payment. You can schedule exams up to six weeks in advance, or as late as one working day prior to the date of the exam. You can cancel or reschedule your exam if you contact the testing center at least one working day prior to the exam.

Although subject to space availability, same-day registration is available in some locations. Where same-day registration is available, you must register a minimum of two hours before test time.

What to Expect at the Testing Center

As you prepare for your certification exam, it may be helpful to know what to expect when you arrive at the testing center on the day of your exam. The following information gives you a preview of the general procedure you'll go through at the testing center:

- You will be asked to sign the log book upon arrival and departure.
- You will be required to show two forms of identification, including one photo ID (such as a driver's license or company security ID), before you may take the exam.
- The test administrator will give you a Testing Center Regulations form that explains the rules you will be expected to comply with during the test. You will be asked to sign the form, indicating that you understand the regulations and will comply.
- The test administrator will show you to your test computer and will handle any preparations necessary to start the testing tool and display the exam on the computer.
- You will be provided a set amount of scratch paper for use during the exam. All scratch paper will be collected from you at the end of the exam.
- The exams are all closed-book. You may not use a laptop computer or have any notes or printed material with you during the exam session.

- Some exams may include additional materials, or exhibits. If any exhibits are required for your exam, the test administrator will provide you with them before you begin the exam and collect them from you at the end of the exam.

- Before you begin the exam, the test administrator will tell you what to do when you complete the exam. If the test administrator doesn't explain this to you, or if you are unclear about what you should do, ask the administrator before beginning the exam.

- The number of items on each exam varies, as does the amount of time allotted for each exam. Generally, certification exams consist of about 50 to 100 items (unless you are taking a CAT exam) and have durations of 60 to 90 minutes. You can verify the number of items and time allotted for your exam when you register.

Because you'll be given a specific amount of time to complete the exam once you begin, if you have any questions or concerns, don't hesitate to ask the test administrator before the exam begins.

As an exam candidate, you are entitled to the best support and environment possible for your exam. In particular, you are entitled to:

- A quiet, uncluttered test environment

- Scratch paper

- The tutorial for using the online testing tool, and time to take the tutorial

- A knowledgeable and professional test administrator

- The opportunity to submit comments about the testing center and staff, or the test itself

The Certification Development Team will investigate any problems or issues you raise and make every effort to resolve them quickly.

Your Exam Results

Once you have completed an exam, you will be given immediate, online notification of your pass or fail status. You will also receive a printed Examination Score Report indicating your pass or fail status and your exam results by section. (The test administrator will give you the printed score report.) Test scores are automatically forwarded to Microsoft within five working days after you take the test. You do not need to send your score to Microsoft.

If you pass the exam, you will receive confirmation from Microsoft, typically within two to four weeks.

If You Don't Receive a Passing Score

If you do not pass a certification exam, you may call the testing center to schedule a time to retake the exam. Before retaking the exam, you should review the appropriate Exam Preparation Guide and focus additional study on the topic areas where your exam results could be improved. Please note that you must pay again for each exam retake.

One way to determine areas where additional study may be helpful is to review your individual section scores carefully. The section titles in your score report generally correlate to specific groups of exam objectives listed in the Exam Preparation Guide.

Here are some specific ways you can prepare to retake an exam:

- Go over the section-by-section scores on your exam results, noting objective areas where your score could be improved.

- Review the Exam Preparation Guide for the exam, with a special focus on the tasks and objective areas that correspond to the exam sections where your score could be improved.

- Increase your real-world, hands-on experience and practice performing the listed job tasks with the relevant products and technologies.

- Consider taking or retaking one or more of the suggested courses listed in the Exam Preparation Guide.

- Review the suggested readings listed in the Exam Preparation Guide.
- After you review the materials, retake the corresponding Assessment Exam.

For More Information

To find out more about Microsoft Education and Certification materials and programs, to register with a testing center, or to get other useful information, check the following resources. Outside the United States or Canada, contact your local Microsoft office or testing center.

- **Microsoft Certified Professional Program:** **(800) 636-7544.** Call for information about the Microsoft Certified Professional program and exams, and to order the *Microsoft Certified Professional Program Exam Study Guide* or the Microsoft Train_Cert Offline CD-ROM.
- **Sylvan Prometric Testing Centers: (800) 755-EXAM.** Call to register to take a Microsoft Certified Professional exam at any of more than 700 Sylvan Prometric testing centers around the world, or to order the *Microsoft Certified Professional Program Exam Study Guide.*
- **Virtual University Enterprises Testing Centers:** **(888) 837-8616.** Call to register to take a Microsoft Certified Professional exam at any of the over 160 different Virtual University Enterprises testing centers around the world.
- **Microsoft Sales Fax Service: (800) 727-3351.** Call for Microsoft Certified Professional Exam Preparation Guides, Microsoft Official Curriculum course descriptions and schedules, or the *Microsoft Certified Professional Program Exam Study Guide.*

- **Education Program and Course Information:
(800) SOLPROV.** Call for information about Microsoft
Official Curriculum courses, Microsoft education
products, and the Microsoft Solution Provider Authorized
Technical Education Center (ATEC) program, where you
can attend a Microsoft Official Curriculum course, or to
order the *Microsoft Certified Professional Program Exam
Study Guide.*

- **Microsoft Certification Development Team:
Fax (425) 936-1311.** Use this fax number to volunteer for
participation in one or more exam development phases
or to report a problem with an exam. Address written
correspondence to: Certification Development Team,
Microsoft Education and Certification, One Microsoft Way,
Redmond, WA 98052.

- **Microsoft TechNet Technical Information Network:
(800) 344-2121.** Call for support professionals and system
administrators. Outside the United States and Canada, call
your local Microsoft subsidiary for information.

- **Microsoft Developer Network (MSDN): (800) 759-5474.**
MSDN is the official source for software development kits,
device driver kits, operating systems, and information
about developing applications for Microsoft Windows and
Windows NT.

- **Online Services: (800) 936-3500.** Call for information
about Microsoft Connection on CompuServe, Microsoft
Knowledge Base, Microsoft Software Library, Microsoft
Download Service, and Internet.

This section contains excerpts from the Microsoft Certified Professional Exam Study Guide
(Microsoft Corporation, 1998), reprinted with permission.

Preface

Welcome to *MCSE NT Server 4.0 Ace It!* This book is intended to help you hone your existing knowledge and gain a greater understanding of Windows NT Server 4.0 so you have the ability to pass Microsoft Certified Professional Exam No. 70-67: Implementing and Supporting Microsoft Windows NT Server 4.0.

Consider this book your strategy guide as you prepare for the exam. It supplements any other materials you already have and helps you decide how to make best use of your study time leading up to the exam. Throughout this book I assume you are familiar with Windows NT Server 4.0 concepts, or that you have other study materials to help you understand these concepts. With that in mind, I cover Windows NT Server 4.0 to the depth of the exam objectives, but not beyond that point.

How to Use This Book

The chapters of this book are designed to be studied sequentially. In other words, it would be best if you complete Chapter 1 before you proceed to Chapter 2. A few chapters could probably stand alone, but all in all, I recommend a sequential approach.

For best results (and we both know that the only acceptable result is a passing score on the Windows NT Server 4.0 exam), I recommend the following plan of attack as you use this book. First, take the Are You Prepared? self-test at the beginning of the chapter to see if you've already mastered the topic. Next, if your self-test score tells you that you need more study, read the chapter and the Test Tip and Test Trap highlights, paying particular attention to the Inside Scoop section for pointers on what topics to concentrate on. Then use the Have You Mastered? and Practice Your Skills sections to see if you really have the key concepts under your belt. If you don't, go back and reread the section(s) you're not clear on. If your self-test score indicates you are prepared on this topic, you may want to move on to the next chapter.

After you've completed your study of the chapters, reviewed the Have You Mastered? questions, and done the Practice Your Skills exercises, take the Practice Exam included in the back of the book. The Practice Exam will help you assess how much you've learned from your study and will familiarize you with the types of questions you'll face when you take the real exam. Once you identify a weak area, you can use the cross-references to the corresponding chapters (including the Have You Mastered? questions) to improve your knowledge and skills in that area.

Before you take the Windows NT Server 4.0 exam, tear out the *Ace Card* and use its quick run-down of essential concepts to refresh your memory and focus your review just before the test.

Prerequisites

This book is an exam preparation guide, but it does not start at ground zero. I do assume you have the following knowledge and skills at the outset:

1. Basic terminology and basic skills to use a Microsoft Windows product. (This could be Windows 95, Windows for Workgroups, or a Windows NT product.)

2. Networking knowledge or experience equal to the scope required to pass the Microsoft Certified Professional Networking Essentials Exam (Exam No. 70-58).

3. Some hands-on experience with Windows NT Server, or the aptitude to jump into this material with a running start.

If you meet these prerequisites, you're ready to begin this book.

If you don't have the basic Windows experience or mouse skills, I recommend you either take a one-day Windows application course or work through a self-study book to acquire these skills *before* you begin this book.

What You Learn

MCSE NT Server 4.0 Ace It! gives you the quickest review of all the essential topics on Exam 70-67. Here's a rundown of what you learn:

- **Installation:** How to install NT servers using various methods

- **Disk systems:** Methods of managing disk storage and fault tolerance methods
- **Configuration:** Setting up a Windows NT server for hardware platforms and network communication
- **People resources:** Fundamentals of managing users and groups in stand-alone and domain configurations
- **Environments:** Providing roaming or predefined user work environments on compatible platforms
- **Printing:** Planning and implementing solutions for shared printers
- **Security:** Providing a secure environment for file protection of local and remote resources
- **Network protocols:** Installing and configuring Windows NT Server communication protocols for a networked environment
- **NetWare:** Communicating with and migrating from NetWare servers
- **Remote Access Service:** Providing remote access solutions to mobile and remote users through Windows NT Server
- **Performance:** Monitoring and improving performance using standard Windows NT tools
- **Troubleshooting:** Fundamentals of solving common Windows NT problems

Let's Get Started!

That concludes the owner's manual on how to operate this book. It's time to get started, and get you on your way to passing the Windows NT Server 4.0 exam. Now, let's get certified!

Acknowledgments

If it's true what they say — life is a roller coaster — sometimes I feel like I'm on a ride at a traveling carnival where no one is sure if all of the bolts are put in each time it packs up and moves to the next city. Without the support of my family and friends, I would certainly be a bigger mess than I am today.

First, I would like to thank Alan Carter for his supreme wisdom in getting me to talk with IDG Books. Without his intervention, I would not be here today.

My appreciation goes out to the entire team at IDG Books who worked on this book tirelessly for several months, especially to BC Crandall, lead development editor; Jennifer Rowe, development editor; Tracy Thomsic, acquisitions editor; Brian MacDonald, copy editor; and the graphics and production staff. I wish to send thanks to Tony Houston for his efforts in technically reviewing this book, and my sincerest appreciation to Associate Publisher Steve Sayre.

Of course, I also want to thank all of my family and friends who supported me during this tremendous effort. To my wife, your support and understanding were paramount in finishing this project.

Contents
at a Glance

Contents

Installing Windows NT Server

hat better way of getting started than jumping into installing Windows NT Server? In this chapter I explore the basics of the Windows NT Server 4.0 operating system and a take a brief look at workgroups and domains. To prepare you for the Windows NT Server exam, I examine the most common ways to install Windows NT Server, including network-based installations. I then move on to take a look at using the Network Client Administrator and how to troubleshoot common installation problems. So let's get started!

Exam Material in This Chapter

Based on Microsoft Objectives

Installation and Configuration

- Install Windows NT Server on Intel platforms.
- Install Windows NT Server to perform various server roles. Server roles include:
  - Primary domain controller
  - Backup domain controller
  - Member server
- Install Windows NT Server by using various methods. Installation methods include:
  - CD-ROM
  - Over-the-network
  - Network Client Administrator

Troubleshooting

- Choose the appropriate course of action to take when the installation process fails.

Based on Author's Experience

- You need to know the hardware requirements for installing Windows NT Server on Intel and Alpha platforms.
- You should be familiar with the command-line switches for the Windows NT setup program, including how to start an unattended installation.
- You should expect a few questions about converting NTFS and FAT partitions and what the restrictions are in doing so.

- You definitely need to be familiar with Windows NT Server's licensing modes and domain server roles, including restrictions for renaming or moving domain controllers between domains.

- You need to know how to use the Network Client Administrator to create setup and installation disks.

Are You Prepared?

Do you have what it takes? Try out these self-assessment questions to see if you have prepared for the material in this chapter or if you should review problem areas.

1. **Which command-line option for** `Winnt.exe` **enables you to start your installation without creating the startup disks?**

   ☐ A. `Winnt.exe /S`
   ☐ B. `Winnt.exe /F`
   ☐ C. `Winnt.exe /B`
   ☐ D. `Winnt.exe /X`
   ☐ E. `Winnt.exe /C`

2. **What is the purpose of an installation disk set?**

   ☐ A. To install an operating system, such as Windows NT, over the network.
   ☐ B. To install the network drivers to connect to an NT Server and download the installation disks.
   ☐ C. It contains the files required to install client software, such as TCP/IP for Windows for Workgroups.
   ☐ D. It installs client operating systems on an NT Server to enable clients to install from the server.

3. What is the minimum free disk space that is required to install Windows NT Server?

- [ ] A. 210MB
- [ ] B. 430MB
- [ ] C. 50MB
- [ ] D. 124MB
- [ ] E. 12MB

Answers:

1. C   *The /B command line switch configures Windows NT to install without creating startup disks. This should only be used on computers that are in the HCL. See the "Installation Process" section.*

2. C   *An installation disk set contains installation files for client software for most DOS environments and can contain services such as TCP/IP for Windows for Workgroup computers. An installation disk set cannot be made for installing whole operating systems such as Windows NT. See the "Using Network Client Administrator" section.*

3. D   *Windows NT Server requires a minimum of 124MB of free disk space to install. If you use the /B switch for a disk-less installation, the amount of required hard disk space increases. See the "Hardware Requirements for Installation" section.*

The Windows NT Server Operating System

The Microsoft Windows NT Server 4.0 is a powerful 32-bit operating system that is optimized as a network file, print, or application server.

The minimum hardware required to run Windows NT Server consists of an Intel-based computer with a 486/33 processor, 16MB of RAM, 124MB of free hard disk space, and a VGA graphics card. Windows NT Server does not support Plug and Play.

Windows NT Server supports most MS-DOS applications, most 16-bit and 32-bit Windows-based applications, POSIX 1.*x* applications, and most OS/2 1.*x* applications. It does not support applications that require direct hardware access, which could compromise Windows NT Server's security. It also does not support software applications that require a *terminate-and-stay-resident* (TSR) program or a virtual device driver. Windows NT Server is the operating system of choice for the Microsoft BackOffice products, including SQL Server, Exchange Server, and SNA Server.

Windows NT Server is a high-end, powerful operating system that supports multiple processors for true multiprocessing. Windows NT Server also supports preemptive multitasking for all software applications that run on Windows NT Server.

Windows NT Server is a high-security operating system. User logon and authentication are required in order to use the Windows NT Server operating system and in order to access local or network resources. Security is controlled and administered via a domain directory database.

Workgroups versus Domains

Before this overview of Microsoft Windows NT Server (from here on often referred to as simply Windows NT or NT) can progress much further, it's important that you get good and comfortable with two key concepts: workgroups and domains.

Workgroups and domains are two prevalent methods of grouping networked computers for common purposes. Computers and their users may be grouped based on common usage requirements or on departmental or geographical traits. For example, all the members of an accounting department or all the computers on the third floor of a building may be grouped together.

Workgroups

A *workgroup* is a logical grouping of networked computers in which one or more of the computers has one or more shared resources, such as a shared folder or a shared printer.

In a workgroup environment, security and user accounts are all maintained individually at each separate computer. Resources and administration are distributed throughout the computers that make up the workgroup. In a workgroup configuration, there is no centrally maintained user accounts database, or any centralized security. Figure 1-1 illustrates how security is distributed throughout a workgroup environment. Notice that security is maintained individually at each separate computer in the workgroup.

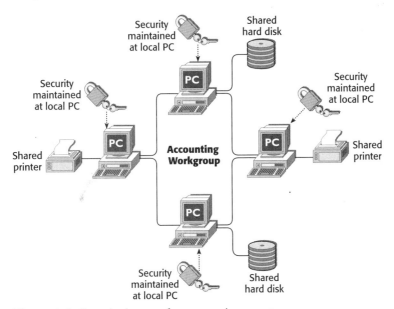

Figure 1-1 *Security in a workgroup environment*

Typically, all of the computers in a workgroup run desktop operating systems, such as Windows NT Workstation or Windows 95.

Domains

A *domain* is a logical grouping of networked computers in which all of the computers share a common, central domain directory database that contains user account and security information.

One distinct advantage of using domains (or a *domain model,* as it is sometimes called), particularly on a large network, is that administration and security for the entire network can be managed from a centralized location. Figure 1-2 illustrates how security is centralized in a domain environment. Note that all user account security is maintained at the domain controller.

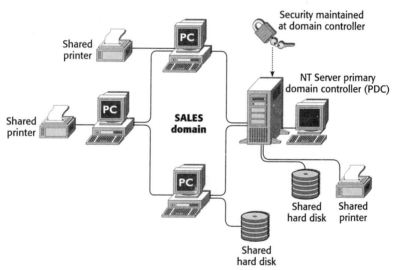

Figure 1-2 *Security in a domain environment*

In a Windows NT domain, at least one of the networked computers is a server computer that runs Windows NT Server. The server computer is configured as a *primary domain controller* (PDC), which maintains the domain directory database. A domain may contain only one PDC. Typically, there is at least one additional server computer that also runs Windows NT Server. This additional computer is usually configured as a *backup domain controller* (BDC). There is no limit to the number of

BDCs in an NT Domain. The other computers on the network normally run Windows NT Workstation or Windows 95 (although they may utilize Windows NT Server or other operating systems).

Choosing Between the Workgroup and Domain Models

Choosing the appropriate model of grouping computers and managing shared network resources depends upon the size and security needs of the network.

Often, small- to medium-sized networks (two to twenty computers) can be managed fairly easily by using the workgroup model, with the user of each computer controlling the security of the specific resources that are shared by that user's computer.

In a larger network environment, administration and security become harder to manage; thus, the domain model, which provides centralized account administration and greater security, is usually the preferred choice.

POP QUIZ True or False?

1. A Windows NT workgroup has a PDC. F
2. In large corporate networks, Windows NT Servers should participate in workgroups rather than domains because workgroups have a common directory service. F
3. A Windows NT Domain may have only one PDC and more than one BDC. T
4. Windows NT Server supports applications that require direct hardware access. F
5. You can run most OS/2 1.x applications on Windows NT Server. T

Answers: *1. False 2. False 3. True 4. False 5. True*

Hardware Requirements for Installation

Before you can install NT, you need to make sure you have the appropriate hardware. To avoid problems, only use hardware that appears on the Windows NT *Hardware Compatibility List* (HCL). The HCL, which is updated periodically, ships with the NT products.

Table 1-1 shows the minimum hardware required for installing Windows NT Server. The requirements listed apply only to Intel-based platforms. Windows NT can also be installed on DEC Alpha AXP, PowerPC, and MIPS R4000 platforms, but additional hardware may be necessary, depending on the type of processor(s) you plan to use.

TABLE 1-1 Minimum Hardware Required for Installation of Windows NT Server 4.0

Hardware Component	Minimum Requirement
Processor	486/33
Memory	16MB of RAM
Hard disk space	124MB
Display	VGA or better
Floppy disk drive	3.5-inch high-density
CD-ROM drive	Required (If your computer does not have a CD-ROM drive, you can still install NT Server by using an over-the-network installation.)
Network adapter	Optional (Required for over-the-network installation)
Mouse	Optional

TEST TRAP

As you prepare for the Windows NT Server exam, make sure you know the minimum hardware requirements to install Windows NT Server. You need to know what the installation requirements are for both Intel and Alpha platforms.

Do you know exactly what hardware you have in your computer? You can use the *NT Hardware Qualifier* (NTHQ) utility that comes with Windows NT to examine and identify your hardware configuration. NTHQ helps you determine if Windows NT can detect your hardware, and it identifies the hardware settings used for each adapter. To use NTHQ, you must create an NTHQ diskette, which you then use to boot your computer. (You can create an NTHQ diskette with a blank, formatted 3.5-inch floppy diskette by running `Makedisk.bat` from the `\support\hqtool` directory on the Windows NT compact disc.)

The Installation Process

Now that you know the minimum hardware required to install Windows NT Server and have all the information required to perform the installation, you're ready to move on to the actual installation process.

Starting Setup

There are three ways to start the installation process: from a CD-ROM drive, by using `Winnt.exe`, and by using `Winnt32.exe`. Installation can be done locally, from a CD-ROM drive; or over the network.

Starting from a CD-ROM drive

To start the installation from a CD-ROM drive, your computer must be configured with a local CD-ROM drive that is on the HCL. Place the Windows NT Server compact disc in the CD-ROM drive. Then boot the computer from the Windows NT Setup Boot Disk.

Using Winnt.exe

You can use `Winnt.exe` to start the installation from an unsupported CD-ROM drive (a CD-ROM drive that is not listed on the HCL), or to start the installation over the network. First boot the computer to MS-DOS, and then load either the CD-ROM drivers or network drivers (depending on the type of installation you're doing). Then use `Winnt.exe` to start the install.

`Winnt.exe` has several command-line switches that enable you to customize the setup process. Table 1-2 lists these switches and describes

Winnt.exe has several command-line switches that enable you to customize the setup process. Table 1-2 lists these switches and describes their functions.

TABLE 1-2 Winnt.exe Command-Line Switches

Switch	What the Switch Does
/S[:]sourcepath	Specifies the source location of NT files. You must specify a full path, in the form x:\[path] or \\server\share[\path]. The default sourcepath is the current directory.
/T[:]tempdrive	Specifies the drive that contains NT's temporary setup files during installation. If not specified, Setup uses the first drive it finds (that it thinks has enough free space) for the tempdrive.
/I[:]inffile	Specifies the filename (no path) of the file containing setup information. The default inffile is DOSNET.INF.
/OX	Instructs Setup to create the Setup Boot Disk set.
/X	Instructs Setup *not* to create the Setup Boot Disk set.
/F	Instructs Setup not to verify files as they are copied to the Setup Boot Disk set (during the creation of the Setup Boot Disk set).
/C	Instructs Setup to skip the disk free space check during the creation of the Setup Boot Disk set.
/B	Enables you to install NT without using the Setup Boot Disk set. Requires you to specify the source path by using the /S switch.
/U	Enables you to perform an unattended NT installation and use an optional script file. Requires you to specify the sourcepath by using the /S switch.

Switch	What the Switch Does
/R	Specifies an optional directory to be installed during installation.
/RX	Specifies an optional directory to be copied to the local hard drive during installation.
/E	Specifies a command to be executed at the end of the installation/setup process.
/UDF	Specifies that a Uniqueness Database File is used during an unattended NT installation.

KNOW THIS **Command-Line Switches**

The most common command-line questions are about the /U, /B, /X, and /I. Make sure you understand their purpose and how to use them in various scenarios.

The syntax for the Winnt.exe command is:

```
WINNT [/S[:]sourcepath] [/T[:]tempdrive] [/I[:]inffile
[/OX] [/X | [/F] [/C]] [/B] [/U[:scriptfile]]
[/RX]:directory] [/E:command]
```

To illustrate how the switches are used, suppose that you want to install Windows NT from a network drive (named drive K:) without using the Setup Boot Disk set. (This is often referred to as a disk-less installation.) To accomplish this, use the following command:

```
K:\I386\Winnt /B /S:K:\I386
```

Notice the /B switch is used to permit you to perform a disk-less installation, and the sourcepath switch, /S, is used to specify that the location of the NT files that will be installed on your computer: network drive K:, directory I386.

Using Winnt32.exe

Winnt32.exe functions the same as Winnt.exe, except that Winnt.exe is designed to run on MS-DOS-based or Windows-based computers, whereas Winnt32.exe is designed to be used on Windows NT computers. All Winnt32.exe command-line options are the same as Winnt.exe, with the exception of /F and /C, which are not supported by Winnt32.exe. Additionally, Winnt32.exe performs functions much more quickly because it can launch multiple threads in Windows NT. As a result, your installation time will be shorter if you use Winnt32.exe.

POP QUIZ · True or False?

1. Winnt.exe performs an installation faster than Winnt32.exe.

2. Winnt.exe works only on Windows NT computers.

3. The /U command line switch allows you to specify a script file to use during the installation.

4. You must have at least 12MB of RAM to install Windows NT Server.

5. The /B command line switch allows you to perform a disk-less installation.

Answers: *1. False 2. False 3. True 4. False 5. True*

Setup Flow

The installation of Windows NT Server takes place in four or five phases, depending on whether you install from a CD-ROM or you use Winnt.exe or Winnt32.exe. These phases are: the Pre-Copy Phase, Phase 0, and Phases 1–3. During each phase, you perform specific tasks and enter requested information. The Windows NT installation program (Setup) causes the computer to reboot after the Pre-Copy Phase, and again after Phase 0.

Pre-Copy Phase (Winnt.exe and Winnt32.exe only)

The Pre-Copy Phase is the initial phase of the installation process. This phase applies only when the `Winnt.exe` or `Winnt32.exe` installation option is used. The Windows NT Setup program creates a set of three floppy disks to use during the installation process. The floppy disks are not created if the `/B` or `/U` switches are used. Setup creates a `$Win_NT$.~ls` folder on the first local drive with enough free space, and then copies the installation files from the source directory to this folder. The installation program deletes this folder after the installation is complete.

Phase 0

Phase 0 begins when you boot the computer with the Setup Boot Disk, or when you reboot the computer after starting `Winnt.exe` using either the `/B` or `/U` switch. Setup confirms all SCSI and CD-ROM adapters and allows you to add any necessary adapter drivers from the disks supplied by the manufacturer. Setup then verifies the hardware and software components in the computer. You are then prompted to choose the disk partition on which to install Windows NT, and choose the type of file system to use on this partition.

FAT and NTFS

Windows NT supports two file system types:

- The *file allocation table* (FAT) file system is supported by Windows NT and many other operating systems, including MS-DOS, OS/2, Windows 3.*x*, and Windows 95. To dual boot between Windows NT and one of these other operating systems (and both operating systems are located on the same hard disk partition), choose the FAT file system. The FAT file system supports neither extended attributes nor file-level security.

Continued

- The *Windows NT file system* (NTFS) is supported only by Windows NT. In general, choose NTFS if you do not want your computer to dual boot between Windows NT and another operating system and you want the added advantages provided by NTFS, including extended attributes and file-level security.

  You can select FAT as the file system to be used during installation of Windows NT, and then later choose to convert the file system to NTFS. However, if you choose NTFS as the file system during installation of Windows NT and then later want to convert to FAT, the process isn't so easy: You need to back up all files, repartition and format the drive, reinstall Windows NT, and then restore all the files from backup.

  Windows NT 4.0 does not support the *high performance file system* (HPFS) used by OS/2. If you want to install Windows NT 4.0 on a computer that uses HPFS, you must backup all data, repartition and format the computer's drive with FAT or NTFS, and then restore all the files from backup before you can install Windows NT 4.0.

Phase 1

In Phase 1, the NT Setup Wizard starts. The Setup Wizard gathers information from you about your computer and specific installation details, including your name, the name of your organization, your CD key number, and which Licensing mode you want to use. Windows NT Server has two licensing modes: *per server* and *per seat*:

- **Per server:** In the per server licensing mode, you must have one client access license for each concurrent connection to the server. For example, if you have 150 client computers (workstations), but only 100 of them will be logged on to the Windows NT Server computer at any one time, you need 100 client access licenses. Enter the number of client access licenses you have purchased for this server in the box next to concurrent connections in the Choose Licensing Mode dialog box.

- **Per seat:** In the per seat licensing mode, you must have one client access license for each client computer that will ever connect to the Windows NT Server computer.

You are then prompted to enter you computer name and select what role the server will play. Choose one of the following server types:

- **Primary Domain Controller:** Choose *primary domain controller* (PDC) if you want the server to participate in a domain instead of a workgroup, and if you have not already installed any servers in this domain.

- **Backup Domain Controller:** Choose *backup domain controller* (BDC) if you want the server to participate in a domain instead of a workgroup, and if you have already installed a server in this domain. Additionally, you need to enter the administrator's user account name and password to complete the installation of a BDC.

- **Member Server:** Choose member server if you want the server to join a domain but do not want the server to have to expend its resources authenticating user logon requests in the domain. Or, choose member server if you plan to move this server from one domain to another. If you want the server to be a member server in a domain, you will also need to enter the administrator's user account name and password to complete the installation.

- **Stand-Alone Server:** Choose stand-alone server if you want the server to participate in a workgroup instead of a domain.

Server Roles

You need to choose the role this server will play on the network. Planning is very important here, because once a server is installed as either a *primary domain controller* (PDC) or a *backup domain controller* (BDC), it can't

Continued

become a stand-alone server or a member server. Also, once a computer is installed as a domain controller in a domain, the domain controller cannot migrate to another domain without a complete reinstall of Windows NT Server.

TEST TRAP

If a stand-alone server later joins a domain, it becomes a member server at that point (and is no longer a stand-alone server). If, at some point after that, this member server no longer participates in a domain (it "un-joins" a domain), it reverts to stand-alone server status.

Phase 2

In Phase 2, Setup installs and configures the networking components. To accomplish this, you provide information on how (or if) the computer connects to the network and whether to install Microsoft Internet Information Server (IIS). You also configure which network adapters are installed in your computer, choose the network protocol(s) you want to use, and enter related information depending on the protocol(s)selected.

KNOW THIS

Network Protocols

- **TCP/IP:** The *TCP/IP* protocol provides the most capability of the three protocols. It is routable, fast, and has powerful network-wide name resolution capabilities. It can be used on much larger networks than either of the other protocols. TCP/IP is the most commonly supported protocol. It is supported on many operating systems, including Windows NT, Windows 95, UNIX, MS-DOS, Macintosh, and IBM Mainframes. TCP/IP is the protocol used on the Internet. The main drawback to using TCP/IP is that it requires substantial planning and configuration to implement.

- **NWLink IPX/SPX Compatible Transport:** *NWLink IPX/SPX Compatible Transport* was developed by Novell for use on NetWare servers. NWLink IPX/SPX is a routable protocol, but has some limitations when used on large NetBIOS-based networks such as Windows NT. It has no name resolution capabilities, so all broadcasts are forwarded across routers. NWLink IPX/SPX is very easy to configure, and is a good choice for a small, routed network. NWLink IPX/SPX should be used on any network that has NetWare servers on it if Windows NT computers on the network need to access the NetWare servers. You should choose autodetect for the frame type selection, unless you know which frame types you want to support.

- **NetBEUI:** The NetBEUI protocol is designed for small, nonrouted networks. It does not require any configuration, and has minimal overhead. NetBEUI is included primarily to provide backward compatibility with earlier networking software that uses NetBEUI as its only protocol.

Phase 3

In Phase 3, Setup completes the installation. You enter specific IIS setup and publishing directory information, and configure the date, time, and time zone information. You are also given the opportunity to make an Emergency Repair Disk.

What Is Server-Based Deployment?

Server-based deployment is a process that involves automating the installation and setup of Windows NT, other operating systems (Windows 95 and Windows for Workgroups), and applications on multiple computers on a network. This process is primarily designed for rolling out large networks quickly and efficiently.

In server-based deployment, source files are placed on a centrally located Windows NT Server computer. Then floppy disks are created that, when run on the computers that need to be set up, cause these computers to automatically connect to the server and to run a partially or fully automated installation and setup routine.

 Using server-based deployment can save you a significant amount of time. Consider using it when you have five or more identical installs to perform.

Preparing for Server-Based Deployment

To prepare a Windows NT Server computer for server-based deployment, you need to place the appropriate files on this server in a prescribed format. To begin the preparation, copy the Clients folder, including all files and subfolders, from your Windows NT Server compact disc to one of the drives on the Windows NT Server computer. This drive must have enough free space to hold the entire contents of the Clients folder and the source files for any additional operating systems and applications you want to install using server-based deployment.

Then share the Clients folder on the Windows NT Server computer as CLIENTS. At this point, if the only operating system you want to deploy is Windows 95, you are finished preparing your Windows NT Server computer. To deploy Windows NT, create a subfolder in the Clients folder named Winnt and create a subfolder in the Clients\Winnt folder named Netsetup. Copy the Windows NT installation files and subfolders from the I386 folder on your Windows NT compact disk to the Netsetup folder.

Once the Windows NT Server computer is prepared, you're ready to use the Network Client Administrator to proceed with the server-based deployment process.

Using Network Client Administrator

Network Client Administrator is a Windows NT Server tool that you can use to create an *installation disk set* to install network clients or services on client computers.

You can also use Network Client Administrator to create a *network installation startup disk*. A network installation startup disk, when run on a computer that needs to be set up (the *target computer*), causes the target computer to automatically connect to the server and start an interactive installation/setup routine.

 Network Client Administrator is only included with Windows NT Server — it is not available on Windows NT Workstation computers.

Creating an Installation Disk Set

You can use Network Client Administrator to create an installation disk set to install network clients or services on client computers. For example, suppose you want to install TCP/IP on several Windows for Workgroups computers. You can use Network Client Administrator to create a TCP/IP installation disk set, and then use this disk set on each computer on which you want to install TCP/IP.

You can create an installation disk set for several network clients and services, including:

- Network Client 3.0 for MS-DOS and Windows
- Remote Access 1.1a for MS-DOS
- TCP/IP 32 for Windows for Workgroups 3.11
- LAN Manager 2.2c for MS-DOS
- LAN Manager 2.2c for OS/2

Creating a Network Installation Startup Disk

Use Network Client Administrator to create a single disk that you can use on each of the new client computers to automatically begin an interactive, over-the-network installation of Windows NT Workstation.

 Installation Disks

A Network installation startup disk is used to boot a computer, load the MS-DOS network client software and start an installation automatically. These disks are generally used for computers that do not have an existing OS or are not bootable.

Network installation startup disks can be used to install any of the following operating systems: Windows for Workgroups, Windows 95, Windows NT Workstation, and Windows NT Server. (A separate disk is required for each different operating system.)

 True or False?

1. The Clients folder is automatically installed on NT Server computers when they are first installed.

2. A network installation disk set is used to copy network client software to a computer.

3. Network Client Administrator is only included with Windows NT Server.

4. An installation disk set can be used to install RAS on MS-DOS client computers.

5. A network installation startup disk works only on computers that have identical network adapters installed in them.

Answers: *1. False 2. False 3. True 4. True 5. True*

Troubleshooting Common Installation Problems

Most installation problems occur because of hardware incompatibilities. Therefore, your first troubleshooting step should be to ensure that all of your hardware is on the HCL or is supported by the manufacturer. Table 1-3 lists some common Windows NT installation problems and their possible causes and solutions.

TABLE 1-3 Troubleshooting Common Installation Problems

Problem	Possible Cause/Solution
You have the recommended amount of free disk space, but still run out of disk space during installation.	The recommended amount of disk space is based on the expectation that you are using 16K sectors on your hard disk. If you have a very large partition, you could be using 32K or 64K sectors. You would then need significantly more free disk space to complete your installation.
A blue screen or STOP message is displayed during installation or after a reboot.	This can be caused by several things. The most common causes are a *corrupt boot sector* or a *boot sector virus*, which you can usually repair by using Fdisk /mbr from MS-DOS (many virus scanners can also repair this error); and *hardware conflicts*, which you can check for by using NTHQ to examine all of your hardware settings. Look for two pieces of hardware with the same I/O port, interrupt, or DMA address. Reconfigure hardware so that there are no hardware conflicts.

Continued

23

TABLE 1-3 *Continued*

Problem	Possible Cause/Solution
You can't install from your CD-ROM drive.	This could be caused by an unsupported CD-ROM drive or by an unsupported SCSI adapter. Some SCSI adapters, such as PC card SCSI adapters, are not supported during installation, but you can install the drivers for them after the installation is complete. Try installing using Winnt.exe.
You can't join a domain during installation	Make sure that all network settings, both hardware and software, are correct. Confirm that you have correctly typed in the domain name and the administrator's user account name and password. (All passwords in Windows NT are case-sensitive.) Check the network cable and connections and verify that the PDC is up and accessible on the network.
Network services don't start correctly.	Verify that all network adapter and network protocol settings are correct, including interrupt, I/O port, and transceiver type. Confirm that the newly assigned computer name is unique—that it does not match any other computer, domain, or workgroup name used on the network. If you are installing a PDC, ensure that the new domain name is unique—that it does not match any other computer or domain name used on the network.

Have You Mastered?

Now it's time to apply what you've learned in this chapter by testing your mastery of the material. These questions provide you with a means to determine if you are ready to move on to the next chapter or if you need to review the material again.

1. You are upgrading a Windows NT Server 3.51 computer to Windows NT Server 4.0. You want to increase the speed of the upgrade. What can you do?

- ☐ A. Run NTHQ before starting the upgrade.
- ☐ B. Start the upgrade with Winnt32.exe.
- ☐ C. Start the upgrade with Winnt.exe.
- ☐ D. Remove all of the network components in NT 3.51 before starting the upgrade.

The correct answer is B. Winnt32.exe performs installations and upgrades faster because it can start multiple threads of the installation simultaneously, rather than sequentially as Winnt.exe does. Winnt32.exe can only be run on computers that are already running Windows NT, so it can only be used to increase performance during upgrades and installations to different directories on a Windows NT computer. For more information, see the "Installation Process" section.

2. You planning a new network that will have 15 Windows NT Server computers. You want to manage user accounts and security privileges centrally for all of the computers. What type of network should you implement?

    ☐ A. Create a Workgroup and place all of the computers in the Workgroup.

    ☐ B. Create a Workgroup, place all of the computers in the Workgroup, and configure one of the Windows NT Server computers as a PDC.

    ☐ C. Create a Domain, place all of the computers in the Domain, and configure all of the Windows NT Server computers as a PDC.

    ☐ D. Configure one of the Windows NT Server computers as a PDC and place all of the other computers in its domain.

The correct answer is **D**. To manage user accounts and security privileges centrally, you must have an NT Domain. Additionally, a Domain can only have one primary domain controller (PDC) at a time. The other computers can be configured as backup domain controllers or member servers. A workgroup does not support central user accounts because there is no common directory for the computers. For more information, see the "Workgroups versus Domains" section.

3. You are installing Windows NT Server on a new computer. Your network consists of 5 Windows NT Server computers and 200 Windows NT Workstation client computers. You have 200 client access licenses for the Windows NT Workstation users to access the Windows NT Servers. You want to use the licensing mode that will enable all 200 client computers to access any of the Windows NT Servers and be in compliance with your licensing requirements. What should you do?

    ☐ A. Configure the Windows NT Server computers to use per-seat licensing.

    ☐ B. Configure the Windows NT Server computers to use per-server licensing.

☐ C. Configure the Windows NT Workstation computers to use per-seat licensing.

☐ D. Configure the Windows NT Workstation computers to use per-server licensing.

The correct answer is A. Per-seat licensing assigns a client access license to each client computer and enables that client to connect to an unlimited number of Windows NT Server computers. The per-server licensing mode assigns a concurrent number of permitted clients for that server, so with 200 licenses, it is possible that a client may exceed the license allocation for a server. For more information, see the "Installation Process" section.

4. **You are preparing to deploy Windows NT Workstation to 40 new computers on your network. What can you do to enable the computers to boot up, access a shared folder on an NT Server, and install Windows NT Workstation?**

☐ A. Use the Windows NT Setup Manager to create a boot disk.

☐ B. Use the Network Client Administrator on a Windows NT Server computer to create a boot disk.

☐ C. Use the Network Client Administrator on a Windows NT Workstation computer to create a boot disk.

☐ D. Use the contents of the clients folder to create a boot disk.

The correct answer is B. The Network Client Administrator (NCA) can create a bootable disk to startup a computer and begin the installation of Windows NT Workstation without installing drivers or software on the PC first. The NCA is available only on a Windows NT Server computer. The NT Setup Manager is used to create an unattended installation file. For more information, see the "Using Network Client Administrator" section.

5. **You are the network administrator of a network that contains a Windows NT Server domain. You want to create a new domain, and want to use the BDC computer in the existing domain as the PDC for the new domain. What should you do?**

☐ A. Change the domain settings for the BDC.
☐ B. Promote the BDC to a PDC and place it in the new domain.
☐ C. Reinstall Windows NT Server on the computer and configure it as the PDC for the new domain.
☐ D. You must use a new computer; the BDC can not be used in the new domain.

The correct answer is C. Once Windows NT Server has been configured as a primary or backup domain controller, you cannot change its domain configuration. You must reinstall Windows NT Server and configure the new domain settings and server role. For more information, see the "Installation Process" section.

6. **What are the minimum processor, amount of RAM, and hard disk space required to install Windows NT Server on an Intel-based computer?**

☐ A. Processor: 386/33; RAM: 8MB; Hard disk: 500MB
☐ B. Processor: 486/33; RAM: 16MB; Hard disk: 124MB
☐ C. Processor: 486/66; RAM: 12MB; Hard disk: 220MB
☐ D. Processor: Pentium/100; RAM: 16MB; Hard disk: 330MB

The correct answer is B. Microsoft Windows NT Server does not support the Intel 386 processor and the minimum amount of free space is 124MB, depending on the options installed. For more information refer to the "Hardware Requirements for Installation" section.

7. What file system types does Microsoft Windows NT Server 4.0 support?

☐ A. FAT
☐ B. FAT32
☐ C. HPFS
☐ D. NTFS
☐ E. POSIX

The correct answers are A and D. Windows NT Server 4.0 supports older FAT partitions and as well as newer NTFS partitions. NT Server 4.0 does not support the newer FAT32 file system that ships with Windows 98, nor can it use HPFS drives. POSIX is a computing subsystem, not a file system. For more information, see the "Installation Process" section.

8. You are adding a new Windows NT Server computer to your network. You want this new server to be part of an existing network and participate in the domain directory services. You do not want the server to replicate the security database to the local computer. What role should this computer take in the domain?

☐ A. Primary domain controller
☐ B. Backup domain controller
☐ C. Member server
☐ D. Stand-alone server

The correct answer is C. Servers configured as a PDC or BDC contain either the master copy or a replicated version of the domain directory. Stand-alone servers do not participate in domain-based directory services. For more information, see the "Installation Process" section.

9. You are installing Windows NT Server on a test computer. You want to evaluate how Windows NT Server will communicate between servers on your network and how well it will run your customized client-server software. You want to configure Windows NT Server to use a protocol that is designed for small, nonrouted networks, does not require any configuration, and has minimal overhead. What protocol should you use?

☐ A. TCP/IP
☐ B. NWLink IPX/SPX Compatible Transport
☐ C. NetBEUI
☐ D. DLC

The correct answer is C. NetBEUI is a nonroutable protocol that is excellent for small networks and peer to peer communications. It has very little protocol overhead and travels efficiently over local networks because of its small size. TCP/IP and NWLink IPX/SPX Compatible Transport are designed for large routed networks and require configuration parameters. For more information, see the "Installation Process" section.

10. You are installing applications on your Windows NT Server computer. You want to use applications that are compatible with Windows NT Server's multitasking process. What type of multitasking does Windows NT Server provide?

☐ A. Cooperative
☐ B. Preemptive
☐ C. Parallel
☐ D. NUMA

The correct answer is B. Windows NT Server multitasks Win32 applications in a preemptive environment where the micro-kernel controls how long an application has access to the processor. In a cooperative multitasking environment, it is up to the individual application to cooperatively volunteer the processor up for other applications to use. For more information, see the "Windows NT Server Operating System" section.

Practice Your Skills

Here is a chance to apply your practical hands-on experience and material from this chapter. These exercises are designed not only for you to apply the material in the book, but also for you to gain greater experience and exposure to the product. These exercises are a critical part of understanding the product and gaining valuable experience for using the product and passing the certification exam. For each of the following problems, consider the given facts and determine what you think are the possible causes of the problem and what course of action you might take to resolve the problem.

1. Planning NT Server groups

EXERCISE You are installing 50 new Windows NT Server computers to your network. You create a Workgroup called NT Computers and place all of the Server computers in the Workgroup. When users try to access network shares on other computers they get access denied errors. What is the problem and what can you do to resolve it?

ANALYSIS Workgroups do not provide a central directory service or security management. When the computers are added to the workgroup, there is no sharing of user accounts between the computers. To resolve the issue, the computers should be added to a Windows NT Domain, and managed by a Windows NT Domain Controller that provides a central account directory.

2. Planning for fault tolerance

EXERCISE You are planning a new Windows NT domain. Your network contains 15 Windows NT Server computers and 200 Windows NT Workstation computers. You want to ensure that you have the highest level of fault tolerance as it relates to your domain directory. What roles should the computers take in the new domain?

ANALYSIS If the servers will not be heavily loaded and there is a need for the highest level of fault tolerance possible, configure one of the NT Servers as a primary domain controller and the remaining systems as backup domain controllers.

3. Troubleshooting Windows NT installation problems

EXERCISE You are installing Windows NT Server 4.0 to your new computer. During the installation, the process stops and you see a blue screen containing error information on your display. What should you do to determine and resolve the problem?

ANALYSIS The most likely cause of the problem is a hardware compatibility problem. Try removing all add-on devices that are not required for the installation and attempt the installation again. If the error occurs again, try installing from a new compact disk or another location. If the problem still occurs, check the HCL to ensure that Windows NT supports your computer hardware.

4. Joining domains

EXERCISE You are installing Windows NT Server 4.0 to your new computer. During the installation you try to join a domain and an error message is displayed stating that the domain controller for this domain cannot be located. What should you do to join the domain?

ANALYSIS Click the Back button in the installation dialog boxes until you are returned to the Network configuration dialog. Verify all of your network configuration information and alternatively, select an additional supported protocol. Proceed with the installation to determine if the domain controller is now accessible. If not, make a quick scan of the physical network components, status LEDs and cable, and ensure the domain controller is online.

5. Server installations

EXERCISE Your organization has been using a network installation startup disk to install Windows NT Workstation. You recently purchased some new computers and you are attempting to install Windows NT Workstation using the same network installation startup disk. When you boot the new computers with the disk, you are unable to access the network. What is the most likely problem?

ANALYSIS Network installation startup disks are specific to a particular network adapter. The new computers most likely have a different network adapter card or are configured differently than the previous computer types. You may need to create a new disk set or update the settings on the current set to reflect the configuration changes.

Configuring Disks

One of the most challenging sections of the Windows NT Server 4.0 exam involves configuring and supporting hard disks. You will be tested on the strengths, limitations, and special features of the two file systems that Windows NT supports: FAT and NTFS. Are you prepared? Do you know how to convert from FAT to NTFS and vice versa? Do you know how to establish disk mirroring, volume sets, and stripe sets? The chapter wraps up with a look at how to recover from single or multiple drive failures as well as how to use an Emergency Repair Disk.

Exam Material in This Chapter

Based on Microsoft Objectives

Planning

- Plan the disk drive configuration for various requirements. Requirements include:
  - Choosing a file system
  - Choosing a fault-tolerance method
- Configure hard disks to meet various requirements. Requirements include:
  - Allocating disk space capacity
  - Providing redundancy
  - Providing security
  - Formatting

Based on Author's Experience

- You need to know the three types of fault tolerant disk configurations Windows NT Server provides and their limitations. You also need to know which of these methods can be used on boot and system partitions.

- You should know which types of partitions are supported by Windows NT, Microsoft Windows 3.x, Windows 9x, and MS-DOS.

- You should know how FAT and NTFS handle partitions of various sizes.

- Watch for questions about NTFS file-level security.

- The exam will present scenarios to test your understanding of how to convert a FAT partition to NTFS, and how to convert NTFS to a FAT partition.

- You should be aware of the function of the Emergency Repair Disk and how to create one.

Are You Prepared?

Do you have what it takes? Try out these self-assessment questions to see if you have prepared for the material in this chapter or if you should review problem areas.

1. **You are configuring the hard disks in your Windows NT Server computer. Which type(s) of fault tolerance can be used on disks containing the boot partition?**

   - ☐ A. Volume sets
   - ☑ B. Stripe sets
   - ☐ C. Stripe sets with parity
   - ☑ D. Mirror sets

2. **You have configured your boot disk to be mirrored onto a second hard disk. You create a fault tolerance boot disk and copy the required files to the floppy. Which file must be edited to configure the floppy disk to boot the proper hard disk?**

   - ☐ A. `Ntldr`
   - ☐ B. `Ntdetect.com`
   - ☑ C. `Boot.ini`
   - ☐ D. `Recover.dat`

3. When configuring Windows NT Server to provide disk fault tolerance, which levels of RAID protection can NT Server provide?

    ☑ A. RAID 0
    ☑ B. RAID 1
    ☐ C. RAID 2
    ☐ D. RAID 3
    ☐ E. RAID 4
    ☑ F. RAID 5

Answers:

1. D   *Windows NT Server does not support configurations where the boot or system partition is part of a volume or stripe set. The boot partition can reside in a mirrored set, though. For more information, refer to the "Disk Configurations" section.*

2. C   *When a disk in a mirror set fails and it contains the boot partition, a fault tolerance boot disk is required to boot the computer and load the OS from the remaining good mirror. For the floppy to locate the proper drive and OS, the* boot.ini *file needs to be updated so the boot ARC points to the second disk in the mirror. For more information, refer to the "Disk Configurations" section.*

3. A, B, and F

   Windows NT can provide mirror sets, stripe sets, and stripe sets with parity. Only mirror sets can contain the boot or system partition. RAID levels 2 though 4 cannot be provided by the NT Server OS. This is covered in the "Disk Configurations" section.

File Systems

Before you attempt to configure disks in a Windows NT environment, you should have a clear understanding of the different file systems that NT supports. Windows NT Server 4.0 supports three file systems: the *file allocation table* (FAT) *file system*, the *Windows NT file system* (NTFS), and the *Compact Disc Filing System* (CDFS). Windows NT 4.0 does *not* support the *high performance file system* (HPFS), although earlier versions of NT did. (If you are upgrading from an earlier version of Windows NT that used HPFS, you must convert to NTFS before performing the upgrade.) Table 2-1 shows which file systems are supported by various operating systems.

TABLE 2-1 File System Support by Operating System

Operating System	File Systems Supported
Windows NT 4.0	FAT, NTFS, CDFS
Windows NT 3.51 (and earlier versions)	FAT, NTFS, CDFS, HPFS
Windows 98	FAT, FAT32, CDFS
Windows 95	FAT, CDFS
Windows 3.x and 3.1x	FAT, CDFS
OS/2	FAT, CDFS, HPFS
MS-DOS	FAT, CDFS

FAT

The *file allocation table* (FAT) *file system* used on Windows NT is a modified version of the FAT file system used by MS-DOS. FAT is the only hard disk file system supported by Windows 3.x, Windows 3.1x, Windows 95, Windows 98, and MS-DOS. So, if you want to configure a Windows NT computer to dual boot between Windows NT and Windows 3.1x, Windows 95, Windows 98, or MS-DOS, your computer's first partition must use the FAT file system.

Don't confuse the FAT file system with the FAT32 file system. Windows NT does not support the FAT32 file system (an enhanced rendition of FAT) that is supported in the original equipment manufacturer (OEM) version of Windows 95 that includes Service Pack 2 and in Windows 98.

FAT

The ability to dual boot between Windows NT and any other Microsoft OS requires that the C: drive be formatted as FAT. Most of the file-system-related questions deal with FAT vs. NTFS file system security. This is the area that you should focus on!

Security

The FAT file system does *not* support file and folder security in Windows NT. Because file and folder security is not supported on a FAT partition, any user who is logged on locally to a computer has full control of all of the files and folders located in the FAT partition(s) on that computer. This applies only to local access.

However, you can use share permissions to control users' access to shared folders over the network. Share permissions affect only the access of files and folders over the network, not when someone is logged on locally. So if you need local file and folder security, you should use an NTFS partition instead of a FAT partition.

Speed of access to files

Access speed to files on a FAT partition depends on many factors, including file type, file size, partition size, number of files in a folder, and fragmentation.

Windows NT accesses files on FAT partitions smaller than 500MB faster than it accesses files on other similar-sized file system partitions discussed here. Additionally, NT accesses certain types of files on FAT partitions more efficiently than on partitions formatted with other file systems.

On very large partitions, however, or when there is a large number of files in a folder, Windows NT accesses files on NTFS partitions much faster than it accesses files on a FAT partition of similar size.

Windows NT usually accesses files on a highly fragmented FAT partition slower than it can access files on an NTFS partition of similar size.

Partition size

The maximum size of a FAT partition is 4GB. The maximum size of a file in a FAT partition is 4GB. The FAT file system does *not* support file compression.

NTFS

The *Windows NT file system* (NTFS) is the most powerful file system supported by Windows NT. Only Windows NT supports NTFS — no other operating systems currently support this file system.

When it comes to security, naming conventions, speed of access to files, and partition size, NTFS has its own unique characteristics. Additionally, NTFS has some features not supported by the FAT file system.

Security

NTFS provides file and folder security for both local and remote users on a network. NTFS is the only file system discussed here that permits the assigning of permissions to individual files and folders.

NTFS security controls access to files on an NTFS partition by utilizing the user's *security identifier* (SID) to determine which files that user can access. Each file and folder on an NTFS partition has an *access control list* (ACL) associated with it. The ACL is a list that contains user and group SIDs, with the associated privileges of each user and group.

Naming conventions

Like the FAT file system, NTFS supports the use of long filenames. Names of files and folders (including extensions) can be up to 255 characters long.

NTFS preserves upper- and lowercase in filenames. Filenames are not case-sensitive (except when used by a POSIX application). For example, a Win32 application does not distinguish between Money.DOC, MONEY.DOC, and money.doc — it treats all three names as though they were the same file.

The POSIX subsystem, however, is case-sensitive with respect to filenames, because it does not translate a request for a file into all uppercase letters as the Win32 and other subsystems do. A POSIX application treats the filenames in the previous paragraph as though they were three separate files: Money.DOC, MONEY.DOC, and money.doc. You must use a POSIX application if you want to access these three different files — if you attempt to access Money.DOC with a Win32 application (no matter how you type the filename) you will normally retrieve the MONEY.DOC file because the Win32 Subsystem translates file requests into all uppercase letters.

Speed of access to files

NTFS usually provides faster access to files stored on a large partition that contains many files than the FAT file system does. NTFS is able to access files in this situation faster than the FAT file system because NTFS uses an enhanced binary tree to locate files. A binary tree search is a faster mechanism for searching through a large number of filenames than the sequential read mechanism used on FAT partitions.

Partition size

The maximum theoretical size of an NTFS partition is 16 exabytes (an *exabyte* is one billion billion bytes, or a giga-gigabyte). However, when you actually implement NTFS on current standard industry hardware, there is a functional limitation of 2 terabytes.

Additional features not supported by the FAT file system

NTFS has several other unique attributes and features that are not found in, nor supported by, the FAT file system.

- NTFS supports a compression attribute for each file. You can choose which files to compress and which ones to leave uncompressed. The compression algorithm NTFS uses is similar to the one used by Drivespace in MS-DOS. Using compression provides an approximately 40 to 50 percent increase in hard disk space.

- NTFS is a highly reliable, recoverable file system. It is not necessary to periodically run `Chkdsk.exe` on an NTFS partition.

Compression can cause some performance degradation on partitions with substantial write activity. Additionally, accessing uncompressed files is faster than accessing compressed files.

True or False?

1. FAT partitions access files faster than NTFS partitions when they are under 500MB in size.
2. Only NTFS can use long file names with up to 255 characters.
3. Windows NT supports drives formatted as FAT32.
4. FAT partitions may be as large as 16 exabytes.
5. Files on a FAT partition are case-sensitive.

Answers: *1. True 2. False 3. False 4. False 5. False*

Converting from FAT to NTFS

In Windows NT you can format a new partition with either FAT or NTFS. But what do you do when you want to change the file system on an existing partition?

You can change an existing FAT partition, and retain the data on it, into an NTFS partition by using `Convert.exe`. This is a fairly simple procedure. However, it is a one-way process — there is no way to convert an NTFS partition into a FAT partition without first backing up, reformatting the disk, and restoring the data.

There is no way to convert an NTFS partition into a FAT partition without first backing up, reformatting the disk, and restoring the data. Remember this as it is very likely to appear on the Windows NT Server exam.

Disk Configurations

Fault tolerant configurations enable an administrator to configure a Windows NT Server to survive during a hard disk failure. When a hard disk fails in a non-fault tolerant computer, the operating system and computer stop responding and usually require reinstallation and restoration of data. When using Windows NT Server as a centralized service for a network, the time it takes to recover from a hard disk failure is a luxury most companies don't have. To guard against this type of failure, Windows NT Server provides four different disk configurations, offering various degrees of fault tolerance.

Disk Mirroring

Disk mirroring is a fault tolerance method that enables operations to continue when one hard disk fails.

The term *disk mirroring* is somewhat of a misnomer. It should be called *partition mirroring*. Any partition can be mirrored, including the system partition and the boot partition. In disk mirroring, Disk Administrator makes an exact replica of the partition being mirrored on a *separate* hard disk. You can't make a replica of a partition on the same physical disk—the mirror image must be produced on a different hard disk.

Disk mirroring is a fault tolerance method that enables operations to continue when one hard disk fails. After a disk fails in a mirror, you must eventually break the mirror and replace the failed hard disk.

Disk mirroring is fairly expensive, as fault tolerance methods go, because twice the normal amount of disk space is required. However, you get a high level of fault tolerance for your money. Disk mirroring is used in situations where the integrity of data is more important than minimizing costs. For example, a financial institution might decide that disk mirroring is cost-effective for their company because the extra safety provided by disk mirroring outweighs the cost of additional disk space.

Disk mirroring does not provide fault tolerance in the event of multiple disk failure, and it does not guarantee continued operations if a server goes down. Disk mirroring is also known as RAID level 1. (RAID stands for *Redundant Array of Inexpensive Disks.*)

Figure 2-1 shows the Disk Administrator main dialog box. Notice that there are two drives of the same size with the same drive letter, located on different hard disks. The mirrored partitions are highlighted in the color that corresponds to the mirror set box at the bottom of the dialog box.

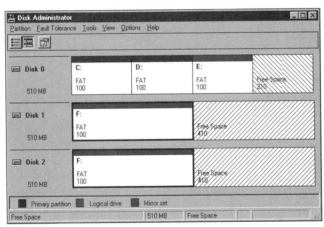

Figure 2-1 *Mirrored set*

A fault tolerance boot disk should be used in case the original disk in the mirror set (the disk that is mirrored) fails.

Creating a Fault Tolerance Boot Disk

A *fault tolerance boot disk* is a floppy disk that enables you to boot your computer in the event that one of the disks in your computer's mirror set fails. The fault tolerance boot disk should be created *before* the disk failure occurs.

If the original disk in a mirror set fails, and if that disk contains the original boot partition, you will not be able to reboot your computer because the Boot.ini file will be pointing at the failed hard disk and partition.

When this happens, you need to use a fault tolerance boot disk that points at the mirrored disk and partition that are still functional to boot your computer.

Using a Windows NT formatted floppy disk, copy the ntldr, Ntdetect.com, and Boot.ini files to the floppy disk. Then edit the Boot.ini file on the floppy disk (not the Boot.ini file on your hard drive) to point at the mirrored disk and partition that still function, instead of at the disk and partition that failed.

The Boot.ini file is a read-only file in the root of the active partition on the first hard disk in the computer. To edit the Boot.ini file, you can use any text editor, such as Notepad. To understand the structure and syntax of the Boot.ini file, Listing 2-1 shows a sample file.

Listing 2-1 *Sample* Boot.ini *file*

```
[boot loader]
timeout=30
default=multi(0)disk(0)rdisk(1)partition(1)\WINNT
[operating systems]
multi(0)disk(0)rdisk(1)partition(1)\WINNT="Windows NT
     Server Version 4.00"
multi(0)disk(0)rdisk(1)partition(1)\WINNT="Windows NT
     Server Version 4.00 [VGA mode]" /basevideo /sos
C:\="Microsoft Windows"
```

The `Boot.ini` file is a big-time target for the exam! You should expect a few questions about how to configure the `boot.ini` target ordinals. Also, you need to know how to make changes to the file and where it is located.

The first section, [`boot loader`], contains two entries. The first entry, `timeout`, determines how long, in seconds, the boot loader screen (or boot menu) is displayed when the computer boots. The default timeout is thirty seconds. The second entry, `default`, specifies which operating system loads if no selection is made within the timeout period.

The second section of the `Boot.ini` file, [`operating systems`], first lists entries consisting of ARC (*Advanced RISC Computing*) pathnames to various operating systems. Only Windows NT uses ARC pathnames in the `Boot.ini` file to indicate which partition, physical disk, and folder contains the files used to start the operating system. Next, the drive letter and path to any other operating systems are listed. The operating system named at the end of each operating systems entry, after the = sign (whether it is an ARC pathname entry or not), is displayed in the boot loader screen.

There are two types of ARC pathname entries: *multi* and *scsi*. The terms multi and SCSI refer to the type of hard disk that is listed in the ARC pathname.

SCSI disks require a device driver to be loaded before the operating system can access the disk. The Windows NT installation program copies the device driver for a SCSI adapter to the root of the system partition, and renames the file as `Ntbootdd.sys`.

Disk Identifiers

All hard disks that can be detected by the computer's BIOS, or by the BIOS on a SCSI adapter, are referred to as *multi*. All hard disks connected to SCSI adapters that do not have their BIOS enabled are referred to as *SCSI*.

The syntax of operating systems entries that begin with multi is as follows:

```
multi(W)disk(X)rdisk(Y)partition(Z)\path
```

where:

- W is the ordinal number of the adapter. It should always be zero.
- X is not used for multi. It is always zero.
- Y is the ordinal for the hard disk on the controller. It is always 0 or 1 for disks connected to the primary controller, including SCSI adapters that have their BIOS enabled. It is 0, 1, 2, or 3 on dual channel EIDE controllers.
- Z is the partition number. The range of Z is usually 1 to 4.

The syntax of operating system entries that begin with scsi is as follows:

```
scsi(W)disk(X)rdisk(Y)partition(Z)\path
```

where:

- W is the ordinal number of the adapter.
- X is the SCSI ID of the disk.
- Y is the logical unit number (LUN) of the disk. It is usually zero.
- Z is the partition number. The range of Z is usually 1 to 4.

Operating systems entries that begin with scsi are typically used in three types of situations:

- When the hard disk containing the system partition is on a SCSI adapter that does *not* have its BIOS enabled
- When the hard disk containing the system partition is on a SCSI adapter *and* has an SCSI ID greater than one
- When the hard disk containing the system partition is on a SCSI adapter *and* there is an IDE or EIDE controller in the system

Questions relating to the operating system syntax in the `boot.ini` file are very likely to appear on the exam. You should expect to be asked about how to resolve boot failures using the `boot.ini` and how to recover from failed disks.

Stripe Sets

In a *stripe set*, which is made up of 2 to 32 hard disks, data is stored, a block at a time, evenly and sequentially among all of the disks in the set. Stripe sets are sometimes referred to as disk striping. *Disk striping* alludes to the process in which a file is written, or striped, one block at a time; first to one disk, then to the next disk, and then to the next disk, and so on, until all of the data has been evenly distributed among all of the disks.

 Neither the boot nor the system partition can be in a stripe set. If the boot or system partition were allowed to be on a stripe set, and if one of the disks failed, there would be absolutely no way of recovering from the failure – save for reinstalling Windows NT Server.

A stripe set is referenced using a single drive letter, as if all of its disks were combined into a single drive. A stripe set is created from identical amounts of free space on each of the disks that belong to the set.

Stripe sets provide faster disk access than volume sets or large individual hard disks because the stripe sets store a single file across multiple disks. The various pieces of the file can be read nearly simultaneously from the multiple disks, thus increasing performance. Access speed is the primary advantage and common reason for using a stripe set. The trade-off or downside to using a stripe set is that the potential disk failure rate is increased because there are more possible points of failure when a file is accessed across several disks.

Stripe sets have no additional cost associated with them because they use the same amount of disk space in which that data would normally be stored. However, stripe sets do not provide any fault tolerance. If one partition or disk in a stripe set fails, all data on the stripe set is lost.

A stripe set (or disk striping) is also known as RAID level 0.

Figure 2-2 shows a stripe set. Note that the stripe set uses the drive letter H: on Disks 1, 2, and 3. (The stripe set is not yet formatted, so Disk Administrator lists the file system type as Unknown.)

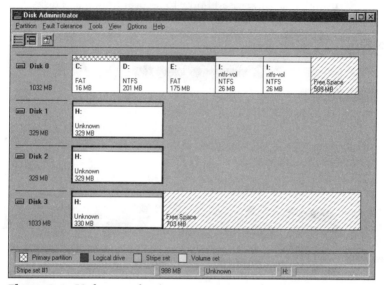

Figure 2-2 *Unformatted stripe set*

Stripe Sets with Parity

A *stripe set with parity* is similar to a stripe set, but it provides a degree of fault tolerance that the stripe set cannot. In a stripe set with parity, data is not only distributed a block at a time, evenly and sequentially among all the disks in the set, but parity information is also written across all of the disks in the set.

A stripe set with parity is made up of 3 to 32 hard disks. Like stripe sets, stripe sets with parity are created from identical amounts of free space on each disk that belongs to the set.

A stripe set with parity provides the same read performance as a stripe set, but its write performance is a little slower.

If a single disk in a stripe set with parity fails, the parity information contained in the other disks is used to regenerate the data from the failed disk. (Recovering from a single disk failure in a stripe set with parity is discussed later in this chapter.) You cannot recover your data in a stripe set with parity if more than one disk fails.

Stripe sets with parity (sometimes called *striping with parity*) are also known as RAID level 5.

Stripe Set Limitations

Neither the boot nor the system partition can be on a stripe set with parity. You will likely encounter a few questions on the Windows NT Server exam asking you about which types of partitions cannot belong to a stripe set.

Volume Sets

A *volume set* is a combination of free space areas over 2 to 32 hard disks that is treated as a single drive. (The free space areas do not need to be of identical size.)

The primary purpose and use of a volume set is to access disk space on more than one hard disk by using a single drive letter. A volume set is sometimes used when a drive becomes full and you want to enlarge its capacity.

Volume Set Limitations

Neither the boot nor the system partition can be on a volume set. Again, be on the lookout for exam questions relating to placing the boot or system partition in a volume or stripe set – it is not allowed.

A volume set is similar to a stripe set. However, a file in a volume set is usually fully contained on a single hard disk, instead of being striped over multiple hard disks.

Volume sets do not involve additional cost, because no additional hard disks are required over the number normally needed to store data.

Volume sets, like stripe sets, do not perform any fault tolerance function. If one disk in a volume set fails, all data on
the volume may be lost, because Windows NT can't access
data unless all of the disks that make up the volume set are
functional.

Volume sets are said to be *created* when areas of free space only (not
existing volumes) are combined into a volume set. Volume sets are said
to be *extended* when an existing NTFS partition is enlarged.

Figure 2-3 shows the status of a volume set. Note that the volume set
uses the drive letter F: over Disks 1, 2, and 3. Drive 0 contains a separate
volume set using drive I:.

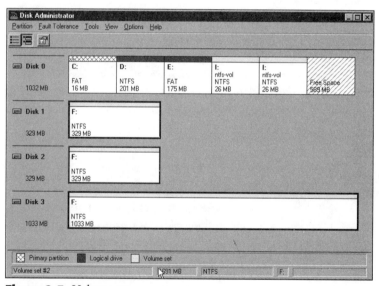

Figure 2-3 *Volume set*

True or False?

1. The Windows NT system partition can be part of a
   stripe set.

2. You can only convert from FAT to NTFS, but not from
   NTFS to FAT.

3. An extended partition can be used for a bootable system drive.

4. A stripe set is created from an equal amount of free space on multiple disks.

5. A volume set is usually striped over multiple physical drives.

Answers: *1. False 2. True 3. False 4. True 5. True*

Emergency Repair Disk

The *Emergency Repair Disk* is a floppy disk used to restore the Windows NT Registry to the configuration that existed when the Emergency Repair Disk was created (or updated).

If you have made any changes to your computer's system configuration since the Emergency Repair Disk was created or last updated, those changes will be lost during the emergency repair process. For this reason, you should update your Emergency Repair Disk *every time* you make a change to your computer's system configuration, including any changes to your disk configuration. Windows NT will prompt you to update your Emergency Repair Disk every time you make a change to your disk configuration in Disk Administrator.

The Emergency Repair Disk is initially created during the installation of Windows NT. To update it at any time after installation (or to create an Emergency Repair disk after installation if one was not created at that time), you must use the `Rdisk.exe` utility.

If you use the Update Repair Info command button in the Repair Disk Utility dialog box, `Rdisk.exe` will save all of your Registry (with the exception of the Security hive and the Security Accounts Manager [SAM] database) to the `<winntroot>\repair` directory. `<winntroot>` is the directory that was specified for the installation of Windows NT, usually `C:\winnt`. After `Rdisk.exe` saves your Registry configuration information, it will ask if you want to create an Emergency Repair Disk.

A second way you can update your Emergency Repair Disk is to use the one command line switch that can be used with `Rdisk.exe`, the `/S` switch. The `S` stands for security. Using the `/S` switch causes the entire

Registry, including the Security hive and the SAM database, to be backed up. When you run Rdisk.exe with the /S switch, Rdisk.exe automatically begins saving your Registry information to the repair directory, and then prompts you to create the Emergency Repair Disk.

It's a good idea to use the Rdisk.exe utility with the /S switch. This will provide you with a backup of the SAM database in addition to the one on your regularly scheduled tape backup.

Have You Mastered?

Now it's time to apply what you've learned in this chapter by testing your mastery of the material. These questions provide you with a means to determine if you are ready to move on to the next chapter or if you need to review the material again.

1. **You are installing Windows NT Server onto a new computer. You want to protect against a disk failure by implementing a disk fault tolerance scheme. You also want to balance the level of fault tolerance with the need for high-speed access to the disk. What fault tolerance method should you use?**

   ☐ A. Stripe set
   ☐ B. Stripe set with parity
   ☐ C. Volume set
   ☐ D. Mirror set

   The correct answer is B. A stripe set with parity offers the highest level of fault tolerance while still offering high-speed access to the hard disk. A mirror set offers the highest level of fault tolerance but provides a comparatively slow access to the hard disk. Neither volume nor stripe sets offer fault tolerance in the event of a disk failure. For more information, see the "Disk Configurations" section.

2. **You are configuring a mirror set on your Windows NT Server computer. You configure NT Server to mirror disk 1 and disk 2. You create a fault tolerant boot disk and edit the `boot.ini` file. You want to change the ARC for the `boot.ini` file on the floppy**

disk so that you can boot the server if disk 1 fails. How should you configure the ARC?

☐ A. `multi(0)disk(1)rdisk(0)partition(1)`
`\WINNT="Windows NT Server Version 4.00"`
☐ B. `multi(0)disk(2)rdisk(0)partition(1)`
`\WINNT="Windows NT Server Version 4.00"`
☐ C. `multi(0)disk(0)rdisk(1)partition(1)`
`\WINNT="Windows NT Server Version 4.00"`
☐ D. `multi(0)disk(0)rdisk(2)partition(1)`
`\WINNT="Windows NT Server Version 4.00"`

The correct answer is D. The ARC syntax describes the rdisk value as the reference to the physical disk for BIOS-detected hard disks. In this case, if disk 1 fails, you could boot the server using the emergency repair disk, which would load the operating system from disk 2 as indicated in the boot.ini on the floppy disk. The ARC *disk* entry is not used for *multi* devices. For more information, see the "Creating a Fault Tolerance Boot Disk" section.

3. **You are installing Windows NT Server on a new computer. Users who access the server will be storing sensitive company documents that need to be protected. What type of file system should be used on the drives containing the sensitive documents to ensure that only authorized users have access to them?**

☐ A. NTFS
☐ B. FAT32
☐ C. FAT
☐ D. HPFS

The correct answer is A. NTFS is the only file system that can set access permissions on the local hard disks and files. NTFS file permissions are in effect even for users who have direct access to the Windows NT Server computer. FAT32 and FAT do not have any means of applying access permissions at the file system level. Windows NT Server does not provide support for HPFS volumes. For more information, see the "File Systems" section.

4. **You are configuring a Windows NT Server 4.0 computer. The computer has a 3GB hard disk configured as a FAT partition and is nearing its capacity. You need to increase the amount of information stored on the hard disk. What can you do to increase the capacity of the computer?**

☐ A. Enable Windows NT compression for the hard disk.
☐ B. Convert the disk to NTFS and enable Windows NT compression for the hard disk.
☐ C. Repartition the drive into three FAT partitions and use a stripe set.
☐ D. Repartition the drive into three NTFS partitions and use a stripe set.

The correct answer is B. Windows NT only supports compression on NTFS volumes. The use of a stripe set would do nothing to increase the amount of usable disk space because you have to have at least two disks to create a stripe set. For more information, see the "File Systems" section.

5. **You are installing Windows NT Server on your computer. You have a 2GB disk installed in your computer and you would like to configure your disk for optimal performance. You want to separate your NT system files from your user files. Which of the following steps should you take to configure your disk?**

☐ A. Create a 500MB C: drive and format it as FAT.
☐ B. Create a 500MB C: drive and format it as NTFS.
☐ C. Place the NT System Files on the C: drive.
☐ D. Create a 1.5GB D: drive and format it as FAT.
☐ E. Create a 1.5GB D: drive and format it as NTFS.
☐ F. Place the NT System Files on the D: drive.

The correct answers are A, C, and E. Because FAT is faster then NTFS when working with volumes 500MB and smaller, you get the best performance by having a 500MB C: drive with your NT system files for faster access. The D: drive performs better as an NTFS partition because of the large size of the partition and additional features found in NTFS. For more information, see the "File Systems" section.

6. You have three hard drives of different capacities in your Windows NT Server computer. You have two partitions on each of the drives. The C: drive partition contains the Windows NT system files. You want to use the remaining space as a single drive letter, rather than having three more drive letters to use. What can you do without wasting any possible storage space?

☐ A. Create a stripe set that spans the remaining partitions.

☐ B. Create a stripe set that spans all of the drive partitions.

☐ C. Create a volume set that spans the remaining partitions.

☐ D. Create a volume set that spans all of the drive partitions.

The correct answer is C. A volume set can span multiple partitions, each of which can be different sizes, whereas a stripe set must use partitions of equal size. Also, the system and boot files cannot be on a volume or stripe set. For more information, see the "Disk Configurations" section.

7. You are configuring the hard disks in your Windows NT Server computer. The computer has three 4GB drives and will be used for graphics-intensive applications that need quick access to files on the hard drives. You also have a 2GB disk you use to store the Windows NT Server boot and system partitions. You want to increase the performance of your disks. What should you do?

☐ A. Configure the 4GB disks as a stripe set.

☐ B. Configure the 4GB disks as a volume set.

☐ C. Configure each of the disks as a standalone NTFS volume.

☐ D. Configure each of the disks as a standalone FAT volume.

The correct answer is A. A stripe set spans an equal space on multiple disks to create a high-performance drive. The resulting stripe set is accessed as a single drive, although the files are distributed throughout the disks. A volume set will not give you the best performance for this scenario. For more information, see the "Disk Configurations" section.

8. **You are configuring the hard disks in your Windows NT Server computer. You want to protect the boot and system files on drive C: in case of a hard disk failure. Which NT fault tolerance method can use on this disk?**

   ☐ A. Stripe set
   ☐ B. Volume set
   ☐ C. Stripe set with parity
   ☐ D. Mirror set

The correct answer is D. Windows NT cannot have the boot or system files as part of a volume or stripe set. A mirror set is the only form of fault tolerance that Windows NT can provide for the boot and system files. This is separate from any hardware fault tolerance, which is automatically supported by Windows NT if it is on the HCL. For more information, see the "Disk Configurations" section.

Practice Your Skills

Here is a chance to apply your practical hands-on experience and material from this chapter. These exercises are designed not only for you to apply the material in the book, but also for you to gain greater experience and exposure to the product. These exercises are a critical part of understanding the product and gaining valuable experience for using the product and passing the certification exam. For each of the following problems, consider the given facts and determine what you think are the possible causes of the problem and what course of action you might take to resolve the problem.

1. File permissions

EXERCISE You are using a Windows NT Server computer. When you attempt to open some files from a directory called Company Documents, you are unable to successfully retrieve the document. When you attempt to open a file anywhere else, you have no problem. What is most likely causing this to happen?

ANALYSIS The problem is mostly because the partition is formatted as NTFS and has permissions set on the Company Documents directory that are preventing you from accessing the files. To resolve the problem, you will need NTFS file access permissions to these files.

2. Recovering from disk failures in a stripe set

EXERCISE You have created a stripe set across three hard disks in your Windows NT computer. What will happen to the files in the stripe set when one of the hard disks fails?

ANALYSIS Because a stripe set spans multiple disks and the data is spread evenly among them, all of the data in the set will be lost.

3. Fault tolerance

EXERCISE A volume set does not offer any fault tolerance if a hard disk in the set fails. What, then, is the primary purpose of a volume set?

ANALYSIS A volume set contains unused fragments of disk space across as many as 32 hard disks. It not only provides access to these previously unused areas, it also provides access to them with a single drive letter, which makes all of the fragmented spaces appear as one large one.

Configuring NT Server

P reparing for the Windows NT Server exam also requires a thorough knowledge of how to configure Windows NT Server to perform common network tasks and optimize performance. In this chapter I take a look at some of the tools provided in the Windows NT Server Control Panel. I also explore configuring network adapters and protocols for optimal performance. The chapter then takes a look at managing the server service through the control panel and setting up the directory replication service. The chapter wraps up with a look at troubleshooting common configuration problems.

Exam Material in This Chapter

Based on Microsoft Objectives

Installation and Configuration

- Configure protocols and protocol bindings. Protocols include:
  - TCP/IP
  - NWLink IPX/SPX Compatible Transport
  - NetBEUI
- Configure network adapters. Considerations include:
  - Changing IRQ, IOBase, and memory addresses
  - Configuring multiple adapters
- Configure Windows NT Server core services. Services include:
  - Directory Replicator
  - License Manager
- Configure peripherals and devices. Peripherals and devices include:
  - Communication devices
  - SCSI devices
  - Tape device drivers
  - UPS devices and UPS service
  - Mouse drivers, display drivers, and keyboard drivers

Troubleshooting

- Choose the appropriate course of action to take to resolve configuration errors.

Based on Author's Experience

- You need to know how to manage system resources using the Windows NT Server Control Panel.

- You need to know the requirements for adding or moving a Windows NT Server into a domain. You also need to know what the restrictions are for moving domain controllers between domains.

- You should be familiar with optimizing Windows NT Server performance using bindings and network access ordering.

- You definitely need to know how to use the *Server* Control Panel and how to configure Directory Replication. You also need to know the requirements and user rights required for the Directory Replication account.

- The exam is likely to ask about setting application performance and configuring virtual memory on a Windows NT Server computer.

Are You Prepared?

Do you have what it takes? Try out these self-assessment questions to see if you have prepared for the material in this chapter or if you should review problem areas.

1. **If you want a system device to start only after another device has started, how should you configure the startup value for the device?**

   - ☐ A. System
   - ☐ B. Automatic
   - ☐ C. Boot
   - ☐ D. Manual
   - ☐ E. Disabled

2. **What can you do to improve the performance of the workstation service?**

   - ☐ A. Optimize the network bindings.
   - ☐ B. Change the startup properties for the workstation service.
   - ☐ C. Install more than one network protocol.

3. **You are configuring replication on your Windows NT Server, which is a PDC. Which global groups should the replicator user account be a member of? (Choose two.)**

   - ☐ A. Backup
   - ☐ B. Power Users
   - ☐ C. Replicator
   - ☐ D. Administrators

Answers:

1. D *Unless the device is specifically written to be dependant on another device, or you use some of the Windows NT Server resource kit utilities, there is no way to configure when a device will be started, or in what order. Because all devices configured as boot, system, and automatic will automatically start when the system is booted, none of these will work in this scenario. For more information, refer to the "Managing Services" section.*

2. A *The network bindings order dictates in which order the computer will attempt to access and locate resources on the network. More than one protocol will actually slow things down as the server will attempt to communicate with each device through each protocol if it has difficulty locating the device. This is covered in the "Networking" section.*

3. A and C

The Directory Replicator service requires that a domain account be created for the service to use and that the account must be a member of the Backup and Replicator groups. This ensures that the service will have sufficient access permissions when connecting and copying files between replication servers. For more information, refer to the "Managing the Server" section.

Control Panel Overview

Windows NT Control Panel is a collection of mini-applications, sometimes called *applets*. These applications, which are automatically installed during installation of Windows NT Server, are used to install and/or configure various options, hardware, protocols, and services.

Each Control Panel application is used for a different task. Some software packages and some installable services include their own Control Panel icon, which is displayed in the Control Panel dialog box after the new application or service is installed.

Managing Peripherals and Devices

This section examines the Control Panel applications that are used to install or configure options, hardware, and hardware drivers.

Devices

The *Devices* application is used to start and stop device drivers, to configure the startup behavior of device drivers, to view the status of a device driver, and to enable or disable a device driver within a hardware profile.

The startup behaviors (or types) available in this application include *boot, system, automatic, manual,* and *disabled.* If you choose boot, system, or automatic, Windows NT starts the device driver automatically every time the computer is booted. If you choose manual, a user (or another device driver) must start the device driver. If you select disabled, the device driver can't be started by a user.

 One of the most common mistakes is not understanding how the device startup properties work. Be sure to thoroughly review this section before proceeding on with the chapter.

Use extreme caution when using the Devices application. Changing the startup type or disabling a device driver, such as Atdisk, can leave your computer in an unbootable state.

Display

The *Display* application is used to configure a computer's desktop background, screen saver options, desktop appearance, Microsoft Plus! options, and display adapter settings. You can also configure the display to use large fonts, large icons, and a high-contrast color scheme to accommodate a visually challenged person. The Display application can also be accessed by right-clicking the desktop and selecting Properties from the menu that appears.

Modems

The *Modems* application is used to install and configure modems and to configure dialing properties.

When you install a modem, you can instruct Windows NT to detect your modem automatically, or you can select your modem manually from a list. If you choose to select your modem manually and your modem does not appear on the list, you can choose from the list of standard modem types. When you troubleshoot modem connection problems, consider configuring Windows NT to record a log file of your modem connection activity (Figure 3-1). This log file will contain a detailed record of all commands sent to and from your modem starting from the time that you enable this feature. Windows NT saves this log file in your Windows NT installation directory as ModemLog_*your modem name*.txt. You can use any text editor to view this file.

Figure 3-1 *Configuring the Modems application to record a log file*

You can use the Modems application to configure dialing properties, including the area code you are calling from, the country you are in, special instructions on how to access an outside line, whether to dial using a calling card, instructions on how to disable call waiting, and to specify tone or pulse dialing. To access the Dialing Properties dialog box, double-click Modems in Control Panel, and then click the Dialing Properties command button in the Modems Properties dialog box.

SCSI Adapters

The *SCSI Adapters* application is used to install, configure, and manage SCSI adapters. SCSI adapter drivers are usually installed and configured during the installation of Windows NT. The SCSI Adapters application, however, is a convenient tool to add additional SCSI adapters after installation, and to view the operational status, configuration, and resources used by your SCSI adapters.

Figure 3-2 shows the two SCSI adapters installed in my desktop computer (a dual-channel IDE controller and an Adaptec SCSI adapter), and the devices connected to each adapter. (Note: Windows NT treats dual-channel IDE controllers as SCSI adapters.) After I click the Properties button in the SCSI Adapters dialog box, the IDE CD-ROM dialog box is displayed, which shows the driver status and other information about the IDE controller.

 Remember that any item that can be used to view configuration information is usually fair game for troubleshooting questions!

Tape Devices

The *Tape Devices* application is used to install drivers for tape backup devices and to view the status of tape backup devices connected to your computer. This application functions much like the PC Card (PCMCIA) and SCSI Adapters applications.

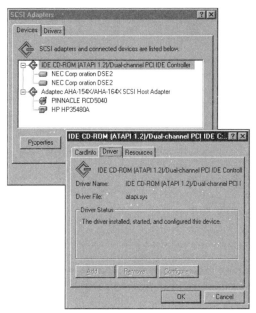

Figure 3-2 *SCSI adapters installed in a computer*

You must install a driver for your tape backup device before you can access it in the Windows NT Backup application.

UPS

The *UPS* application is used to install, configure, and manage an uninterruptible power supply. The Windows NT UPS application is adequate for managing an inexpensive UPS that does not include Windows NT-compatible UPS application software.

Figure 3-3 shows the configuration options available in the Windows NT UPS application. Note that you can configure the UPS interface voltages, expected battery life, the name of an executable program to run thirty seconds before shutdown, and other settings.

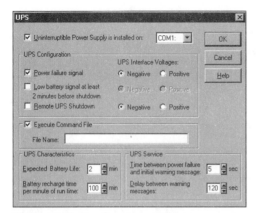

Figure 3-3 *Configuring a UPS*

Most of the UPS devices on the market connect with a server through a serial communications port. As a result, many of the problems with premature UPS shutdowns or failure to shut down have to do with a serial port problem.

Licensing

The *Licensing* application is used to manage licensing on your Windows NT Server computer. Normally, a licensing mode (Per Server or Per Seat) is chosen and the number of client access licenses is configured during the installation of Windows NT Server. However, if you purchase additional client licenses, or decide after installation to change your licensing mode, you can use the Licensing application to accomplish this.

Windows NT Server has two licensing modes: *per server* and *per seat*.

- **Per server:** In the per server licensing mode, you must have one client access license for each concurrent connection to the server. For example, if you have 150 client computers (workstations), but only 100 of them would be logged on to the Windows NT Server computer at any one time, you would need 100 client access licenses. You should enter the number of client access licenses you have purchased for this server in the box next to concurrent connections in the Choose Licensing Mode dialog box.

- **Per seat:** In the per seat licensing mode, you must have one client access license for each client computer that will ever connect to a Windows NT Server computer.

In addition, you can use the Licensing application to replicate licensing information to a centrally located (enterprise) server on your network.

True or False?

1. A device configured as a System device will only start when a user starts the device.

2. Windows NT Server does not have an automatic modem detection process.

3. You should always use the Windows NT UPS software, regardless of the manufacturer's software.

4. The SCSI application allows you to view every device connected to a SCSI adapter in your computer.

5. If you are not sure what a Windows NT Server device is, you should disable it.

Answers: *1. False 2. False 3. False 4. True 5. False*

Networking

The *Network* application is used to control all aspects of networking services on the Windows NT computer, including changing the computer/domain/workgroup name, installing and configuring protocols and services, configuring bindings and network access order, and configuring network adapters.

Changing the Computer/Domain Name of a Domain Controller

Normally you will not change the computer or domain name of a Windows NT Server computer that is configured as a domain controller. However, you may need to change one or both of these names to conform to a naming convention standard that is developed or changed *after* the server is installed. If you want to change a computer or domain name of a domain controller, you can use the Network application to accomplish this.

The Network dialog box has five tabs: Identification, Services, Protocols, Adapters, and Bindings. The Identification tab is on top initially. If you click the Change command button, the Identification Changes dialog box is displayed, as shown in Figure 3-4.

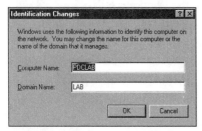

Figure 3-4 *Making identification changes on a Windows NT Server domain controller*

If you change the domain name of one domain controller in a domain, you *must* change the domain name of all other domain controllers, member servers, and Windows NT Workstation computers in that domain to match the new domain name you assign.

Notice that in the Identification Changes dialog box you can change the computer name or change the name of the domain.

Moving Domain Controllers

You *cannot* change a domain controller's domain membership by changing its domain name. For example, if you have two domains on your network named EAST and WEST, you can't move a domain controller from the EAST domain to the WEST domain simply by changing the EAST domain controller's name to WEST. You have to reinstall Windows NT Server to move this domain controller from the EAST domain to the WEST domain. However, if you just want to change the name of the EAST domain to the FAR_EAST domain, you can do this by changing the domain name of all of the domain controllers, member servers, and Windows NT Workstation computers in the EAST domain to FAR_EAST.

Changing the Computer/ Domain/Workgroup Name of a Stand-Alone or Member Server

Occasionally you may want to change the computer, domain, or workgroup name, or change the domain membership status of a stand-alone or member server. For example, you might need to change the computer name of a stand-alone server that is assigned to a new employee to match the new user's name, instead of the name of the previous employee who used that computer.

On a stand-alone or member server you can use the Identification Changes dialog box to change the computer name or change the domain or workgroup the computer belongs to. A Windows NT computer must belong to either a workgroup or a domain.

If you select the Workgroup option button, you can accept the workgroup name that is displayed, or, if no name is displayed, you must type in a workgroup name. A Windows NT computer can be a member of any existing workgroup, or it can be the only computer in a new workgroup.

If you select the Domain option button, you must either accept the domain name that is displayed or type the name of any existing domain on the network. To be a member of a domain, a Windows NT computer must have a computer account in that domain. If a computer account does not exist in the domain for the computer you are configuring, you must check the Create a Computer Account in the Domain check box, and you must supply the administrator's user account name and password (or any other user account that has the right to add computer accounts to the domain). This entire process is called *joining a domain*.

Once a Windows NT computer has joined a domain, a user can log on to this computer interactively (locally) by using a user account in the domain directory database via a process known as *pass-through authentication*.

 Remember that a Windows NT computer **must** have a computer account in the domain it is configured to participate in. You can either create the account using the Server Manager application or create it when joining the domain.

Protocols

Windows NT supports a variety of protocols and services. Table 3-1 identifies each protocol and service that ships with Windows NT Server and briefly describes the functionality of each.

TABLE 3-1 Windows NT Server protocols

Protocol	Description
DLC Protocol	This protocol is a datalink protocol. In an NT environment, DLC is primarily used by Windows NT computers to communicate with Hewlett-Packard printers and IBM mainframe computers.
NetBEUI Protocol	This protocol is designed for small, non-routed networks. It doesn't require any configuration and has minimal overhead. NetBEUI is included with NT 4.0 primarily to provide backward compatibility with earlier networking software that uses NetBEUI as its only protocol.

Protocol	Description
NWLink IPX/SPX Compatible Transport	This protocol is a routable protocol usually associated with NetWare networks. NWLink is fully supported for Windows NT networking.
Point-to-Point Tunneling Protocol	This protocol is used to provide a secure network communications path between computers over the Internet.
Streams Environment	Some applications require Streams for correct network functionality
TCP/IP Protocol	Of the protocols listed here, TCP/IP provides the most robust capabilities for Windows NT networking. It is a fast, routable enterprise protocol. TCP/IP is the protocol used on the Internet. TCP/IP is supported by many other operating systems, including Windows 95, Macintosh, UNIX, MS-DOS, and IBM mainframes. Its only drawback is the extensive configuration required to implement it.

Configuring Bindings and Network Access Order

Bindings and *network access order* specify which protocol or service Windows NT will use first when it attempts to connect to another computer.

Bindings and network access order don't have much effect on the speed of performance of the Server service on Windows NT. (The Server service is normally installed by default.) The Server service's performance is not affected because the Server service replies to the client computer that contacted it by using the same protocol the client computer used. For example, if a client computer uses NetBEUI to contact a server, the server will reply by using NetBEUI, even if TCP/IP is the server's first bound protocol.

Bindings and network access order *can* be very important to the performance of the Workstation service on Windows NT. (The Workstation service is also normally installed by default.) The workstation service's performance can be affected because the workstation service will try each of the protocols installed, in the order they are bound, when attempting to connect to another computer. Figure 3-5 illustrates the network bindings order on a computer. Notice that the WINS Client (TCP/IP) is the first protocol listed for the Workstation service, and that NWLink NetBIOS is listed second.

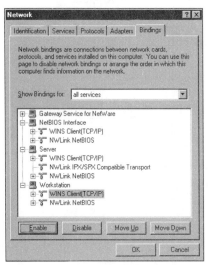

Figure 3-5 *Bindings order on a Windows NT computer*

Network Bindings

If a Windows NT computer is primarily used as a client computer, you should configure the protocols and services that are used most often to be at the top of the bindings and network access order lists.

Occasionally you may want to disable network services on one or more network adapters in your server. For example, if you have a server that has two network adapters, one of which is connected to your local network, and the other connected to the Internet, you might want to disable the Server service on the network adapter that is connected to the Internet so that users on the Internet can't connect network drives to your server. To disable a network binding, start the Network application in Control Panel, select the Bindings tab, highlight the protocol or service on which you want to disable the bindings, and click the Disable command button.

Disabling services on an Internet connection is a very likely scenario. When taking the Windows NT Server exam, be on the lookout for questions on what to do to prevent users from connecting to a Windows NT Server from over the Internet.

When configuring bindings, the primary emphasis is on ordering protocols. When configuring network access order, the primary emphasis is on ordering network service providers, such as Microsoft Windows Network, or NetWare or Compatible Network. Figure 3-6 shows the network access order on a computer. Notice that Microsoft Windows Network is the first provider listed in the Network Providers list, and that NetWare or Compatible Network is listed second.

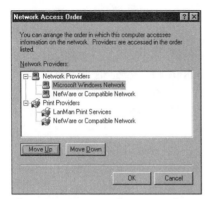

Figure 3-6 *Network access order on a Windows NT computer*

Assume that you use the computer that has the network access order shown in Figure 3-6 primarily to connect to NetWare servers. If this is the case, you should move NetWare or Compatible Network to the top of the Network Providers list. Making this configuration change will improve the performance of the Workstation service on this computer.

Configuring Network Adapters

Occasionally you may need to configure a network adapter. For example, assume that you install an additional card (of any kind) in your computer. You might have to change the settings on your network adapter to resolve an interrupt or an I/O port address conflict between the existing network adapter and the newly installed card.

Configuring a network adapter in Windows NT is usually a two-step process. First, you must manually configure the hardware settings of the network adapter. This can include setting jumpers or switches, or using a manufacturer-supplied configuration program. Second, you must configure the network adapter driver settings used in Windows NT by using the Network application in the Control Panel.

To configure the driver settings for a network adapter, start the Network application in Control Panel. Select the Adapters tab in the Network dialog box. Highlight the adapter you want to configure and click the Properties command button. An adapter setup dialog box appears. Figure 3-7 shows a setup dialog box for a 3Com Etherlink III network adapter. Notice that you can modify the I/O port address, interrupt, and transceiver type.

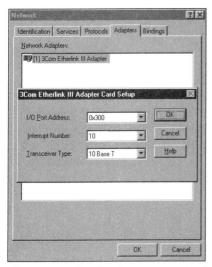

Figure 3-7 *Configuring a network adapter*

 True or False?

1. A Windows NT computer must belong to either a workgroup or a domain.

2. In order for a Windows NT computer to participate in a workgroup, it must have a computer account created for it.

3. You can improve the performance of the server by optimizing the network bindings.

4. You can selectively disable or enable services and protocols on a per adapter basis.

5. You can not improve the performance of the Server service.

Answers: *1. True 2. False 3. True 4. True 5. False*

Managing Services

The *Services* application is used to start and stop services, to configure the startup type of services, to view the status of a service, and to enable or disable a service within a hardware profile.

The startup types available in this application include automatic, manual, and disabled. If you choose automatic, Windows NT starts the service automatically every time the computer is booted. If you choose manual, a user must start the service. If you select disabled, the service can't be started by a user.

Managing the Server

The *Server* application is used to view user sessions (including the resources that users are accessing), disconnect users from the computer, view the status of shared resources, configure directory replication, and configure administrative alerts.

Most of the functions within the Server application are fairly intuitive and straightforward, but directory replication deserves an in-depth discussion.

Directory replication was designed to copy logon scripts from a central location (usually the primary domain controller [PDC]) to all domain controllers, thus enabling all users to execute their own logon scripts no matter which domain controller validates their logon. Directory replication is also used extensively by Microsoft Systems Management Server.

Replication involves copying all subfolders and their files from the source folder on the source server to the destination folder on all Windows NT computers on the network that are configured as replication destinations.

The source replication folder, by default, is `<winntroot>\system32\repl\export`, where `<winntroot>` is the Windows NT installation folder, which by default is `c:\winnt`. During installation, Windows NT creates a folder named `scripts` in the `export` folder. The `scripts` folder is the default source location for logon scripts.

Only subfolders and their files in the `export` folder are replicated. Individual files within the `export` folder are *not* replicated. The `export` folder is shared as the administrative share REPL$. This share is not visible in a network browse list.

The destination replication folder, by default, is <winntroot>\ system32\repl\import. The <winntroot>\system32\repl\import\ scripts folder is shared as NETLOGON. All client computers look to the NETLOGON share on the domain controller that validates their logon for their logon scripts. The NETLOGON share is visible in a network browse list.

Replication is configured between source and destination computers. Because of its central location, the primary domain controller (PDC) is usually configured as the source export server, even though any Windows NT Server computer can be configured as the source export server. It seems obvious that the PDC is configured as the export server and that all backup domain controllers (BDCs) are configured as import servers. What is not so obvious is that the PDC should also be configured to import from its *own* export folder. In other words, the PDC should be configured to replicate to itself. If the PDC is not configured this way, users that are validated by the PDC won't be able to access their logon scripts.

KNOW THIS Configuring the Replicator Service

- The user account for the Directory Replicator service must be a member of the Backup Operators group and the Replicator group.

- The user account must be granted the "Log on as a service" user right, and must be configured so that its password never expires.

- The startup type of the Directory Replicator service should be configured as Automatic.

- Configure the Directory Replicator service to log on using the user account you created for it.

- Configure replication by using the Server application in Control Panel. Figure 3-8 shows a PDC configured for replication. Notice that the PDC (named PDCLAB) is configured to export to all computers in the LAB domain, and that the PDC is configured to import from its own export folder.

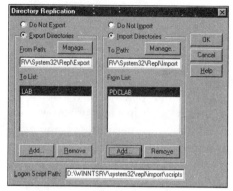

Figure 3-8 *Configuring replication on a PDC*

Managing the System

The *System* application is used to configure foreground application performance, virtual memory, system and user environment variables, startup and shutdown behavior, hardware profiles, and user profiles.

You can use the System application to set the performance boost for the foreground application and to configure your virtual memory paging file(s).

Foreground application performance involves giving a higher priority to the application running in the foreground than to other applications. The purpose of assigning a higher priority is to make the foreground application more responsive to the user.

To configure the foreground application priority, double-click the System icon in the Control Panel, and select the Performance tab. Adjust the slide bar for the amount of performance boost you want.

Virtual memory is implemented in Windows NT by the use of paging files. You should consider both performance and recoverability when configuring virtual memory paging files.

Configuring Paging Files

If you want to configure your system for maximum paging file performance, you should put a small paging file on each physical disk, except on the disk that contains the Windows NT boot partition. This will provide the highest performance for virtual memory.

If you want to configure your system for optimum system recovery, you must put a paging file on the Windows NT boot partition that is at least as large as the amount of RAM in your computer. This paging file is used by Windows NT as a normal paging file, and, additionally, this paging file is required to enable Windows NT to write a memory.dmp file when the operating system crashes.

It's up to you to consider the tradeoffs between performance and recoverability, and then to determine the best configuration for your paging files.

You can configure virtual memory paging files by using the System application. On the Performance tab, click the Change command button in the Virtual Memory section. Then configure paging files on each drive as desired.

Troubleshooting Configuration Problems

Configuration problems are common and usually arise in three major areas: hardware, directory replication, and protocols. Troubleshooting configuration problems can be difficult, because it's easy to overlook a simple configuration issue, and to look instead for some complicated (and usually nonexistent) cause.

Some of the most common hardware configuration problems occur when two cards installed in the same computer are configured to use the same interrupt, I/O port address, or DMA address. To resolve this type of problem, you must reconfigure one of the cards to use a nonconflicting setting.

Another common hardware configuration problem occurs when a card is physically configured in one way (via switches or jumpers), and the software driver for that card is configured with different settings. To resolve this type of problem, you must either change the hardware settings or the software driver settings so that both use the same settings.

Directory replication is fairly straightforward to troubleshoot. Verify that each step necessary to configure replication has been properly completed. Ensure that the replication user account is a member of the Backup Operators and Replicator groups, has the "Log on as a service" user right, and is configured so that its password never expires. Make sure the Directory Replicator service is configured to start automatically, and that it is configured to log on by using the replication user account. Verify the password for the replication user account, and ensure that this password is being used by the Directory Replicator service. Verify that the source and destination servers are configured for replication. Finally, make sure to stop and restart the Directory Replicator service on all replication servers.

Troubleshooting protocols can be a detailed, painstaking task.

TCP/IP, for example, is easy to configure improperly. Several settings must be typed on each computer that uses this protocol, including IP address, subnet mask, and default gateway. The best way to prevent configuration problems in a TCP/IP environment is to use a DHCP server to configure TCP/IP automatically on each computer on the network. If you don't use DHCP, you should manually verify that the settings are correctly entered on each computer that experiences a network communications problem.

NWLink IPX/SPX Compatible Transport also has several configuration settings, and thus is prone to human error during protocol configuration. Verify that all of the settings for this (and every) protocol are correctly entered on each computer that experiences a network communications problem.

Have You Mastered?

Now it's time to apply what you've learned in this chapter by testing your mastery of the material. These questions provide you with a means to determine if you are ready to move on to the next chapter or if you need to review the material again.

1. **You are configuring directory replication on your Windows NT PDC Server. You configure the PDC to export to all of the other Windows NT Servers in the domain. What directory should be used when exporting to other servers?**

   ☐ A. `<winntroot>\system32\repl\import`
   ☐ B. `<winntroot>\system32\repl\export`
   ☐ C. `<winntroot>\import`
   ☐ D. `<winntroot>\export`

   The correct answer is B. Normally the export folder in the `repl` folder is used when exporting to other servers. This folder isn't used by default, but good practice and consistency dictates that this folder should be used. For more information, see the "Managing the Server" section.

2. **You are combining two Windows NT Server domain networks together. You want the PDC and BDC servers from the MKT domain to be BDCs in the CORP domain. What must you do?**

   ☐ A. Use the Network application in Control Panel to change the domain name of the MKT servers.
   ☐ B. Change the computer names and domain groupings of the PDC and BDCs at the same time.

☐ C. Create computer accounts for the servers in the
CORP domain, change the domain configuration,
and reboot the servers.

☐ D. Remove and reinstall Windows NT Server and configure the domain setting as CORP.

The correct answer is D. Windows NT Server computers that are
configured as BDC or PDCs cannot join another domain. You must
reinstall Windows NT Server. Just changing the domain configuration will not allow the servers to join the CORP domain. For more
information, see the "Networking" section.

3. **You are configuring your Windows NT Server 4.0 computer. You
have two network adapters, one connected to your corporate
network and the other connected to the Internet. What can you
do to prevent people from accessing your shared folders over
the Internet?**

☐ A. Change the network access order, so Microsoft
Networks is last.

☐ B. Place the computer in a Workgroup rather than an
NT Domain.

☐ C. Disable the Server service on the network adapter
connected to the Internet.

☐ D. Disable the NetBEUI protocol on the network
adapter connected to the Internet.

The correct answer is C. By disabling the server service, Windows
NT does not broadcast or accept connection requests for shared
folders and shared printers. The network access order has nothing to
do with accepting requests. For more information, see the
"Networking" section.

4. **You have been experiencing problems with your modem when it
is connecting to your Internet Service Provider. What can you do
to view historical information on the modem connections?**

☐ A. Use the Windows NT Event Viewer.

☐ B. Use the Windows NT Performance Monitor.

☐ C. Configure the modem to record a log file.

☐ D. Use the Server icon in Control Panel.

The correct answer is C. The only way to view historical information on the status and performance of modem connections is with a log file. Neither the Event Viewer nor the Performance Monitor can view the performance information of a modem. For more information, see the "Managing Peripherals and Devices" section.

5. **You are working on your Windows NT Server and you notice that someone appears to be accessing sensitive files on the server. You want to disconnect only the user accessing the sensitive files. What should you do?**

☐ A. Change the network access order.

☐ B. Disable the Server service on the network adapter interface.

☐ C. Disable the Workstation service on the network adapter interface.

☐ D. Use the Server icon in Control Panel to view the user connection and disconnect it.

The correct answer is D. Since you only want to disconnect the one user, the Server icon in Control Panel is the best choice, because it enables you to view each user connection and what file they are accessing. Disabling the Server service will disconnect all of the users, not just the unauthorized user. For more information, see the "Managing the Server" section.

6. **You are configuring your Windows NT Server computer. You want to increase the performance of the paging file on your computer. How should you configure the page file settings on the computer?**

☐ A. Configure one large page file on the partition that contains the Windows NT boot files.

☐ B. Configure one page file for each disk in the computer, including the Windows NT boot partition.

☐ C. Configure one page file for each disk in the computer, except the Windows NT boot partition.

☐ D. Configure one large page file on a partition other than the Windows NT boot partition.

The correct answer is C. By spreading the page files over multiple disks, Windows NT can access the files in parallel, rather than waiting for a file to be read. Also, by not placing a page file on the boot partition, Windows NT has faster access to the boot and system files without having to contend with page file access. For more information, see the "Managing the System" section.

7. **You are configuring your Windows NT Server computer that has 128MB of RAM. You want to ensure that this computer is configured for optimum system recovery, so that it can provide a high up-time of resources to the network. How should you configure the page files on this computer?**

☐ A. Configure a 128MB page file on a partition other than the Windows NT boot partition.

☐ B. Configure a 128MB page file on the Windows NT boot partition.

☐ C. Configure a 64MB page file on a partition other than the Windows NT boot partition.

☐ D. Configure a 64MB page file on the Windows NT boot partition.

The correct answer is B. If the paging file is at least as large as the amount of RAM in the computer and is placed on the boot partition, Windows NT can use the paging file to create a memory dump when a critical system error occurs. For more information, see the "Managing the System" section.

8. You are installing Windows NT Server. After the installation you notice that it takes longer to access Windows NT computers than it does to access NetWare servers. You use Windows NT resources more often than NetWare servers. What can you do to improve the performance of accessing Windows NT resources?

- ☐ A. Change the application performance setting to increase Foreground application speed.
- ☐ B. Configure the network bindings.
- ☐ C. Change the Network access order.
- ☐ D. Disable the Server service for the network adapter.

The correct answer is C. By configuring the Network access order, you determine which Network Operating System will be used first for each communications. Rather than waiting for the NetWare network to timeout and then using the Windows NT network, you can configure the Windows NT network to be used first. For more information, see the "Networking" section.

9. Which of the protocols that ship with Windows NT Server is a fast, routable enterprise protocol that is used on the Internet and is supported by many operating systems, including Windows NT, Windows 95, Macintosh, UNIX, MS-DOS, and IBM mainframes?

- ☐ A. NetBEUI
- ☐ B. TCP/IP
- ☐ C. NWLink IPX/SPX Compatible Transport
- ☐ D. DLC

The correct answer is B. The TCP/IP protocol is a scalable, routable protocol that has support or more platforms than any other protocol available. In addition, TCP/IP can be used across many different networks and topologies, including the Internet. For more information, see the "Networking" section.

10. You are the network administrator for a network that contains a single Windows NT Server domain. Your company was recently purchased and it has changed its name to Widgets, Inc. Your manager wants to reflect the name change on the network by naming the Windows NT domain Widgets. What should you do?

☐ A. Remove and reinstall Windows NT Server on all of the domain servers and create the new domain name.

☐ B. Change the PDC domain name to Widgets and then change all the other domain servers and members to the Widgets domain.

☐ C. Install the RPC Configuration service on all of the servers in the domain.

☐ D. Configure the servers to be members of both the old domain and the Widgets domain.

The correct answer is B. Because there is only one Windows NT Server domain, and all of the servers need to be changed to the new domain name, you can simply move all of the servers to the new domain. The important thing to remember is that they are not moving to an existing domain that has been in existence and has established relationships with all the servers. Since all of the servers have existing relationships, they will maintain those through the domain name change as long as the current PDC remains the PDC. For more information, see the "Networking" section.

Practice Your Skills

Here is a chance to apply your practical hands-on experience and material from this chapter. These exercises are designed not only for you to apply the material in the book, but also for you to gain greater experience and exposure to the product. These exercises are a critical part of understanding the product and gaining valuable experience for using the product and passing the certification exam. For each of the following problems, consider the given facts and determine what you think are the possible causes of the problem and what course of action you might take to resolve the problem.

1. Networking

EXERCISE You are changing the network configuration on a Windows NT Server computer. The server has been participating in a Windows NT workgroup and you want the server to join a Windows NT Domain. During the change, you enter your name and password to create a domain account for the server. You are unable to complete the change. What is most likely the problem?

ANALYSIS Most of the time this happens because the username and password you specified does not belong to the Domain Admins group or does not have "Add a Computer to the Domain" access rights. Usually specifying a domain admin account to use for the change will resolve the problem.

2. Network access order

EXERCISE You are troubleshooting communications problems between a Windows NT Server computer and other Windows NT computers on the network. The other computers on the network use various protocols to communicate with each other, such as TCP/IP, NetBEUI, and the NWLink IPX/SPX Compatible Transport. What determines which protocol your Windows NT Server computer will use to respond to network requests from other computers?

ANALYSIS Windows NT uses the Server service for sharing resources on the network. When the Server service receives a request from a computer, the response is sent using the same protocol as the request was received on. So Network access order and bindings have no impact on which protocol will be used when responding. However, these configuration parameters do affect the performance of the Workstation service, which is used to originate requests to other computers.

3. Managing peripherals and devices

EXERCISE You have added an IDE CD-ROM drive to your Windows NT Server computer. After starting Windows NT, you look in Windows Explorer and do not see the CD-ROM drive. What should you do to determine if Windows NT saw the new CD-ROM and the controller it is attached to?

ANALYSIS The SCSI icon in the control panel shows a view of the SCSI and IDE devices that have been detected by Windows NT. If the device is not displayed, either the device is not operative or is not supported by Windows NT. If the default driver set does not support it, you can add the manufacturer's driver files to Windows NT in this dialog box as well.

4. Configuring paging files

EXERCISE Your Windows NT Computer has three hard drives, configured so that the first drive is partitioned as drives C: and D:, and the remaining two drives each have a single partition, defined as drives E: and F:. Windows NT is installed on drive D: and drive C: is used to boot the computer. How should you configure the paging file setting for Windows NT for the best performance?

ANALYSIS To achieve the best performance, avoid placing the paging file on the boot partition, drive D:, and configure a small paging file on the remaining three drive partitions. Placing the paging file on the boot partition can cause excessive drive activity resulting in a system bottleneck and slower performance.

Managing Users and Groups

Y
ou need to understand how to create and manage user accounts to be successful in passing the NT Server exam. This chapter looks at the steps in creating a user account and configuring specific Windows NT user account properties. Are you prepared for exam questions on local and global groups? Do you know what the limitations are when using a local or global group? This chapter looks at built-in groups as well as user profiles, and wraps up with a look at password restrictions and account lockout features.

Exam Material in This Chapter

Based on Microsoft Objectives

Managing Resources

- Manage user and group accounts. Considerations include:
  - Managing Windows NT users
  - Managing Windows NT user rights
  - Managing Windows NT groups
  - Administering account policies
  - Auditing changes to the user account database

Based on Author's Experience

- You definitely need to know how to configure auditing, what rights are required to establish auditing, and how to view the audit log.

- You need to understand that a user must be assigned dialin permission before they are allowed to connect to a Windows NT Remote Access Server.

- Watch for exam questions about renaming user accounts and whether they retain local and network permissions.

- You need to know the limitation of local groups and which types of groups can contain others.

- You should understand the purpose of the six built-in account groups and what their permissions are.

- You should be familiar with user profiles, their purpose, and how they are created.

- You need to know the various user properties available for user accounts and their uses in a networked environment.

- Expect a few questions about configuring and using account password restrictions and lockout features.

Are You Prepared?

Do you have what it takes? Try out these self-assessment questions to see if you have prepared for the material in this chapter or if you should review problem areas.

1. **What Windows NT feature can you use to increase the security level for users who connect to a Windows NT Remote Access Server?**

   - ☐ A. Configure Call Back permissions as Preset To.
   - ☐ B. Configure Call Back permissions as Set By Caller.
   - ☐ C. Place the user accounts in the Everyone group.
   - ☐ D. Define user account profiles.

2. **What happens to the network security permissions for a user account when it is renamed?**

   - ☐ A. All of the network and user account rights are lost.
   - ☐ B. All of the network permissions are lost, but the account rights are maintained.
   - ☐ C. All of the permissions are retained.
   - ☐ D. All of the network permissions are retained, but the account rights are lost.

3. You are assigning permissions to a printer on a Windows NT Server computer, which is a BDC for your Windows NT Server domain. You assign a local group permission to the printer. When assigning user permissions for the printer, which Windows NT group can't you add to this local group?

☐ A. The Everyone group
☐ B. The Domain Admins global group
☐ C. Any global group
☐ D. Any local group

Answers:

1. A *Once a user has authenticated himself, call back security will hang up the connection and call the user back. If the administrator presets the number, you can increase the security because even if a hacker guessed your username and password, it is very difficult to steal your phone number. If the caller is allowed to set a call back number once they are connected, this does not increase the security, but it does centralize long distance phone card charges. For more information, refer to the "User Account Properties" section.*

2. C *When a user account is renamed, all of the permissions and rights assigned to it are maintained. If the account is deleted and re-added, even with the same name, all of the permissions are lost. This is covered in the "Renaming and Deleting User Accounts" section.*

3. D *Windows NT local groups cannot contain other local groups. Local groups can contain global groups from domains that they are servers or members of. For more information, refer to the "Groups" section.*

User Accounts

User accounts are records that contain unique user information, such as user name, password, and any logon restrictions. User accounts enable users to log on to Windows NT computers or domains.

There are two types of user accounts: built-in user accounts, and user accounts that you create. You can configure various user account properties, including group memberships, profile, and the dial-in permission.

Built-in User Accounts

There are two built-in user accounts in Windows NT: *Administrator* and *Guest*. Built-in accounts are created automatically during the installation of Windows NT.

The Administrator account has all of the rights and permissions needed to fully administer a Windows NT computer. The Administrator account can be used to perform numerous tasks, including creating and managing users and groups, managing file and folder permissions, and installing and managing printers and printer security. In addition, members of the Administrators local group have the right to take ownership of any file, folder, or printer. The Administrator account's rights and permissions are due solely to its membership in the Administrators local group.

 Membership in the Administrators local group is a prime target for exam questions. Be on the lookout for questions where someone is unable to perform a task; most likely it will be because he or she is not in the Administrators local group.

The Administrator account, because of its powerful capabilities, can pose a security risk to your network if an unauthorized user is able to guess the password for the account. For this reason, you should consider renaming the Administrator account.

The Guest account is designed to permit limited access to network resources to occasional users that don't have their own user account. For example, a client visiting your office might want to connect a laptop computer to the network to print a document. The client can log on using the Guest account. You can specify which network resources are available to this account by assigning the appropriate file, folder, and printer permissions to the Guest account. The Guest account is disabled by default.

User Account Properties

User accounts have numerous options that can be configured. These options are called *user account properties*. User account properties that you can configure include group memberships, profile, logon scripts, logon hours, workstation logon restrictions, account expiration, and dialin permission. User account properties are configured in the User Properties dialog box in User Manager for Domains.

Figure 4-1 shows the User Properties dialog box for Administrator in User Manager for Domains on a Windows NT Server computer configured as a primary domain controller (PDC). Notice the Groups, Profile, Hours, Logon To, Account, and Dialin command buttons along the bottom of the dialog box.

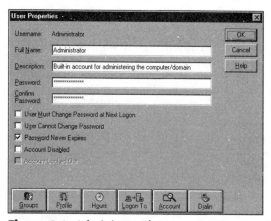

Figure 4-1 *Administrator's user properties on a domain controller*

Groups

The Groups command button in the User Properties dialog box is used to configure which group(s) a user is a member of. Assigning users to

Groups

The Groups command button in the User Properties dialog box is used to configure which group(s) a user is a member of. Assigning users to groups is an efficient way to manage permissions for multiple users.

When you click the Groups command button in the User Properties dialog box, the Group Memberships dialog box appears. Figure 4-2 shows the Group Memberships dialog box for Administrator.

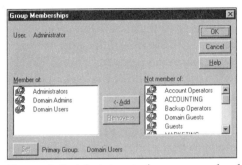

Figure 4-2 *Administrator's group memberships*

Profile

The Profile command button in the User Properties dialog box is used to configure the user's environment. You can configure the user profile path, logon script name, and home directory location.

When you click the Profile command button in the User Properties dialog box, the User Environment Profile dialog box appears. Figure 4-3 shows the User Environment Profile dialog box for Administrator.

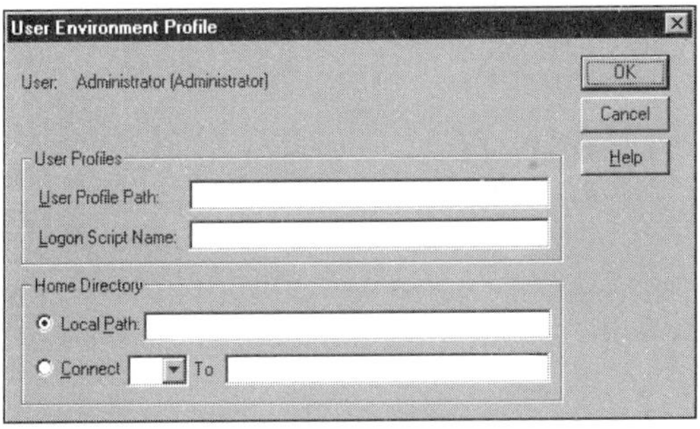

Figure 4-3 *Administrator's environment profile*

The user profile path is used to assign a location for the user's profile. A user's profile contains the user's unique desktop settings, such as screen color, screen saver, desktop icons, fonts, and so on. The default location for a user's profile is the `<winntroot>\Profiles\`%USERNAME% folder. User profile paths must include the complete path to the folder that contains the user's profile, in the format of `\\Server_name\Share_name\Folder\Subfolder`. If no path is entered in the User Profile Path text box, Windows NT uses the default location.

The Logon Script Name text box is an optional configuration that enables you to enter the user's logon script filename, if the user has one. *Logon scripts* are batch files that run on a user's computer during the logon process. Many Windows NT installations don't use logon scripts. If you choose to use logon scripts, enter the user's logon script filename in the Logon Script Name text box. You should place a copy of each user's logon script file in the Netlogon share on every domain controller in the domain, or use directory replication to replicate the logon script file.

The Home Directory section of the User Environment Profile dialog box is used to configure either a local home directory on the user's computer, or a server-based home directory.

A *home directory* (either local or server-based) is a user's default directory for the Save As and File Open dialog boxes in most Windows-based applications. Using server-based home directories enables the network administrator to easily backup user-created data files, because the user-created files are stored by default on the server instead of on individual computers. For security reasons, I recommend you place server-based home directories on an NTFS partition.

If you select the option button next to Local Path, you can enter the user's home directory in the format of `Drive_Letter:\Folder\`*Subfolder*. This assigns a user's home directory to a folder on the user's local computer.

If you want to use a server-based home directory, select the option button next to Connect. Then select a drive letter to use for the user's home directory. The default drive letter is Z:. Next type a complete path in the form of `\\Server_name\Share_name\Folder\Subfolder` in the To text box. If the last folder in the path you type in this box does not yet exist, Windows NT will create it.

The most common way of assigning a server-based home directory is to first create a shared folder named Users on the server, and then to assign the path *Server_name*\Users\%USERNAME% as each user's home directory location. When the %USERNAME% variable is used in a path, Windows NT creates a home directory/folder (that is named using the user's account name) in the Users shared folder. Using this variable can simplify administration when creating a large number of user accounts because you can enter the same path for each new user, and Windows NT creates a unique home directory/folder for each user account.

Hours

The Hours command button in the User Properties dialog box is used to configure the hours that a user is permitted to log on. This command button is only available when managing Windows NT Server computers that are configured as domain controllers.

The logon hours configuration only affects the user's ability to access the domain controller — it does not affect a user's ability to log on to a Windows NT Workstation computer or other non-domain controller.

Restricting a user's logon hours does not disconnect a user from a domain controller when the user's logon hours expire. A logon hours restriction only *prevents* a user from logging on to the domain controller during certain specified hours. If you want to forcibly disconnect users when their logon hours expire, additional steps must be taken.

To forcibly disconnect all users from the domain controller(s) when their logon hours expire, select Policies ⇨ Account in the User Manager dialog box. In the Account Policy dialog box, select the check box next to "Forcibly disconnect remote users from server when logon hours expire."

Logon To

The Logon To command button in the User Properties dialog box is used to configure the names of computers from which a user can log on to the domain. This command button is only available on Windows NT Server computers that are configured as domain controllers.

Account

The Account command button in the User Properties dialog box is used to configure account expiration and user account type. This command button is only available on Windows NT Server computers that are configured as domain controllers.

You might want to configure a user account expiration date for an employee working on a temporary or short-term basis. To set an account expiration, select the option button next to "End of," and then enter the date you want the user's account to expire. The user will not be forcibly disconnected from the domain controller when the account expires, but will not be able to log on after the account expiration date. You can't set an account expiration date on the two built-in user accounts, Administrator and Guest.

There are two options for account type: *global account* and *local account*. By default, all user accounts are configured as global accounts. A global account is designed for regular user accounts in this domain. Users can log on to the domain using a global account. Most Windows NT installations only use global accounts.

A local account is designed to enable users from untrusted domains to access resources on the domain controller(s) in this domain. Users can't log on using a local account.

Dialin

The Dialin command button in the User Properties dialog box is used to configure dialin permission for a user account. The dialin permission allows a user to log on by using a Dial-Up Networking connection.

When you click the Dialin command button in the User Properties dialog box, the Dialin Information dialog box, which is shown in Figure 4-4, appears. Notice that by default a user account is not granted the dialin permission.

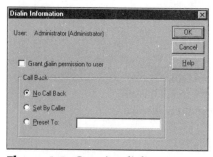

Figure 4-4 *Granting dialin permission to a user account*

The dialin permission should be granted to every user that needs access to the network by using a Dial-Up Networking connection. For example, traveling sales representatives need to access e-mail and other network resources from their laptop computers, and employees whom occasionally work from home may need to be able to dial in to access network resources from their home computers.

To grant a user the dialin permission, select the check box next to Grant dialin permission to user.

 This is a prime target for NT exams, as most environments use Remote Access Server. Look for a scenario where users cannot connect because they do not have dialin permission, or Call Back is set and they are at a different phone number than Call Back was configured for.

There are three options in the Call Back section: No Call Back, Set By Caller, and Preset To. The default setting is No Call Back.

If you select No Call Back, the user can dial in to the server, but the user can't request that the server break the connection and call the user back. Selecting No Call Back ensures that the user dialing in — not the server — is billed for any long distance telephone charges.

If you select Set By Caller, the server prompts the user for a telephone number. The server breaks the connection and calls the user back using this number, and thus the server incurs the bulk of any long distance telephone charges.

If you select Preset To, you must enter a telephone number that the server will always use to call back this user when the user dials in. This setting reduces the risk of unauthorized access to network resources, because the server always calls a preset telephone number, such as a user's home telephone number. An unauthorized user might be able to dial in and guess a password, but will not be able to direct the server to call back at any other number than the number specified in Preset To, and thus will not be able to connect to the network.

 True or False?

1. Any user account can belong to the Administrators local group.
2. Users cannot specify a call back number when connecting to a Windows NT RAS server.

3. A home directory can only exist on a Windows NT Workstation computer.

4. The Guest account is enabled by default.

5. The Administrator and Guest accounts cannot be deleted.

Answers: *1. True 2. False 3. False 4. False 5. True*

Renaming and Deleting User Accounts

Occasionally you may want to rename or delete a user account. Renaming a user account retains all of the account properties, including group memberships, permissions, and rights for the new user of the account. You might want to rename a user account when a new staff member replaces an employee who has left the company.

Deleting a user account is just what it sounds like — the user account is permanently removed, and all of its group memberships, permissions, and rights are lost. Normally you only delete a user account when you never plan to use the account again.

 ## Deleting User Accounts

When you rename a user account, it retains its security ID used throughout the network. That means anything that the user had access to before, he or she still has access to after the renaming process. When you delete a user, the security ID is never reused, even for a new account with the same name. Once you delete a user account, all of the permissions required for the account must be reapplied. The two built-in accounts, Administrator and Guest, can't be deleted, although they can be renamed.

Groups

The remainder of this chapter is dedicated to groups. Using groups is a convenient and efficient way to assign rights and permissions to multiple users.

Groups are collections of user accounts. There are four types of groups in Windows NT: *local groups, global groups, built-in groups*, and *special groups*.

Local Groups

Local groups are primarily used to control access to resources. In a typical Windows NT configuration, a local group is assigned permissions to a specific resource, such as a shared folder or a shared printer. Individual user accounts and global groups (discussed later in this chapter) are made members of this local group. The result is that all members of the local group now have permissions to the resource. Using local groups simplifies the administration of resources, because permissions can be assigned once, to a local group, instead of separately to each user account.

In Windows NT, all domain controllers (within a single domain) maintain identical copies of the same directory database, while each non-domain controller maintains its own separate directory database. All user accounts and group accounts are stored in the directory database in which they are created. For example, if you create a local group in the LAB domain, it is stored in the LAB domain directory database. If you create a local group on a Windows NT Workstation computer, it is stored in the NT Workstation computer's local directory database.

Local groups can be created on any Windows NT computer. A local group in the directory database on a domain controller can be assigned permissions to resources on any domain controller in the domain. However, a local group in the directory database on a domain controller cannot be assigned permissions to resources on any non-domain controller. (Remember that non-domain controllers include stand-alone servers, member servers, and all Windows NT Workstation computers.) A local group in the directory database on a non-domain controller can be assigned permissions to resources only on that computer.

A local group can contain various user accounts and global groups, depending on whether the local group is located in the directory database on a domain controller, on a non-domain controller that is a member of a domain, or on a non-domain controller that is not a member of a domain.

Local Groups

A local group in the directory database on a domain controller can contain individual user accounts and global groups from the domain directory database, and can also contain user accounts and global groups from the directory database of any trusted domain. A *trusted domain* is a domain whose users can access resources in the domain that "trusts" it.

A local group in the directory database on a non-domain controller that is a member of a domain (such as a member server or a Windows NT Workstation computer that is a member of the domain) can contain individual user accounts from the local directory database, user accounts and global groups from the directory database of the member domain, and user accounts and global groups from the directory database of any trusted domain.

As you prepare for the Windows NT Server exam, remember that local groups cannot contain other local groups. You are likely to encounter at least one exam question on this topic.

Global Groups

Global groups are primarily used to organize users that perform similar tasks or have similar network access requirements. In a typical Windows NT configuration, user accounts are placed in a global group, the global group is made a member of one or more local groups, and each local group is assigned permissions to a resource. The advantage of using global groups is ease of administration — the network administrator can manage large numbers of users by placing them in global groups.

Suppose when the network was first installed, the administrator created user accounts, and placed these user accounts in various global groups depending on the users' job functions. Now, the network administrator wants to assign several users permissions to a shared printer on a member server. The administrator creates a new local group on the member server and assigns the new local group permissions to the shared printer. Then the administrator selects, from the domain directory database, the global groups that contain the user accounts that need access to the shared printer. The administrator makes these global groups members of the new local group on the member server. The result is that all domain user accounts that are members of the selected global groups now have access to the shared printer.

Global Groups

A global group can only be created on a domain controller, and can only contain individual user accounts from the domain directory database that contains the global group. Global groups can't contain local groups, other global groups, or user accounts from other domains.

Comparison of Local and Global Groups

Local and global groups are complex topics that can be confusing. To help simplify the important information about each type of group, Table 4-1 summarizes the basic characteristics of local and global groups. Remember that the table is only a summary — you should refer to the detailed descriptions of local and global groups in the previous sections for complete coverage of these topics.

TABLE 4-1 Comparison of Local and Global Groups

Characteristic	Local Groups	Global Groups
Primary purpose/use	Used to control access to network resources.	Used to organize users that perform similar tasks or have similar network access requirements.
Where created	On any Windows NT computer.	Only on a domain controller.
Can contain	User accounts and global groups. (The specific user accounts and global groups that can be contained in a local group depend on the type of computer on which the Directory Services database that contains the local group in question is located.)	User accounts from the domain directory database that contains the global group.
Can't contain	Other local groups.	Local groups, other global groups, or user accounts from other domains.
Can be assigned permissions to	Resources on any domain controller in the domain, if the local group is created on a domain controller; otherwise, only resources on the local computer.	Not a preferred practice, but can be assigned permissions to a resource on any computer in the domain, or on any computer in any trusting domain.

Built-in Groups

Built-in groups are groups with preset characteristics that are automatically created during the installation of Windows NT. The actual built-in groups created during installation depend on whether the computer is configured as a domain controller or a non-domain controller.

The members of built-in local groups have the rights or permissions to perform certain administrative tasks. You can assign users to the built-in local groups that most closely match the tasks that the users need to perform. If there isn't a built-in local group that has the rights or permissions needed to perform a specific task or access a specific resource, you can create a local group and assign it the necessary rights or permissions to accomplish the task or access the resource.

You can use built-in global groups to organize the user accounts in your domain. As you recall from the previous section, you can also create additional global groups to further organize your domain's user accounts by task or network access requirements.

You can assign permissions to and remove permissions from built-in groups. (An exception is the built-in Administrators group — this group always has full rights and permissions to administer the computer or domain.) You can also assign users to and remove users from built-in groups. Built-in groups can't be renamed or deleted. Table 4-2 lists the various built-in groups on Windows NT Server computers, and gives a brief description of each group's purpose or function.

TABLE 4-2 Built-in Groups on NT Server Computers

Built-in Group Name	Type of Group	Description
Administrators	Local	Has full administrative rights and permissions to administer the domain; initially contains the Domain Admins global group.
Backup Operators	Local	Has permissions to back up and restore files and folders on all domain controllers in the domain.
Guests	Local	Has no initial permissions; initially contains the Domain Guests global group.
Replicator	Local	Used by the Windows NT Directory Replicator service.
Users	Local	Has no initial permissions; initially contains the Domain Users global group.

Continued

TABLE 4-2 *Continued*

Built-in Group Name	Type of Group	Description
Account Operators	Local	Can create, delete, and modify user accounts, local groups, and global groups, with the exception of Administrators and Server Operators groups.
Printer Operators	Local	Can create and manage printers on any domain controller in the domain.
Server Operators	Local	Has permissions to back up and restore files and folders on all domain controllers in the domain; can share folders on any domain controller in the domain.
Domain Admins	Global	No initial permissions; initially contains the built-in Administrator user account.
Domain Users	Global	No initial permissions; initially contains the built-in Administrator user account; when new user accounts are created, they are automatically made members of this group.
Domain Guests	Global	No initial permissions; initially contains the built-in Guest user account.

Special Groups

Special groups are created by Windows NT and are used for specific purposes by the operating system. These groups don't appear in User Manager. Special groups are only visible in Windows NT utilities that assign permissions to network resources, such as a printer's Properties dialog box, and Windows NT Explorer.

You can assign permissions to and remove permissions from special groups. You can't assign users to special groups, and you can't rename or delete these groups. Special groups are sometimes called system groups. There are five special groups: *Everyone, Interactive, Network, System,* and *Creator Owner.*

Any user who accesses a Windows NT computer, either interactively or over-the-network, is considered a member of the Everyone special group. This includes all users accessing the computer using authorized user accounts, as well as unauthorized users who accidentally or intentionally breach your system security. If your computer is connected to the Internet, over-the-network also means over-the-Internet. Everyone means *everyone.* You should consider limiting the permissions assigned to the Everyone group to those that you really want everyone to have.

Any user who physically sits at a computer and logs on locally to a Windows NT computer is a member of the Interactive special group. If you want to assign permissions to a resource that is limited to users who have physical access to a computer, consider assigning these permissions to the Interactive group. You are only a member of the Interactive group during the time that you are logged on locally.

Any user who accesses resources on a Windows NT computer over-the-network is a member of the Network special group. If you want to assign permissions to a resource that is limited to users who access the computer over-the-network, consider assigning these permissions to the Network group. You are only a member of the Network group during the time that you access resources on a computer over-the-network.

The System special group is used by the Windows NT operating system. The System special group is not normally assigned any permissions to network resources.

A user who creates a file, folder, or a print job is considered a member of the Creator Owner special group for that object. The Creator Owner special group is used to assign permissions to creators of these objects. For example, by default the Creator Owner special group is assigned the Manage Documents permission to a printer when it is first created, so that creators of print jobs sent to this printer are able to manage their own print jobs.

Renaming and Deleting Groups

I apologize if you envisioned a time-saving solution when you read the above heading, but unfortunately, the fact of the matter is you can't rename groups. You can delete user-created groups, but you can't delete built-in or special groups. Deleting a group does not delete the user accounts that the group contains.

POP QUIZ True or False?

1. On Windows NT Server computers, all built-in groups are global groups.

2. Any user who accesses a Windows NT computer, either interactively or over-the-network, is considered a member of the Everyone system group.

3. The Server Operators group can create and modify user and group accounts.

4. You cannot assign permissions to or remove permissions from built-in groups.

5. Where possible, it is better to assign permissions to groups rather than users.

Answers: *1. False 2. True 3. True 4. False 5. True*

Account Policy

The Policies menu provides three main configurable options: Account Policy, User Rights, and Auditing. Only members of the Administrators local group have the necessary rights to manage account policy, user rights, and auditing.

The Account Policy dialog box has two main sections: one enables you to configure password restrictions, and another enables you to set the account lockout policy.

Settings in the Account Policy dialog box apply to *all* users in the domain (or to all users on a computer, if it is not a domain controller).

You can't set individual account policies. The Account Policy dialog box is shown in Figure 4-5.

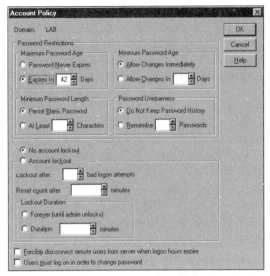

Figure 4-5 *The Account Policy dialog box in User Manager for Domains*

Password Restrictions

The Password Restrictions section of the Account Policy dialog box has four configurable options: Maximum Password Age, Minimum Password Age, Minimum Password Length, and Password Uniqueness.

Maximum Password Age

Maximum Password Age determines the maximum number of days a user may use the same password. Two selections are available in this section: Password Never Expires, or Expires In *xx* Days. The default setting is Expires in 42 Days. When Password Never Expires is selected, users are never required to change their passwords.

When Expires in *xx* Days is selected, Windows NT forces users to change their passwords when the maximum password age setting is exceeded. Normal settings for password expiration are between thirty and ninety days. If users have to change their passwords too frequently, they may be unable to remember their passwords.

KNOW THIS — Expired Passwords

If a user's password expires *and* the check box next to "Users must log on in order to change password" (at the bottom of the dialog box) is selected, the user will *not* be able to change his or her own password — the administrator must change the user's password.

Minimum Password Age

Minimum Password Age determines the minimum number of days a user must keep the same password. Two selections are available in this section: Allow Changes Immediately, or Allow Changes in *xx* Days. The default setting is Allow Changes Immediately.

If Allow Changes Immediately is selected, users can change their passwords as often as they like, without waiting for any time to pass before selecting a new password.

If Allow Changes in *xx* Days is selected, users must use their passwords for at least the number of days specified before Windows NT lets them change their passwords. Normal settings for Minimum Password Age are from one day to the number of days specified as the Maximum Password Age.

If Minimum Password Age is not set, and Password Uniqueness is set at Remember 8 Passwords, then users are often tempted to bypass the Password Uniqueness setting by changing their passwords nine times, in rapid succession, so they can recycle back to their original, favorite, and easily remembered password.

Minimum Password Length

Minimum Password Length specifies the minimum number of characters required in users' passwords. Two selections are possible in this section: Permit Blank Password, or At Least *xx* Characters.

If At Least *xx* Characters is selected, you can specify the minimum number of characters a user's password must contain. Windows NT will not enable users to choose a password with fewer than the required number of characters. Possible settings for password length are from 1 to 14 characters.

Password Uniqueness

Password Uniqueness specifies how many different passwords a user must use before an old password can be reused. Two selections are possible in this section: Do Not Keep Password History, or Remember *xx* Passwords. The default setting is Do Not Keep Password History.

If Do Not Keep Password History is selected, users can cycle back and forth between their two favorite passwords each time they are required to change their passwords.

If Remember *xx* Passwords is selected, users must use at least the number of new passwords specified before they can reuse an old password. Possible settings for Password Uniqueness are between 1 and 24 passwords. Normal settings range between 5 and 12 passwords.

You can multiply the number of passwords specified in Password Uniqueness times the number of days specified in Minimum Password Age to determine the number of days that must pass before a user can reuse an old password.

Account Lockout

The Account lockout section of the Account Policy dialog box specifies how Windows NT treats user accounts after several successive unsuccessful logon attempts have occurred. The default setting is "No account lockout."

When "No account lockout" is selected, user accounts are never locked out. This means no matter how many unsuccessful logon attempts a user makes, the user's account is not locked out.

When Account lockout is selected, users are locked out after the specified number of successive bad logon attempts is reached. Several configuration options exist for Account lockout: Lockout after *xx* bad logon attempts, Reset count after *xx* minutes, and Lockout Duration.

Lockout after *xx* bad logon attempts specifies the number of successive unsuccessful logon attempts that are acceptable before Windows NT will lock out an account. The possible settings are from 1 to 999 bad logon attempts. Normal settings for this configuration are from 3 to 10 bad logon attempts. This counter is reset after each successful logon. Windows NT maintains a separate counter for each user account.

Reset count after *xx* minutes specifies the number of minutes that must pass without a bad logon attempt in order for the bad logon attempts counter to be reset to zero. (Resetting the counter to zero gives users the full number of possible bad logon attempts before account lockout.) The possible settings are from 1 to 99,999 minutes. Normal settings for this configuration are from 30 to 60 minutes.

Lockout duration specifies how long a user account is locked out after the specified number of bad logon attempts occurs. Two possible settings are in this section: Forever (until admin unlocks), or "Duration *xx* minutes."

If Forever is selected *and* the specified number of bad logon attempts occurs, the administrator must unlock the user account in User Manager for Domains before the user can log on.

If "Duration *xx* minutes" is selected, user accounts that are locked out (because the specified number of bad logon attempts have been exceeded) are unlocked automatically by Windows NT after the specified number of minutes elapses. The possible settings are from 1 to 99,999 minutes. Normal settings for this configuration are from 30 to 60 minutes.

Two additional check boxes are in the Account Policy dialog box: "Forcibly disconnect remote users from server when logon hours expire," and "Users must log on in order to change password." By default, both of these check boxes are *not* selected. The "Forcibly disconnect remote users from server when logon hours expire" check box is only available on Windows NT Server computers configured as domain controllers.

If "Forcibly disconnect remote users from server when logon hours expire" is selected, users whose logon hours expire are automatically disconnected from the domain controllers in the domain. Users are *not* disconnected from Windows NT Workstation computers, however, or from member servers in the domain.

If "Users must log on in order to change password" is selected, and a user's password expires, the administrator must change the user's password (because the user cannot log on with an expired password).

A configuration conflict arises when the "Users must log on in order to change password" option is set in Account Policy *and* new users are configured so that User Must Change Password at Next Logon. This combination of settings places users in a catch-22 situation: Users can't log on without changing their passwords, and users can't change their passwords without logging on. The administrator can resolve this problem by changing the users' passwords and clearing the check box next to

User Must Change Password at Next Logon in the users' Properties dialog box in User Manager for Domains.

POP QUIZ

True or False?

1. Windows NT will not allow users to have blank passwords ever.
2. By default, the maximum password age is set to 42 days.
3. Windows NT can only track the last three passwords a user has used.
4. Windows NT will always lock out an account after five unsuccessful logon attempts.
5. Users do not have to be logged in to change their NT account passwords.

Answers: *1. False 2. True 3. False 4. False 5. True*

User Rights

User rights authorize users and groups to perform specific tasks on a Windows NT computer. User rights are not the same as permissions: user rights enable users to *perform tasks*; whereas permissions allow users to *access objects*, such as files, folders, and printers.

Each *user right* authorizes a user or group to perform a specific task. User rights, unlike account policy, can be assigned to individual users and groups.

User rights are listed in the User Rights Policy Dialog box. You can choose to display regular user rights or a combination of regular and advanced user rights in the Right drop-down list box. The default configuration displays only non-advanced user rights.

Table 4-3 lists and describes the most common Windows NT Server user rights. The table also indicates whether each right is an advanced user right.

TABLE 4-3 Common Windows NT Server User Rights

User Right	Advanced User Right?	Description
Access this computer from the network	No	Authorizes a user to access a computer over the network.
Add workstations to domain	No	Authorizes a user to cause workstation computers to join the domain.
Back up files and directories	No	Authorizes a user to back up files and folders. This right supersedes permissions on files and folders.
Bypass traverse checking	Yes	Authorizes a user to change the current folder on the user's computer to a different folder, even if the user or group has no permissions to the newly selected current folder.
Change the system time	No	Authorizes a user to change the time on the Windows NT computer's internal clock.
Force shutdown from a remote system	No	This right is not currently implemented. It is reserved for future use.
Load and unload device drivers	No	Authorizes a user to load and unload device drivers for the Windows NT operating system.
Log on as a service	Yes	Enables a service or application to log on using a specified user account.

User Right	Advanced User Right?	Description
Log on locally	No	Authorizes a user to log on locally (interactively at the computer).
Manage auditing and security log	No	Authorizes a user to view and change the Security Log in Event Viewer. Enables a user to configure auditing of files, folders, and printers. Does *not* enable a user to access the Audit Policy dialog box in User Manager for Domains.
Restore files and directories	No	Authorizes a user to restore files and folders. This right supersedes permissions on files and folders.
Shut down the system	No	Authorizes a user to shut down the Windows NT computer the user is logged on to.
Take ownership of files or other objects	No	Authorizes a user to take ownership of files, folders, and printers.

User Rights

Be sure to be familiar with these rights, as they are likely to be on the exam:

- Add workstations to domain
- Log on as a service
- Log on locally
- Manage auditing and security log

Auditing

When enabled, Windows NT auditing produces a log of specified events and activities that occur on a Windows NT computer. Audited events are written to the Security Log in Event Viewer. Windows NT auditing is divided into two areas: system access and object access. *System access auditing* is configured by using User Manager for Domains. *Object access auditing* is configured in the Properties dialog boxes for files, folders, and printers. By default, auditing is turned off.

The next section explains how to enable system access auditing using the Audit Policy dialog box in User Manager for Domains.

The Audit Policy dialog box is shown in Figure 4-6. The default setting is Do Not Audit. Note the option button next to Audit These Events is selected, and the Success and Failure check boxes for File and Object Access are checked.

 To enable auditing, select the option button next to Audit These Events, *and* select at least one Success or Failure checkbox. On the Server exam you are likely to be asked what the required steps are for enabling auditing.

Figure 4-6 *Enabling auditing*

When a Success check box is selected, Windows NT generates an audit event each time a user successfully performs the audited task.

When a Failure check box is selected, Windows NT generates an audit event each time a user attempts to perform an audited task but fails (usually because of a lack of rights or permissions).

When both success and failure auditing are selected, an audit event is generated each time a user attempts to perform an audited task, whether successfully or unsuccessfully.

Table 4-4 lists and describes the types of audit events that can be selected in the Audit Policy dialog box.

TABLE 4-4 Windows NT Audit Events

Event	Description
Logon and Logoff	A user logs on, logs off, or accesses this Windows NT computer over the network.
File and Object Access	A user accesses a file, folder, or printer configured for auditing.[1]
Use of User Rights	A user exercises an assigned user right, other than the "Log on locally" or "Access this computer from the network" user rights.
User and Group Management	A user account or group is created, changed, or deleted; or, a user account is renamed, disabled, enabled, or its password is changed.
Security Policy Changes	The user rights, audit, or trust relationship policies are modified or changed.
Restart, Shutdown, and System	A user restarts or shuts down the computer, or a system security or Security Log event occurs.
Process Tracking	An event, such as program activation, some forms of handle duplication, indirect object accesses, or process exit occurs. This event is not often selected for audit by administrators.

[1] To audit file, folder, or print events, you must enable file and object access auditing in addition to file, folder, or printer auditing (which is set in Windows NT Explorer or in a printer's Properties dialog box).

Have You Mastered?

Now it's time to apply what you've learned in this chapter by testing your mastery of the material. These questions provide you with a means to determine if you are ready to move on to the next chapter or if you need to review the material again.

1. **You are installing Windows NT Server onto a computer. The first time you try to log on to the system, you use the Guest user account, but you are denied logon access. What is the most likely problem?**

   ☐ A. The Guest account is disabled.
   ☐ B. The Guest account has a user profile configured that cannot be located.
   ☐ C. The computer belongs to a domain, and the local Guest account is not allowed to log on to the computer.
   ☐ D. The Guest account has a home directory configured that cannot be located.

   The correct answer is A. When Windows NT Server is installed, the Guest account is disabled by default. This is to prevent unauthorized access to local and network resources without your consent. If the account had a user profile configured that could not be located, the user could still log on, unless it was a mandatory profile. If the home directory cannot be located, a user account will be allowed to log on as well. For more information, see the "User Accounts" section.

4 : MANAGING USERS AND GROUPS

2. What Windows NT feature can you use to centralize billing for long distance charges for connections made to a Windows NT Remote Access Server?

- ☐ A. Configure the user accounts for Call Back security set as Set By Caller.
- ☐ B. Configure the user accounts for Call Back security set as Preset To.
- ☐ C. Assign the user accounts a mandatory profile.
- ☐ D. Add the user accounts to the Users group.

The correct answer is A. If a user account is configured for Call Back security, the RAS server will hang up the connection and call the user back. If Call Back is configured as Preset To, the user must be at a predefined phone number, or the call back routine will not work. So, by setting Call Back security as Set By Caller, the remote user can input the number for the server to be called back. This allows the central location to incur the bulk of the long distance charges. For more information, see the "User Account Properties" section.

3. You are the network administrator for a network that contains a Windows NT Server domain. You are working with John in the accounting department on a company project. When you try to add the Power Users group from John's Windows NT Workstation computer to the Administrators group on the PDC, you are unable to see John's group. What is the most likely problem?

- ☐ A. You are not a member of John's Administrators group.
- ☐ B. John is not a member of the domain admins group.
- ☐ C. A local group cannot contain local groups from another computer.
- ☐ D. John's Power Users group is a global group.

The correct answer is **C**. Because local groups are contained in the security database of a local computer, they are not accessible by other computers. The only way that the members of John's local group could be members of the local Power Users group on the PDC is to create a global group that contains the members of John's group. For more information, see the "Groups" section.

4. What system group allows users to manage their own print jobs and use the documents that they create?

> ☐ A. The Interactive system group
> ☐ B. The Everyone system group
> ☐ C. The Creator Owner system group
> ☐ D. The System system group

The correct answer is **C**. Whenever a user creates an object, such as a print job or document, the user is automatically made a member of the document's Creator Owner special group. This allows users to manage their print jobs, including deleting and pausing the request. The Interactive system group contains users who are actively logged on to a computer. For more information, see the "Groups" section.

5. You have hired a consultant to work on an important company project. You want to ensure that the consultant is accessing the network during business hours only. Your network contains a Windows NT Server domain. What can you do?

> ☐ A. Configure the consultant's account with logon hours restrictions.
> ☐ B. Configure the consultant's account with an expiration setting.
> ☐ C. Configure the consultant's account to be a member of the *Interactive* special group.
> ☐ D. Configure the consultant's account to be a member of a group that has logon hours restrictions.

The correct answer is A. If you assign the consultant's account with logon hours restrictions, she will be prevented from logging into the domain after the times specified. This does not prevent her from logging into a local workstation or disconnect her if she is already logged onto the network. An expiration setting would only disable the account after a specified date, which can be used to prevent the consultant from accessing the network after her contract is finished. For more information, see the "User Account Properties" section.

6. **A Windows NT Server local group can contain which of the following user and group types?**

    ☐ A. Local groups on other Windows NT computers
    ☐ B. Global groups from the computer's domain
    ☐ C. Local groups from the computer's security database
    ☐ D. User accounts from other Windows NT computers

The correct answers are B and D. Local groups cannot contain any other local group, including groups defined on the computer itself. For more information, see the "Groups" section.

7. **You want to create a location on the network that allows users to store their personal files. You want the users to have access to this location wherever they are on the network, and regardless of which computer they use. What should you do?**

    ☐ A. Configure each user account with a home directory.
    ☐ B. Configure each user account with a mandatory profile.
    ☐ C. Create a user profile for each user and add them to the Replicator global group.
    ☐ D. Create a mandatory user profile for each user and add them to the Power Users group.

The correct answer is A. A home directory is a special configuration that is used to connect users automatically to a shared folder or local folder, to store their personal files. Each time users log on to a Windows NT computer, they are automatically connected to their home directory folders. For more information, see the "User Account Properties" section.

8. **You are the administrator of a stand-alone Windows NT Server computer. You want to prevent the company's intern users from accessing files on the server during the weekend. What can you do?**

   - ☐ A. Configure the interns' accounts with logon hours restrictions.
   - ☐ B. Configure the interns' accounts to be members of a group that has logon hours restrictions.
   - ☐ C. Configure the interns' accounts with an expiration setting.
   - ☐ D. Nothing; you cannot restrict logon hours for accounts on a stand-alone server.

The correct answer is D. You cannot configure the Account, Hours, or Logon To settings on Windows NT Servers that are not configured as domain controllers. The server would need to be configured as a domain controller before these settings would be available to use. For more information, see the "User Account Properties" section.

9. **You are configuring a stand-alone Windows NT Server computer. You want the server to audit access to a set of accounting files that are used for tax purposes. When you attempt to configure the server to audit the files, the server displays an access denied message. What is most likely the problem?**

   - ☐ A. Your account is not a member of the Server Operators local group.
   - ☐ B. Your account is not a member of the Administrators local group.

- [ ] C. Your account is not a member of the Domain Admins global group.
- [ ] D. Stand-alone servers do not support auditing.

The correct answer is **B.** When configuring user rights, account policies, or auditing, you must be a member of the local Administrators group. The server is stand-alone and does not participate in a domain account database, so the domain admins global group cannot be used, as it is not accessible to the server. If your server was a member server, and your account was in the domain admins group, then you would have access, as the domain admins are members of the local Administrators group. For more information, see the "Groups" section.

10. **You are configuring auditing for your network, which contains a Windows NT Server domain. You want to audit the use of the high-cost color laser printers on the network. You configure the properties for each of these printers to audit their use. What else must you do to enable auditing on your network?**

- [ ] A. Configure the System Log properties in Event Viewer for each server.
- [ ] B. Configure the Security Log properties in Event Viewer for each server.
- [ ] C. Use User Manager for Domains to configure an Audit Policy.
- [ ] D. Use User Manager for Domains to configure the account policies to audit user access.

The correct answer is **C.** Before auditing will occur on a Windows NT Server, the computer (or domain) must be configured to enable auditing through the use of an audit policy. This enables you to configure individual objects and resources with audit properties and centrally control when logging will occur. For more information, see the "Auditing" section.

Practice Your Skills

Here is a chance to apply your practical hands-on experience and material from this chapter. These exercises are designed not only for you to apply the material in the book, but also for you to gain greater experience and exposure to the product. These exercises are a critical part of understanding the product and gaining valuable experience for using the product and passing the certification exam. For each of the following problems, consider the given facts and determine what you think are the possible causes of the problem and what course of action you might take to resolve the problem.

1. Managing user accounts

EXERCISE Every time you connect to your Windows NT Remote Access Server and authenticate yourself, the server hangs up. When you call back, the phone number is busy. What is the most likely problem?

ANALYSIS Most likely your account has Call Back security enabled. Because the server is disconnecting after you authenticate yourself, and the phone is busy when you call back, most likely the server is attempting to reach you at a predefined phone number. Either change the Call Back security option or disable Call Back security.

2. Managing group membership

EXERCISE You have a stand-alone Windows NT Server computer on your network. You want to enable the helpdesk users to manage the system, including adding new users and changing passwords. You do not want to enables the helpdesk to change the system's Administrator account or its password. What should you do?

ANALYSIS The Server Operator group enables members to add new accounts and share files and printers, but does not permit them to make changes to the Administrator account or the local Administrators group. This is a lot easier than trying to assign each user the specific user rights they would need to accomplish the tasks required.

3. Managing Groups

EXERCISE Your Windows NT Server computer is a BDC for a Windows NT domain. What must you do so that you can add members of a local group on another computer to one of your local groups?

ANALYSIS Local groups can only be used on the same computer that contains the security database where that local group is defined. As a result, you must create a global group, place the members you want to add in that group, and then add the global group as a member of your local group.

User Profiles and System Policy

One of the areas that you will be tested on in the Windows NT Server exam is managing user properties and configuring a work space for users. To accomplish these tasks, Windows NT Server uses profiles and policies to configure and enforce Windows NT settings for users. To prepare you for the exam, I begin with a look at user profiles and how they are created. The chapter also discusses roaming and mandatory profiles and how they are best used in a network environment. The chapter then moves on to managing system policies and how priority levels can be used to determine how conflicting policy settings are applied to users.

Exam Material in This Chapter

Based on Microsoft Objectives

Managing Resources

- Create and manage policies and profiles for various situations. Policies and profiles include:
  - Local user profiles
  - Roaming user profiles
  - System policies

Based on Author's Experience

- You need to know the difference between roaming and mandatory profiles and where each is best used in a network environment. You should understand the restrictions when using each one.

- You definitely need to know how to create a system policy and where to place it on the network to have clients automatically pick it up during authentication. You should also be familiar with assigning and using priority levels in a policy file.

- You need to understand the order in which user and group policies are applied and when group policies are not applied at all.

- You need to know how the Default User and All User profiles are handled when users have individual and group policies assigned to them.

Are You Prepared?

Do you have what it takes? Try out these self-assessment questions to see if you have prepared for the material in this chapter or if you should review problem areas.

1. **Which of the following account files can prevent a user from logging on to a Windows NT Server computer if the file cannot be located?**

   ☐ A. Logon script
   ☐ B. User policy
   ☐ C. Default computer policy
   ☐ D. Mandatory profile

2. **You have created a system policy that you want all users in your domain to receive when they log onto the network. Where should you place the system policy file?**

   ☐ A. In the `netlogon` share on every domain controller
   ☐ B. In the home directory for each user
   ☐ C. In the `Repl` folder on each domain controller
   ☐ D. In the `<winnt>\system32` folder on each domain controller

3. **What can you do if you want to ensure that users will always receive the same desktop settings, no matter which computer they are using?**

   ☐ A. Configure a home directory.
   ☐ B. Configure a roaming profile.
   ☐ C. Add the user account to the replicator group.
   ☐ D. Add the user account to the Power Users group.

Answers:

1. D *If a user account is configured to use a mandatory profile and it cannot be located, Windows NT will prevent the user from being authenticated and logged on. This is to prevent users from receiving the default user or all users profiles that could enable system access they should not otherwise have. For more information, refer to the "Managing User Profiles" section.*

2. A *The system policy file should be placed in the* netlogon *share on every domain controller that will be authenticating users. This is covered in the "Managing System Policy" section.*

3. B *Roaming profiles allows users to retain their desktop and application settings when using different computers. For more information, refer to the "Roaming User Profiles" section.*

Managing User Profiles

In Windows NT, a *user profile* is a collection of settings and options that specify a user's desktop and all other user-definable settings for a user's work environment. Both users and administrators can benefit from user profiles.

Benefits to users include:

- When a user logs on, the same desktop is displayed as when the user last logged off.

- When there's more than one user on the same computer, a customized desktop is displayed for each at logon.

- Roaming user profiles can be saved on a Windows NT Server computer, and thereby apply to a user no matter which Windows NT computer on the network the user logs on at.

Benefits to administrators include:

- Administrators can develop and assign user profiles that are customized, so each user has a desktop and work environment that complies with established company standards, and can assign user profiles that are suitable for the tasks that each particular user needs to perform.

- If desired or necessary, administrators can forcibly prevent certain users from changing any of their desktop or work environment settings by assigning them mandatory user profiles.

- User profiles make it possible for administrators to assign common program items and shortcuts to all users by customizing the All Users profile folder.

The following sections discuss the contents of a user profile, how a user profile is created, customizing the Default User and the All Users profile folders, and roaming and mandatory user profiles.

Contents of a User Profile

Various settings are saved in a user profile. The contents of a user profile include:

- All user-specific settings for Windows NT Explorer, Notepad, Paint, HyperTerminal, Clock, Calculator, and other built-in Windows NT applications
- User-specific desktop settings, including: screen saver, background color, background pattern, wallpaper, and other display settings
- User-specific settings for applications written to run on Windows NT
- User-specific settings for network drive and printer connections
- User-specific settings for the Start menu, including program groups, applications, and recently accessed documents

A user profile is normally stored in a subfolder of the <winntroot>\Profiles folder on the local computer. Each user's profile is stored in a separate folder named after the user's account. For example, the Administrator's user profile is stored in the <winntroot>\Profiles\Administrator folder.

How a User Profile Is Created

Windows NT automatically creates a user profile for every new user the first time the new user logs on. After that point, an Administrator can create and assign a user profile to an existing user (a user who has previously logged on and been assigned a user profile by Windows NT) by copying an existing user profile over that user's profile.

Roaming Profiles

There is a way to assign a user profile to a new user in Windows NT—the Administrator can assign a new user a *server-based* (roaming) user profile. Roaming user profiles make it possible for the Administrator to copy and assign a user profile to a new user and have that profile be effective the first time the new user logs on.

As mentioned earlier in this section, when a new user logs on for the first time, Windows NT creates a new user profile folder for the user. Windows NT accomplishes this by copying the entire contents of the `Default User` profile folder to a new folder named after the user's account. When Windows NT creates a new user's profile, the new user's initial profile is an exact copy of the `Default User` profile folder.

The `Default User` profile folder can also be customized by an Administrator, as described in the next section.

Customizing the Default User Profile Folder

Administrators can customize the `Default User` profile folder so new users, at first logon, have the appropriate desktop and work environment settings. For example, you might want to place a shortcut to a network application on the desktop of all new users. Or, you might want to add a shortcut that will appear in the Start menu for all new users.

You can customize the local `Default User` profile folder on a Windows NT computer, or you can create a domain-wide `Default User` profile folder for all Windows NT Workstation computers and member servers in a domain. Changes to the local `Default User` profile folder on a Windows NT computer affect only new users that log on to that computer. The domain-wide `Default User` profile folder affects all new domain users when they log on to Windows NT Workstation computers (that are domain members) and member servers.

To customize the local `Default User` profile folder on a Windows NT computer, an Administrator can either copy an existing user profile to the local `Default User` profile folder, or create shortcuts in the `Default User` profile subfolders (see Figure 5-1).

Figure 5-1 *The Default User profile folder*

To create a domain-wide `Default User` profile folder for all Windows NT Workstation computers and member servers in a domain, customize and copy an existing user profile to a subfolder named `Default User` in the `<winntroot>\System32\Repl\Import\Scripts` folder on the primary domain controller (PDC).

If you have configured directory replication on your PDC, copy the existing user profile to the `<winntroot>\ System32\Repl\Export\Scripts\Default User` folder on the PDC, *not* to the `<winntroot>\ System32\Repl \Import\Scripts\Default User` folder. If you copy it to the `Import\Scripts` folder and directory replication is configured, the Directory Replicator service will delete any files or folders in the `Import\Scripts` folder that do not exist in the `Export\Scripts` folder.

When choosing the user that is permitted to use this copied profile in the Choose User dialog box, select the Everyone group, and ensure that the Everyone group is listed in the Permitted To Use section of the Copy To dialog box.

After a `Default User` profile folder is created on the `Netlogon` share on the PDC, the domain-wide `Default User` profile folder is available to all Windows NT computers that are members of the domain. When a Windows NT Workstation computer (that is a member of the domain) or a member server is rebooted, it copies the domain-wide `Default User` profile folder from the PDC to a subfolder named `Default User (Network)` in its local `Profiles` folder. This member computer now has two `Default User` profile folders: one named `Default User` and one named `Default User (Network)`.

The domain-wide `Default User` profile folder is *not* copied to the local `Profiles` folder on any domain controller in the domain. It is only copied to the local `Profiles` folder on *non*-domain controllers that are members of the domain.

Figure 5-2 shows the `Profiles` folder and its subfolders on a Windows NT Workstation computer that is a member of the LAB domain. Notice the `Default User` and `Default User (Network)` folders.

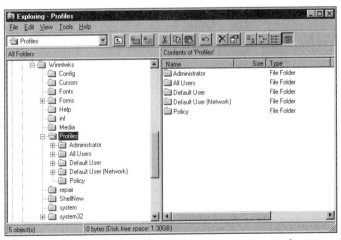

Figure 5-2 *Two Default User profile folders on a member computer*

When a user logs on to a member computer that has two `Default User` profile folders by using a *local user account*, and that user does not have a profile folder on this local computer, Windows NT creates a new user profile for the user on the local computer by using the `Default User` profile folder.

When a user logs on to a member computer that has two `Default User` profile folders by using a *user account from the domain*, and that user does not have a profile folder on this local computer, Windows NT creates a new user profile for the user on the local computer by using the `Default User (Network)` profile folder.

Customizing the All Users Profile Folder

The `All Users` profile folder is a subfolder of the `Profiles` folder on all Windows NT computers. The `All Users` profile folder contains only two subfolders: `Desktop` and `Start Menu`. Figure 5-3 shows the `All Users` profile folder and its subfolders in Windows NT Explorer.

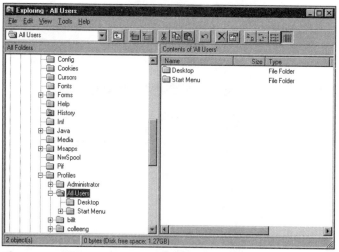

Figure 5-3 *The All Users profile folder*

The purpose of the `All Users` profile folder is to enable an administrator to create shortcuts and install applications that are made available to *all*— not just new — users of a particular Windows NT computer.

Whenever a user logs on to a Windows NT computer, any shortcuts or applications placed in the `Desktop` and `Start Menu` subfolders of the local `All Users` profile folder appear on the user's desktop or Start Menu, as appropriate. Only members of the Administrators group on the local computer can customize the `All Users` profile folder.

Currently, there is no method to create a domain-wide `All Users` profile folder on a server. This means that an Administrator must customize the `All Users` profile folder on each individual Windows NT computer.

To customize the `All Users` profile folder, follow the same steps you would use to customize the `Default User` profile folder, except select the `All Users` profile folder in Windows NT Explorer instead of the `Default User` profile folder.

Roaming User Profiles

Roaming user profiles are user profiles that are stored on a server. Because these profiles are stored on a server instead of a local computer, they are available to users regardless of which Windows NT computer on the network they log on to.

KNOW THIS Benefits of Using a Roaming Profile

The benefit of using roaming user profiles is that users retain their own customized desktop and work environment settings even though they may use several different Windows NT computers.

Roaming user profiles are implemented by first creating a shared folder on a server, and then assigning a server-based user profile path to a user account. You configure the user account by defining the User Environment Profile text box in the account properties. After defining the user account profile properties, the user must log on and log off to create a roaming user profile folder on the server. (When the user logs off, the user's local user profile is saved to the server and becomes the user's roaming user profile.) The roaming user profile is then available to the user from any Windows NT computer to which the user logs on. From this point, every time the user logs off, the user's roaming user profile will be updated with any changes the user has made during the time the user was logged on.

To enable Roaming Profiles, you must choose a shared folder, configure the user account's User Environmental Profile property to point to the shared folder, and then have the user log on and log off.

Both new and existing users can be assigned roaming user profiles. If you assign an existing user a roaming user profile, the next time the user logs on and then logs off, the user's local user profile will be copied, intact, at logoff to the server, and will become the user's roaming user profile.

You can also preconfigure a new or existing user's roaming user profile, so that the next time the user logs on, the properties of the preconfigured server-based roaming user profile are applied to the user. The advantage of using preconfigured roaming user profiles is that the administrator can provide users with all the shortcuts and program items users need to perform their day-to-day tasks.

To preconfigure a user's roaming user profile, assign a server-based profile path to a user account, and then copy an existing user profile (that you have customized with all of the shortcuts and applications you want the user to have) to the user's roaming user profile path.

Mandatory User Profiles

Mandatory user profiles are user profiles that, when assigned to a user, cannot be changed by the user. A user can make changes to desktop and work environment settings during a single logon session, but these changes are *not* saved to the mandatory user profile when the user logs off. Each time the user logs on, the user's desktop and work environment settings revert to those contained in the mandatory user profile.

If you assign a user a mandatory user profile and the profile cannot be accessed or found, the user will be unable to log on to the computer. Avoid using mandatory profiles for administrative accounts for this reason.

In most cases, an administrator permits users to change and customize their own user profiles. There are instances, however, when you might want to use mandatory user profiles:

- When problem users require a significant amount of administrator time
- When an administrator has a large number of users to administer

Occasionally, a problem user modifies his or her profile so that needed shortcuts and applications are deleted, and the administrator must constantly fix the user's profile by reinstalling the necessary items. After repairing the user's profile, the administrator might choose to assign the user a mandatory user profile. To make an individual user's profile (either local or roaming) a mandatory user profile, rename the user's Ntuser.dat file in the user's profile folder as Ntuser.man. The mandatory profile becomes effective the next time the user logs on.

Windows NT system policies provide more control over users' environment settings than mandatory user profiles, but you need to understand the benefits of each when you are preparing for the Server exam.

Sometimes an administrator needs to create a standardized desktop and work environment for a large number of users with similar job tasks. To accomplish this, the administrator can assign a single, customized mandatory profile to multiple user accounts.

True or False?

1. Users are prevented from logging on to a computer if their mandatory profiles cannot be located.

2. By default, all user profiles are configured as roaming profiles.

3. A user profile contains network drive and printer connection settings.

4. An administrator must create a user profile before users can log on for the first time.

5. When using roaming profiles, you can create an `All Users` profile on a domain PDC.

Answers: *1. True 2. False 3. True 4. False 5. False*

Managing System Policy

The Windows NT *system policy* file is a collection of user, group, and computer policies. System policy restricts the user's ability to perform certain tasks on any Windows NT computer on the network to which the user logs on. System policy can also be used to enforce certain mandatory display settings, such as wallpaper and color scheme. You can also create a system policy file that applies to users of Windows 95 or Windows 98 computers.

System policy, like a mandatory profile, enables an administrator to control the work environment of users on the network. System policy, however, gives the administrator many more configurable options than a mandatory profile. Administrators can use system policy to provide a consistent environment for a large number of users, or to enforce a specified work environment for problem users who demand a significant amount of administrator time.

In addition to enabling the administrator to limit the changes users can make to their work environments, system policy can be used as a security measure to limit access to parts of the network; to restrict the use of specific tools, such as the Registry Editor; and to remove the Run command option from the Start menu.

System policy is managed and configured by using the System Policy Editor. You can use System Policy Editor to create Windows NT, Windows 95, and Windows 98 system policy files. The administrator must create a system policy file — a system policy file is not installed by default.

A system policy file should be saved in the `Netlogon` share on each domain controller. When a user logs on to the domain, Windows NT or Windows 95 retrieves the system policy file from the `Netlogon` share on the domain controller that authenticates the user's logon.

Because system policy is made up of user, group, and computer policies, it can be applied to all users and computers; or it can be applied to individual users, groups, and computers.

User Policy

A *user policy* is a collection of settings that restrict a user's program and network options or enforce a specified configuration of the user's work environment. A user policy is created by an Administrator — it does not exist by default.

There are two types of user policies: an individual user policy and the Default User policy.

- An *individual user policy* applies to a single, specific user. Normally, an individual user policy is created only when a user requires a unique policy that differs from any existing Default User or group policy.

- The *Default User policy*, contrary to what its name implies, does not exist by default. Rather, it is created when a system policy file is initially created. When the Default User policy is initially created, it doesn't contain any settings that restrict users. The Administrator must configure any desired user restrictions in the Default User policy.

KNOW THIS Default User Policy

The Default User policy applies to a user only if the user does not have an individual user policy. For the Server exam, you should know the order and process in which policies are applied to a user.

There are a variety of settings that you can configure in a user policy. Figure 5-4 shows all of the configurable options for a Windows NT individual user policy. The same list of configurable options is available for the Default User policy. Notice the options available in the Desktop and Shell sections.

When a user logs on, Windows NT (or Windows 95) permanently overwrites the existing settings in the HKEY_CURRENT_USER section of the Registry on the local computer with the settings contained in the user policy.

Group Policy

A *group policy* is a policy that applies to a group of users. Group policies apply to all users that are members of a group (that has a group policy) and that do not have individual user policies. Group policies have the same configurable options as user policies. Like user policies, group policies don't exist by default — group policies must be created.

A group policy should be created when more than one user requires the same settings. It takes far less time to create one group policy than to create multiple individual user policies.

A user often belongs to multiple groups that have group policies. In this situation, the Administrator can configure group policy priorities. Figure 5-5 shows the Group Priority dialog box in System Policy Editor. Notice the Move Up and Move Down command buttons that are used to arrange the group priority order. The group at the top of the Group Order list box has the highest priority.

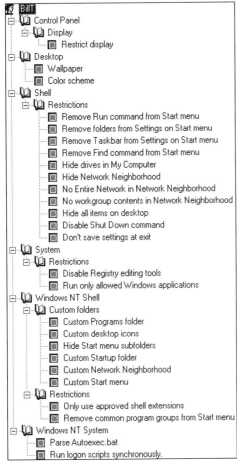

Figure 5-4 *Configurable settings in a Windows NT individual user policy*

Assume that a user named JohnS, a Sales Manager with administrative duties, belongs to three of the groups listed in Figure 5-5: Domain Admins, Managers, and Sales. Also assume that JohnS does *not* have an individual user policy. When JohnS logs on to the domain, the group policy for the Sales group (which has the lowest group priority) is applied first, and then the group policy for the Managers group is applied, and finally the group policy for the Domain Admins group (which has the highest group priority) is applied to JohnS. As each group policy is applied, it overwrites the settings from previously applied group policies. The last group policy applied (the Domain Admins group policy, in this case) takes precedence over the lower priority group policies.

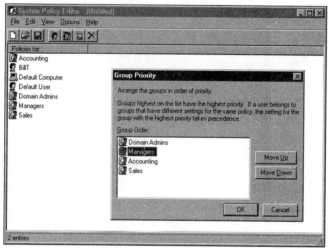

Figure 5-5 *Configuring group priority*

 When a user belongs to multiple groups, each with a separate group policy, group priorities determine which group policy will apply for the user. You definitely need to know that group policies are applied lowest priority first and highest priority last. This enables the highest priority group settings to override any lesser group.

Computer Policy

A *computer policy* is a collection of settings that specifies a local computer's configuration. A computer policy enforces the specified configuration on all users of a particular Windows NT (or Windows 95) computer. A computer policy is created by an Administrator — it does not exist by default.

There are two types of computer policies: an individual computer policy and the Default Computer policy.

- An *individual computer policy* applies to a single, specific computer. Normally, an individual computer policy is created only when a computer requires a unique policy that differs from the Default Computer policy.

- The *Default Computer policy*, like the Default User policy, is created when a system policy file is initially created. The Default Computer policy applies to a computer only if the computer does *not* have an individual computer policy.

There are a variety of settings that you can configure in a computer policy. Figure 5-6 shows the configurable options for a Windows NT individual computer policy. The same list of configurable options is available for the Default Computer policy. Notice the options available in the Windows NT System Logon and File system sections.

When a user logs on, Windows NT (or Windows 95) permanently overwrites the existing settings in the HKEY_LOCAL_MACHINE section of the Registry on the local computer with the settings contained in the computer policy.

POP QUIZ True or False?

1. By default, all Windows NT computers have a computer policy.

2. Group policies are applied only to group members without an individual policy.

3. A Default User profile is applied to all users, regardless of individual policies.

4. A system policy file should be stored in the `<winntdir>\system` folder on domain controllers.

5. Groups with the highest priority setting are applied first.

Answers: *1. False   2. True   3. False   4. False   5. False*

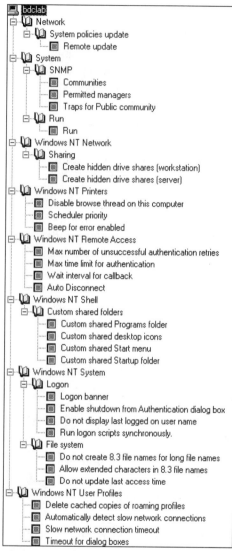

Figure 5-6 *Configurable settings in a Windows NT individual computer policy*

How System Policy Is Applied

A Windows NT system policy is applied to a user or computer in a pre-defined, systematic manner. When a user logs on, the user's roaming or local profile is applied first, and then the system policy is applied. If settings in the system policy conflict with settings in the user profile, the system policy settings take precedence.

Applying System Policy

System policy is applied in the following sequence:

- If a user has an individual user policy, it is applied.
- If a user does *not* have an individual user policy, and the user is a member of a group that has a group policy, the group policy (or policies, if the user is a member of multiple groups that have group policies) is applied.
- If a user does *not* have an individual user policy, the Default User policy is applied. (If a user that does not have an individual user policy has a group policy that conflicts with the Default User policy, the settings in the Default User policy take precedence.)
- If the computer the user logs on to has an individual computer policy, it is applied.
- If the computer the user logs on to does *not* have an individual computer policy, the Default Computer policy is applied.

The end result is that a user has one of the following user/group policy combinations applied: an individual user policy only, a Default User policy only, or a combination of the Default User policy and a group policy (or policies, if the user is a member of multiple groups that have group policies). In addition, the computer to which the user logs on has either an individual computer policy or the Default Computer policy applied.

Have You Mastered?

Now it's time to apply what you've learned in this chapter by testing your mastery of the material. These questions provide you with a means to determine if you are ready to move on to the next chapter or if you need to review the material again.

1. **You want to add an icon to the desktop for all of the users on your Windows NT Workstation computer. All of your users have roaming user profiles assigned to their accounts. Where should you place the icon?**

   ☐ A. In the `<winntroot>\Profiles\All Users\Desktop` folder on each computer

   ☐ B. In the `Profiles\All Users\Desktop` folder on the server containing the roaming profiles

   ☐ C. In the `<winntroot>\Profiles\Default User\Desktop` folder on each computer

   ☐ D. In the `<winntroot>\Profiles\Default User\Desktop` folder on the server containing the roaming profiles

The correct answer is **A.** Because there is no way to define a company-wide roaming All Users profile, you must make the change on each Windows NT computer. The Default User profile is only used when a user logs on to the computer and does not have a local or roaming profile already defined. For more information, see the "Managing User Profiles" section.

2. You have created system policies for your Windows NT Server domain. A few users are having trouble accessing resources on their local Windows NT Workstation computers. You suspect that recent changes you made to the system policies may be causing the problems. You want to determine which policies are being applied and in which order. What can you do?

☐ A. View the priority level of each group policy. The group with the lowest priority is applied first.

☐ B. View the priority level of each group policy. The group with the lowest priority is applied last.

☐ C. The group policies are applied alphabetically, so if needed, change the names to affect the ordering.

☐ D. Only one group policy can be assigned to a single user.

The correct answer is A. Users that belong to more than one group with assigned group policies will have the group with the lowest priority assigned first, so higher priority groups can override any applicable settings. Group policies are applied strictly by priority levels. For more information, see the "Managing System Policy" section.

3. You are logging into a new Windows NT Server computer named ServerA. You do not belong to any special groups and you have never logged into this computer before. ServerA has a computer policy included in the main system policy file. Which profiles and policies will be assigned? (Choose three.)

☐ A. Default computer policy
☐ B. ServerA computer policy
☐ C. Default User profile
☐ D. All Users profile
☐ E. All Users policy

The correct answers are B, C, and D. Because you have not logged onto ServerA before, you will receive the computer's default user profile and the All Users profile. Since ServerA has a computer policy, it will not have the default computer policy applied to it. For more information, see the "Managing User Profiles" section.

4. You have created a network tutorial application that you want
   all new users to run automatically when they log into their
   computers for the first time. However, you do not want them to
   have to run it after the first logon. Where should you place the
   application icon so that it will be started when they log on for
   the first time?

   ☐ A. In the `<winntroot>\Profiles\All
         Users\Startup` folder on each computer.

   ☐ B. In the `Profiles\All Users\Startup` folder on
         the server containing the user account.

   ☐ C. In the `<winntroot>\Profiles\Default
         User\Startup` folder on each computer.

   ☐ D. In the `<winntroot>\Profiles\Default
         User\Startup` folder on the server containing the
         user account.

The correct answer is C. The Default User profile is only used the
first time a user logs on to a computer. From that point forward, the
account has its own profile assigned. This way, when the user completes the tutorial, your program can remove itself from the Startup
menu, but any new users will still receive the tutorial automatically.
For more information, see the "Managing User Profiles" section.

Practice Your Skills

Here is a chance to apply your practical hands-on experience and material from this chapter. These exercises are designed not only for you to apply the material in the book, but also for you to gain greater experience and exposure to the product. These exercises are a critical part of understanding the product and gaining valuable experience for using the product and passing the certification exam. For each of the following problems, consider the given facts and determine what you think are the possible causes of the problem and what course of action you might take to resolve the problem.

1. Using mandatory profiles

EXERCISE You are considering implementing mandatory user profiles for your company. You have several different types of users in your company; some perform just data entry, while others help design software programs. What are some of the benefits and drawbacks to mandatory profiles?

ANALYSIS Mandatory profiles are best suited for environments where the workflow of the user is predictable, such as a data entry clerk who only uses two or three applications. Mandatory profiles usually do not offer enough flexibility for power users, such as engineers and programmers. As a result, there may be a clash between you and your users if you attempt to implement profiles that do not work with their job requirements. When mandatory profiles are used, users are unable to save changes to the desktop settings, but at the same time, they are guaranteed a desktop that is always the same, regardless of any "playing" they may have done previously. The other disadvantage is that if a mandatory profile cannot be located the user will not be allowed to log onto the network.

2. Assigning policy priorities

EXERCISE You are configuring system policies for your corporate network. Most of the user groups contain a lot of the same user accounts. When you are configuring the group policies, why is it important that the System Policy editor enables you to set priority levels for group policies?

ANALYSIS Because users belong to more than one group, they are likely to be subject to multiple group policies. Without priority levels, if the user was first assigned a group policy that prevented him from accessing the Control Panel on his computer, and another group policy granted a group he belonged to access to the Control Panel, the first restriction is effectively overridden. If the policies where assigned priorities, the more restrictive policy would have a higher priority and would be assigned last to allow it to have the final word on the user account settings.

Managing Printing

As you continue your preparation for the Windows NT Server exam, it's important to take a look at using and sharing printers. This is one of the most common areas of use for a Windows NT Server computer, and it plays an important part in your exam. In this chapter I jump right in with a look at print monitors and how they are used to print to devices on a network. Then I move on to look at sharing printers, configuring their properties, establishing permissions, and creating an audit process. The chapter wraps up with a look at printer pools, priorities, and troubleshooting common printing problems.

Exam Material in This Chapter

Based on Microsoft Objectives

Installation and Configuration

- Configure printers. Tasks include:
  - Adding and configuring a printer
  - Implementing a printer pool
  - Setting print priorities

Troubleshooting

- Choose the appropriate course of action to take to resolve printer problems.

Based on Author's Experience

- You need to know the five common print monitors, the platforms they support, and the advantages of each in a networked environment. In Windows NT, the term *print device* refers to the physical device that produces printed output—what is more commonly referred to as a "printer."

- You definitely need to understand how printer permissions behave and how they are similar to file permissions.

- You need to know how to establish printer auditing, the steps involved, and how to view the audit log report.

- You should be familiar with how to create a printer pool and the requirements for print devices in a pool.

- You need to know how to provide printer drivers for client computers when they connect to a shared printer on a Windows NT Server computer.

- You need to be familiar with how to establish printer priorities and how they can benefit heavily used print devices in a networked environment.

Are You Prepared?

Do you have what it takes? Try out these self-assessment questions to see if you have prepared for the material in this chapter or if you should review problem areas.

1. **Your network consists of three network segments connected together with a router. You want to create a shared printer for your network users. The print device has a HP JetDirect device installed. What print monitor should you use on your Windows NT Server computer to connect to the printer?**

   ☐ A. Localmon
   ☐ B. Hpmon
   ☐ C. TCP/IP
   ☐ D. NetWare

2. **A user belongs to the Marketing user group, which has been granted Print permission, and also belongs to the Interns user group, which has been assigned the No Access permission. What is the user's effective permission for the printer?**

   ☐ A. Print permission
   ☐ B. No Access permission
   ☐ C. Manage Documents permission
   ☐ D. Read only permission

3. You want to audit the use of a color plotter in your company's design department. You create the shared printer and configure it to audit successful use of the printer. After several days of use, you check the audit log and do not see any entries. What else must you do to enable auditing?

☐ A. Create a System Policy.
☐ B. Create an Audit Policy.
☐ C. Delete and re-create the shared printer resource.
☐ D. You can not audit shared printers.

Answers:

1. C *Most of the newer JetDirect cards support TCP/IP and DLC, but since the network is connected with a router, DLC cannot be used because it's a nonroutable protocol. See the "Print Monitors" section.*

2. B *Printer permissions behave just like share permissions. They are additive, except that the No Access permission overrides all other permissions. See the "Printer Security" section.*

3. B *When auditing resources on a Windows NT Server computer, you not only need to define the audit properties for each resource, but you also need to configure an audit policy. See the "Printer Security" section.*

Printing Terminology

Before you can fully understand printing with Windows NT, you should first understand a few terms.

In Windows NT, the term *printer* does not represent a physical device that produces printed output. Rather, a printer is the software interface between the Windows NT operating system and the device that produces printed output.

If you are used to working with a different operating system, such as NetWare or UNIX, you may be used to thinking of what Windows NT calls a printer as a combination of a print queue (or print spooler) plus a driver for the device that produces printed output. If you aren't used to working with another operating system, feel free to ignore this note, because it may just be confusing at this point.

In Windows NT, the term *print device* refers to the physical device that produces printed output — what is more commonly referred to as a "printer."

Be sure that you know the Windows NT printing terminology cold. Otherwise, you may become confused when taking the exam. Remember: a *printer* is software, and a *print* (or *printing*) device is hardware.

Print Monitors

Print monitors are software components that run in kernel mode. In Windows NT, print monitors send ready-to-print print jobs to a print device, either locally or across the network. Print monitors are also called *port monitors.*

When you create a printer, you select the port to which the print device is connected. Each port is associated with one specific print monitor.

Localmon

The *Localmon print monitor* sends print jobs to print devices that are connected to hardware ports on a local Windows NT computer (local hardware ports include LPT1: and COM1:).

Localmon is the only print monitor that is installed by default during the installation of Windows NT. All other print monitors require that you install additional Windows NT services or protocols.

Hpmon

The *Hpmon print monitor* sends print jobs to a network print device via a Hewlett-Packard JetDirect adapter. The HP JetDirect adapter may either be installed in the print device, or function as a separate external unit.

Hpmon uses the DLC protocol to communicate with HP JetDirect adapters. Most HP JetDirect adapters support multiple protocols, including: TCP/IP, IPX, AppleTalk, and DLC. However, Hpmon can only communicate by using the DLC protocol.

The DLC protocol is a non-routable protocol. A Windows NT computer that uses Hpmon can only communicate with HP JetDirect adapters that are located on the same network segment. In other words, the DLC protocol will not be forwarded by a network router to another network segment.

If your network supports bridging, however, you can use DLC to communicate to an HP JetDirect adapter on any network segment that is connected by a bridge.

The Hpmon print monitor is not installed by default during the installation of Windows NT. Hpmon is installed automatically when you install the DLC protocol. You must install DLC before you can connect to an HP JetDirect adapter using Hpmon.

Watch for exam questions that deal with printing to network-attached printers, such as HP printers. Make sure you read the scenario carefully, and determine if the question deals with the Hpmon port or the TCP/IP port.

When you configure an Hpmon port, you must configure it as either a job-based or continuous connection. Selecting between a job-based and continuous connection requires some careful planning and consideration.

If a printer isn't shared and you select a continuous connection, only a single user will have access to the HP JetDirect adapter for printing. In this situation, you should generally select a job-based connection.

However, if you share the printer that is associated with the Hpmon port, selecting a continuous connection can make sense. This computer will then function as a print server and manage all print jobs sent to the shared printer. In this situation, all computers on the network that have access to the shared printer, in effect, will have access to the HP JetDirect adapter for printing.

AppleTalk

The *AppleTalk print monitor* sends print jobs to network print devices that support the AppleTalk protocol. The AppleTalk protocol is normally associated with Apple Macintosh computers.

Before you can connect to an AppleTalk print device, you must install Services for Macintosh on your Windows NT Server computer.

AppleTalk is a routable protocol. A Windows NT computer that uses the AppleTalk print monitor can communicate with any AppleTalk print device on any segment of a routed AppleTalk network.

When you select a print device you will be asked if you want to *capture* the AppleTalk print device.

If you choose to capture an AppleTalk print device, it is the same as choosing a continuous connection. The AppleTalk print monitor will monopolize the connection to the AppleTalk print device, and no other computer on the network will be able to access the AppleTalk print device. In addition, the AppleTalk print monitor instructs the AppleTalk print device not to advertise itself on the network. This is called *hiding*.

If you choose not to capture an AppleTalk print device, it is the same as choosing a job-based connection. All computers on the network will be able to access the AppleTalk print device for printing, because the connection to the print device is dropped after each print job. Only one computer can connect to an AppleTalk print device at any given time.

TCP/IP

The *TCP/IP print monitor* sends print jobs to network print devices that both support TCP/IP *and* function as *line printer daemon* (LPD) print servers. TCP/IP and LPD are normally associated with UNIX computers.

TEST TIP *Daemon* is a UNIX term. A UNIX daemon performs the same function as a Windows NT service. Basically, a UNIX daemon is a program that runs in the background and performs an operating system service.

Line printer daemon (LPD) is the print server software used in TCP/IP printing. The client print software used in TCP/IP printing is called *line printer remote* (LPR). To connect to a TCP/IP print server that uses LPD, use a TCP/IP print client that uses LPR.

Before you can connect to a TCP/IP print device, you must install TCP/IP and the Microsoft TCP/IP Printing service on your Windows NT computer.

In addition, to share printers on a Windows NT computer as TCP/IP printers, you must also start the TCP/IP Print Server service. The TCP/IP Print Server service is configured for manual startup by default, so you should configure this service to start automatically.

TCP/IP is a routable protocol. A Windows NT computer that uses the TCP/IP print monitor can communicate with any TCP/IP print device on any segment of a routed TCP/IP network.

Figure 6-1 shows the Add LPR compatible printer dialog box. Notice the IP address of the device providing the LPD service (in this case, an HP JetDirect adapter) and the name of the printer have been entered.

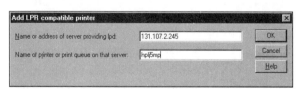

Figure 6-1 *Configuring an LPR port*

Print Monitor

Read the exam question scenarios closely to determine which print monitor port the question is about.

- The Hpmon port monitor uses the DLC protocol to connect with network attached print devices. DLC is not routable and is often the subject of network topology questions involving a router.

- The TCP/IP port monitor uses TCP/IP to connect with network attached print devices. It has a large application, as more vendors support TCP/IP than DLC, and it is a routable protocol.

NetWare

The *NetWare print monitor* sends print jobs to a print queue on a Novell NetWare server. The NetWare server then sends the print job from the print queue to the print device.

 A *print queue* is the NetWare term for a shared printer. A NetWare print queue is designed to handle print jobs that are ready to send to the print device, and that need no additional conversion or formatting.

NWLink IPX/SPX Compatible Transport is a routable protocol. A Windows NT computer that uses the NetWare print monitor can communicate with any NetWare server on any segment of a routed NetWare network.

 Before you can connect to a NetWare print queue, you must install NWLink IPX/SPX Compatible Transport on your Windows NT Workstation computer. In addition, you must install *Gateway Service for NetWare* (GSNW).

True or False?

1. You must install Gateway Service for NetWare before you can connect to a NetWare server.

2. The term *print device* refers to the physical device that produces printed output.

3. The Hpmon port monitor can use either the DLC or TCP/IP protocol to connect to print devices.

4. Use must install the Microsoft TCP/IP Printing service to use the TCP/IP port monitor.

Answers: *1. True 2. True 3. False 4. True*

Sharing a Printer

The purpose of sharing a printer on a Windows NT computer is to enable users of other computers on the network to connect to and to send print jobs to the shared printer. The computer that hosts the shared printer is called a *print server*. The print server performs all of the spooling, print job management, scheduling, and sending of the final print jobs to the print device.

When you share a printer on your Windows NT computer, the types of computers on the network that can access your shared printer are somewhat dependent upon the protocols and services installed in your computer.

When you install Windows NT, Microsoft Windows Networking is installed by default. If you have not installed any other services and you share a printer on your computer, only computers that support Microsoft Windows Networking can access the shared printer.

If you installed Microsoft TCP/IP Printing *and* started the TCP/IP Print Server service (which is installed with Microsoft TCP/IP Printing), and you share a printer on your computer, then computers that support Microsoft Windows Networking and computers that support TCP/IP printing (such as UNIX computers) can access the shared printer.

If you have installed Services for Macintosh on a Windows NT Server computer and you share a printer on your computer, then computers that support Microsoft Windows Networking and Macintosh computers that support Microsoft Windows Networking and Macintosh computers can access the shared printer.

Microsoft TCP/IP Printing and Services for Macintosh both include components that enable you to share printers. These components are called *print server services*. If you have more than one print server service installed and started on your Windows NT computer, and then you share a printer, the printer is shared on *all* running print server services installed on your computer.

Installing Printer Drivers for Shared Printers

When you share a printer on a Windows NT computer, Windows NT permits you to install alternate printer drivers for other versions of Windows NT and Windows 95. You can also install alternate printer drivers for other Windows NT hardware platforms, such as MIPS R4000, PowerPC, and DEC Alpha.

Installing these drivers enables users of Windows NT and Windows 95 computers on your network to automatically download and install the appropriate printer drivers for their operating systems/hardware platforms when they connect to the shared printer. The advantage of being able to install these alternate printer drivers on a shared printer is that the network administrator is spared the time-consuming task of manually installing printer drivers on every computer on the network.

Alternate Print Drivers

You can configure a Windows NT print server to provide print drivers to Windows NT, Windows 95, and Windows 98 client computers. When the client connects to the shared printer, the client can choose to download the printer driver from the server.

Figure 6-2 shows a shared printer, named *managers*, with alternate printer drivers for Windows 95 and Windows NT 4.0 x86 highlighted. The x86 indicates that printer drivers for Intel-based computers that run Windows NT 4.0 will be installed.

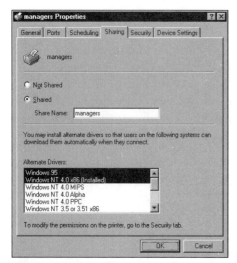

Figure 6-2 *Installing printer drivers for multiple operating systems*

Sharing AppleTalk Printers in Windows NT

When a Windows NT Server computer that has Services for Macintosh installed on it shares a printer, the printer is accessible from Macintosh computers on the network, because Windows NT Server has full AppleTalk print server capabilities.

Shared printers on a Windows NT Server computer that has Services for Macintosh installed advertise themselves to Macintosh computers on the network as Apple LaserWriters. (An Apple LaserWriter is the original laser print device for Macintosh computers. All Macintosh computers have built-in drivers for the Apple LaserWriter.) Windows NT Server converts the PostScript print jobs it receives from Macintosh computers into RAW format print jobs for the print device.

Macintosh computers do not need special drivers to access shared printers on Windows NT Servers running Services for Macintosh. Although you can use the manufacturer's print driver for a Macintosh, computers without the drivers can use the standard Apple LaserWriter driver.

Configuring Printer Properties

In Windows NT you can configure options for a printer in the printer's Properties dialog box. This dialog box is printer-specific, and is titled *Printer_name* Properties.

Printer Security

You can use Windows NT printer security to control access to a printer by assigning printer permissions to users and groups. Printer security is configured on the Security tab in a printer's Properties dialog box. In addition, you can take ownership of a printer and configure Windows NT to audit printer usage in this dialog box.

Printer permissions

Printer permissions control which tasks a user can perform on a specific printer. Table 6-1 lists and describes the Windows NT printer permissions.

TABLE 6-1 Windows NT Printer Permissions

Printer Permission	Description and Functionality
No Access	User or group cannot access the printer.
Print	Enables users to create print jobs, and also to delete their own print jobs.
Manage Documents	Enables users to pause, restart, delete, and control job settings for their own print jobs. The Manage Documents permission does not allow users to print to the printer.
Full Control	User or group can do everything that a user with the Print and Manage Documents permissions can do, and can also assign printer permissions, delete printers, share printers, and change printer properties.

You can assign printer permissions to users and groups. User and group permissions are additive. In other words, if a user has the Print permission, and a group that the user is a member of has Full Control, then the user has Full Control.

There is one exception to this rule. If a user, or any group that a user is a member of, has the No Access permission, then the user's effective permission is always No Access. For example, a user may have the Full Control permission, but a group that the user is a member of may have the No Access permission. The user's effective permission is No Access, and the user cannot access the printer.

Sound familiar? Print permissions behave exactly like Share permissions because they are both shared resources on a Windows NT computer.

Figure 6-3 shows the default printer permissions assigned to a newly created printer in the Printer Permissions dialog box. Note that by default the Everyone group has the Print permission, which effectively enables all users to create and delete their own print jobs on this printer.

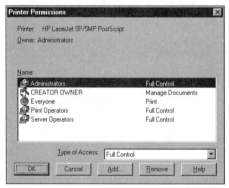

Figure 6-3 *Assigning printer permissions*

True or False?

1. Print permissions for users and groups are not additive.

2. If users have the Manage Documents permission, they can also print to the printer.

3. You can relocate the printer spool directory.

4. If users are granted No Access for a printer, they can still use the printer if they belong to a group that does have access.

Answers: *1. False 2. False 3. True 4. False*

Auditing printers

You can use your printer's Properties dialog box to configure Windows NT to audit a user or group's usage (and/or attempted usage) of a printer. Only members of the Administrators group can configure auditing on a Windows NT computer.

When auditing is enabled, Windows NT adds an entry to the Security Log in Event Viewer every time an audited user or group exercises (and/or attempts to exercise) an audited permission on a specific printer. To gain a better understanding of auditing printers, how about a walk through the process of configuring printer auditing?

Auditing printers is accomplished in two parts: first, auditing is enabled in User Manager for Domains; second, printer auditing is configured in a specific printer's Properties dialog box.

Only members of the local administrators group can configure auditing on a Windows NT Server computer. This includes file and printer auditing.

You must first configure an audit policy using the User Manager for Domains. Figure 6-4 shows the Audit Policy dialog box. You first select the option button next to Audit These Events and then select the events you want to be audited. You *must* select the Success and/or Failure check boxes for File and Object Access to audit printer events.

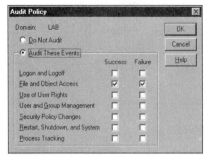

Figure 6-4 *Enabling auditing of file and object access*

Success auditing means that Windows NT will report successful attempts to complete the task or event listed. *Failure auditing* means that Windows NT will report unsuccessful attempts to complete the task or event listed.

After an audit policy has been configured, you configure the audit properties for the printer(s) you want to audit by right-clicking the printer you want to configure. You then select Properties from the menu and click the Security tab in your printer's Properties dialog box.

Figure 6-5 shows the Printer Auditing dialog box. Notice that the check boxes for Success and Failure auditing of Print events are selected for the Everyone group.

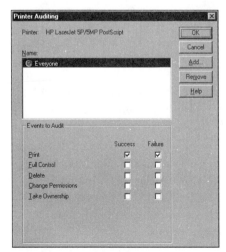

Figure 6-5 *Configuring print events to audit*

To view the events generated by printer auditing, use the Event Viewer. In the Event Viewer dialog box, select the Security Log. A list of audited events is displayed. You can double-click any event for a detailed description of the event.

Printing to Multiple Ports (Printer Pools)

When a printer has multiple ports (and multiple print devices) assigned to it, this is called a *printer pool*. Users print to a single printer, and the printer load-balances its print jobs among the print devices assigned to it.

A printer pool is a useful tool when *both* of the following criteria are met:

- All print devices assigned to the printer use the same print device driver. (Usually, this means that identical print devices are used.)

- All print devices assigned to the printer pool are located physically close to each other.

Figure 6-6 shows the Properties dialog box for a printer that has been configured as a printer pool. Notice that three ports have been selected, and that the check box next to "Enable printer pooling" is checked.

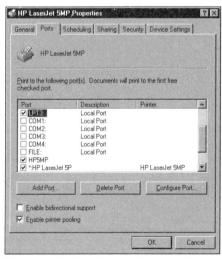

Figure 6-6 *Creating a printer pool*

When a user prints to a printer pool, the print job is sent to the first listed print device in the Port list that is not busy printing another print job. The entire print job is sent to the same port (print device). In a printer pool the print spooler — not the user — determines which print device the print job will be sent to.

Setting Printer Priorities

When more than one printer sends print jobs to the same print device, setting printer priorities may be useful. If two printers are configured to use the same print device, and you configure one of these printers to have a higher priority than the other printer, all print jobs from the higher-priority printer will be sent to the print device before any print jobs from the lower-priority printer are sent.

The highest printer priority is 99, and the lowest printer priority is 1. All printers have a priority of 1 by default.

Here's one situation in which setting printer priorities could be beneficial: Suppose you have two printers on a Windows NT Server computer that both send print jobs to the print device connected to LPT1:. One printer is named *sales*, and the other printer is named *managers*.

The managers at this company, who think their work is more important than everyone else's, tell you — the network administrator — that they want their print jobs printed before anyone else's.

So you decide to configure printer security so that everyone can use the *sales* printer, but only members of the Managers group can use the *managers* printer. Then you set the priority on the *managers* printer to a value higher than 1. Once this is done, the managers' print jobs will take priority. Suppose that there are 100 print jobs waiting to print in the *sales* printer, and a manager sends a print job to the *managers* printer. The current print job from the *sales* printer will finish printing, then the manager's print job will be printed, even though there are one hundred other print jobs in the *sales* printer that were generated before the manager's print job.

Troubleshooting Common Printing Problems

Printing problems can occur on a Windows NT network for several reasons. Some of the most common printing problems involve users who do not have the permissions they need to access the printer, or users who have the Full Control permission or the Manage Document permission accidentally deleting documents that belong to other users. A good first step, when troubleshooting printer problems, is to ensure that users have appropriate printer permissions.

Table 6-2 lists some common printing problems, along with their probable causes and recommended solutions.

TABLE 6-2 Troubleshooting Printing Problems

Problem	Probable Cause/ Recommended Solution
Print jobs are not being sent from the printer to the print device. A print job with a size of 0 bytes is at the top of the print job list for the printer. Other documents are also listed in the print job list, and users can still send print jobs to the printer. There is plenty of free space on the partition that contains your spool folder.	The most likely cause of this problem is a stalled print spooler. Stop and restart the Spooler service, and printing should resume.
No print events are listed in the Security Log in Event Viewer. You recently configured success auditing for print events in the Properties dialog box for the printer. Several days have passed, and hundreds of documents have been printed.	The most likely cause of this problem is that the success option for auditing file and object access has *not* been configured in User Manager. Auditing of printers requires that auditing of file and object access be configured. To resolve the problem, configure the necessary options in User Manager.

Continued

TABLE 6-2 *Continued*

Problem	Probable Cause/ Recommended Solution
A printer that uses the Hpmon print monitor has stopped sending print jobs to its assigned print device.	This problem usually occurs when another computer on the network is configured to use Hpmon to connect to the print device by using a continuous connection. If you want more than one printer to be able to access a print device by using Hpmon, configure a job-based connection for all printers.
You are unable to connect a Windows NT computer to a print device that uses TCP/IP and LPD.	Of the many possible causes for this problem, the most common is an incorrect configuration of a TCP/IP parameter on either the Windows NT computer or on the print device that uses TCP/IP and LPD. Ensure that the IP address, subnet mask, and default gateway parameters on both the Windows NT computer and the print device that uses TCP/IP and LPD are set correctly.
You experience a paper jam in the middle of an important print job. You want to reprint the entire print job, but it is not possible to reprint the job from the application that created it because you deleted the document after you created the print job.	The cause of the paper jam is not important here, but being able to reprint the entire print job is. To solve this problem, I recommend that you: 1. Immediately double-click the printer in the `Printers` folder. 2. The Printers dialog box appears. Select Document ➪ Pause. This pauses the print job. 3. Clear the paper jam at the print device. 4. Select Document ➪ Restart to reprint the entire print job. (Do not select Resume from the Document menu, because this will only print the print job from wherever the printer jammed to the end of the document, and the pages jammed in the print device will very likely be lost.)

Problem	Probable Cause/ Recommended Solution
You receive spooler messages indicating that your print job has been spooled with a size of 0 bytes.	The most probable cause of this problem is that the partition that contains the printer's spool folder does not have enough free space to print the document in question. You should delete some files from this partition, or move the spool folder to a different partition that has more free space.

Have You Mastered?

Now it's time to apply what you've learned in this chapter by testing your mastery of the material. These questions provide you with a means to determine if you are ready to move on to the next chapter or if you need to review the material again.

1. **You are in the process of migrating your NetWare network to a Windows NT network. You want users who have been migrated to Windows NT to be able to print to printers still connected to NetWare servers. You want to create a shared printer on your Windows NT Server that will forward the print jobs to the NetWare servers connected to the printers. What must you do? (Choose two.)**

   ☐ A. Install Gateway Service for NetWare.
   ☐ B. Install NWLink IPX/SPX Compatible Transport.
   ☐ C. Configure a separator page.
   ☐ D. Configure the spool format as RAW.

The correct answers are A and B. Before a Windows NT computer can forward print jobs to a NetWare print queue, the computer must have these two components installed. You do not need to have a separator page defined, nor does the spool format need to be changed in order to forward to a NetWare queue. For more information, see the "Print Monitors" section.

2. **You have installed a print device on your network using a JetDirect card. You want to allow some users to print directly to the print device and bypass the print server. You want the other users to use your Windows NT Server computer as a print server for the print device. The JetDirect card only supports the DLC protocol. How should you configure the printer on the Windows NT Server computer to allow some users to print directly to the print device?**

☐ A. Configure the Hpmon print monitor properties as Continuous.

☐ B. Configure the Hpmon print monitor properties as Job Based.

☐ C. Grant the users who should print directly to the print device Full Control for the printer.

☐ D. This cannot be done using the JetDirect card and Hpmon print monitor.

The correct answer is B. If the Hpmon print monitor is configured as Job Based, a connection to the Jetdirect card is only made when there is a print job waiting. If Continuous is selected, the print server will connect to the JetDirect card and prevent any other devices from connecting to the print device. For more information, see the "Print Monitors" section.

3. **You are the network administrator for a network that contains a Windows NT Server domain. The manager of the Research department has called you because she is unable to print to the department color printer. You check the printer permissions and see that she has been granted the Manage Documents permission. What must you do to allow the manager to use the printer?**

☐ A. Revoke the Manage Documents permission and grant her Print permission.

☐ B. Grant her Print permission.

☐ C. Add her to the Power Users user group.

☐ D. Delete all of the existing documents in the printer queue.

The correct answer is B. The Manage Documents permission does not enable a user to print to the printer, it only enables them to manage the print queue and user documents sent to the printer. While answer A would also work, the question used the word *must*, so since you do not necessarily have to revoke Manage Documents permission, this answer is not correct in this scenario. For more information, see the "Printer Security" section.

4. **You are the network administrator for a network that contains a Windows NT Server domain. You have created a shared printer that connects to a Postscript print device. You want the Macintosh users to be able to access the shared printer on the Windows NT Server. What should you do?**

    ☐ A. Configure the Macintosh computers to have user logons validated by the NT Server domain.
    ☐ B. Configure the Macintosh computers to access the printer using the default LaserWriter print driver.
    ☐ C. Install the print device's AppleTalk print driver on the Macintosh computers.
    ☐ D. Install the print device's AppleTalk print driver on the Windows NT Server computer.

The correct answer is B. When a Windows NT Server computer shares a printer and the server has the Services for Macintosh installed, the client Macintosh computers can use the default LaserWriter print driver to access the shared printer. You would only install a print device's AppleTalk driver on the Macintosh computer if you want the advanced features of the printer. Since many manufacturers do not provide an AppleTalk print driver, you can use the default LaserWriter. For more information, see the "Print Monitors" section.

5. **You are configuring the audit properties for the shared printers on your PDC. You enable all of the audit properties available for the printers. After several days of use, you check the audit log and see no entries. What should you do?**

☐ A. Configure an audit policy that enables auditing for the computers in the domain.

☐ B. Configure each user account to be audited using the User Manager for Domains.

☐ C. Shut down and restart the PDC server.

☐ D. You cannot audit a PDC server; you can only audit on BDC, Member, or Stand-alone servers.

The correct answer is A. Windows NT requires that an audit policy be created before auditing will begin. Even though you configured the individual printers to be audited, there probably wasn't an audit policy in effect, which is why the audit log didn't contain any entries. Auditing can occur on any Windows NT platform, regardless of its role on the network. For more information, see the "Printer Security" section.

6. **You are configuring shared printers on your Windows NT Server computer. You want a print device located in the main office to be used for general printing purposes and to print sales invoices for phone orders. You want the sales reps to have their invoices as soon as possible. What can you do so that the sales invoices will print before any other documents?**

☐ A. Create two printers and set a higher priority for the printer used by the sales reps.

☐ B. Configure the print device as part of a print spool.

☐ C. Enable auditing on the shared printer.

☐ D. Assign the sales reps Full Control permissions for the shared printer.

The correct answer is A. You can create two shared printers, one with a higher priority. The printer with a higher priority will always print its documents before the documents in a printer with a lower priority. This will ensure that the sales reps will have their sales invoices as quickly as possible. For more information, see the "Configuring Printer Properties" section.

Practice Your Skills

Here is a chance to apply your practical hands-on experience and material from this chapter. These exercises are designed not only for you to apply the material in the book, but also for you to gain greater experience and exposure to the product. These exercises are a critical part of understanding the product and gaining valuable experience for using the product and passing the certification exam. For each of the following problems, consider the given facts and determine what you think are the possible causes of the problem and what course of action you might take to resolve the problem.

1. Troubleshooting print jobs

EXERCISE Halfway through a print job, you discover that the print device's paper tray contains letterhead paper, and you need your document printed on white paper. You want to reprint the entire job, but you have already deleted your document from the spreadsheet application you were using. What can you do?

ANALYSIS If the print job is still in the printer queue, you can pause your print job, change the paper in the print device, and restart the print job from the beginning. If the job has already been spooled to the print device, the queue will be empty and you cannot reprint the job unless you still have the file.

2. Using print monitors in a network

EXERCISE Your network consists of several types of client computers and various operating systems, ranging from MS-DOS to UNIX. You want to install print devices that will support the largest variety of platforms possible. Which of the Windows NT print monitors have the greatest pervasiveness for network support?

ANALYSIS In general, you will find that TCP/IP and, to a lesser extent, DLC, are the most pervasively supported platforms for network attached printers. If you purchase print devices or network print servers that support either of these protocols, you will probably be able to meet the printing needs of your users.

3. Configuring printer pools

EXERCISE You have several new high-speed print devices located in a common area. You would like to configure the print devices as one high-speed printer pool for users on the network. What do you need to do before configuring the printer pool for these new print devices?

ANALYSIS Because all of the print devices will be acting as one logical printer for network users, you need to make sure they are all configured the same and support all of the same options. You should ensure that they all have the same language setups, timeouts, default fonts, and so on. If the print devices vary, users will likely experience strange behavior as print jobs are printed on random print devices each time.

Sharing and Securing File Systems

In this chapter, I focus on sharing and securing files and folders on a network. By studying this material closely, you can help improve your readiness for the exam. I start the chapter by getting right to the nitty-gritty of sharing folders. I explain share permissions, including how to assign them, and how user and group permissions combine. Then I explore how to assign NTFS permissions, how NTFS permissions are applied; and how NTFS and share permissions interact. Finally, the chapter wraps up with a look at auditing files and folders on NTFS partitions, and tips for troubleshooting common permission problems.

Exam Material In This Chapter

Based on Microsoft Objectives

Managing Resources

- Manage disk resources. Tasks include:
  - Copying and moving files between file systems
  - Creating and sharing resources.
  - Implementing permissions and security.
  - Establishing file auditing.
- Set permissions on NTFS partitions, folders, and files.

Troubleshooting

- Choose the appropriate course of action to take to resolve resource access problems and permission problems.

Based on Author's Experience

- You should be familiar with the process of sharing folders, assigning share permissions, and how share permissions combine to create a user's effective permission.

- You definitely need to know how user and group permissions combine for both NTFS and share permissions. You also need to know how the No Access permission combines with any other user or group permission.

- You need to know how the Take Ownership permission works, and what the process is for taking the ownership of another user's files.

- You definitely need to understand how NTFS file and folder permissions are handled when files and folders are moved or copied between NTFS partitions

- You need to know how NTFS and share permissions differ, specifically as it relates to effective permissions.

Are You Prepared?

Do you have what it takes? Try out these self-assessment questions to see if you have prepared for the material in this chapter or if you should review problem areas.

1. **You are assigning a user access permissions to a shared folder. You grant his account Full Control. The user belongs to the accounting group, which has been granted Read permissions for the folder, and to the Marketing group, which has been granted the No Access permission for the folder. What are the user's effective permissions for the folder?**

   - ☐ A. Full Control
   - ☐ B. Read
   - ☐ C. No Access
   - ☐ D. Write
   - ☐ E. Special Access

2. **When you move a file from an NTFS volume to another NTFS volume, what happens to the file permissions?**

   - ☐ A. They stay the same.
   - ☐ B. They inherit the access permissions of the new parent folder.
   - ☐ C. The Everyone group is automatically granted Full Control.
   - ☐ D. The Everyone group is automatically granted No Access.

3. You want to become the owner for some files stored on an NTFS volume on your Windows NT Server computer. Which permissions enable you to become the owner of someone else's files? (Choose two.)

        ☐ A. Member of Server Operators
        ☐ B. Member of Administrators group
        ☐ C. Take Ownership user permissions
        ☐ D. Manage Files user rights

Answers:

1. C   *No Access always overrides all other share permissions. If a user has the Full Control permission, but is a member of a group that has the No Access permission, the user's effective permission is No Access. See the "Combining User and Group Permissions" section.*

2. B   *When a file or folder is moved between NTFS volumes, the file permissions are set to match the permissions of the folder containing the file on the new NTFS volume. If the file is moved within the same volume, the permissions remain the same. See the "NTFS Security" section.*

3. B and C
   Only members of the Administrators group or users with Take Ownership permissions can become the owner of other user's files. See the "Taking Ownership" section.

File and Folder Attributes

Windows NT files and folders have various *attributes*, some of which the administrator can use to provide a limited amount of data protection. For example, administrators often use the read-only file attribute to prevent accidental deletion of files, such as application files. Other file and folder attributes are applied by Windows NT system files automatically during installation.

File attributes can be used on both FAT and NTFS partitions, with the exception of the Compress attribute, which is only available on NTFS partitions.

Table 7-1 lists and describes the five Windows NT file and folder attributes.

TABLE 7-1 Windows NT File and Folder Attributes

Attribute	Description
Archive	Indicates that the file or folder has been modified since the last backup. Is applied by the operating system when a file or folder is saved or created, and is commonly removed by backup programs after the file or folder has been backed up. Is normally not changed by the administrator.
Compress	Indicates that Windows NT has compressed the file or folder. Is only available on NTFS partitions. Uses the same compression algorithm as the MS-DOS 6.0 DoubleSpace utility. Can be set on individual files. Is applied by administrators to control which files and folders will be compressed.
Hidden	Indicates that the file or folder can't be seen in a normal directory scan.

Continued

TABLE 7-1 *Continued*

Attribute	Description
Hidden (continued)	Files or folders with this attribute can't be copied or deleted. Is applied to various files and folders by NT automatically during installation.
Read-only	Indicates that the file or folder can only be read. It can't be written to or deleted. Is often applied by administrators to prevent accidental deletion of application files.
System	Indicates that the file or folder is used by the operating system. Files or folders with this attribute can't be seen in a normal directory scan. Files or folders with this attribute can't be copied or deleted. Is applied to various files and folders by NT automatically during installation.

The archive attribute is prime target for exam questions, especially for backup and restore objectives! You should know that the archive bit is set whenever a file is created, modified, or copied onto another partition. The backup application usually removes this bit when the file has been backed up.

File Attributes

Any user who can access a file or folder on a FAT partition can modify that file or folder's attributes. Any user who has the Write (W) NTFS permission (or any permission that includes the Write (W) permission) to a file or folder on an NTFS partition can modify that file or folder's attributes.

On NTFS volumes, when a file or folder has the Read-only attribute, and the file or folder also has the Write (W) NTFS permission for a user or group, the Read-only attribute takes precedence. The Read-only attribute must be removed before the file can be modified or deleted.

Shared Folders

In Windows NT, folders are *shared* to enable users to access network resources. Users cannot access a folder across the network until it is shared or placed within another folder that is shared. Once a folder is shared, users with the appropriate permissions can access the shared folder (and all folders and files that the shared folder contains) over the network.

A shared folder appears in Windows NT Explorer and My Computer as a folder with a hand under it. A shared folder is often referred to as a *share*.

 Only members of the Administrators, Server Operators, and Power Users built-in local groups can share folders. A Windows NT Workstation computer has the Administrators and Power User groups, while a Windows NT Server computer has the Administrators and Server Operators groups.

Sharing a Folder

Only certain users can share folders. Members of the Administrators local group can share folders on any Windows NT computer; members of the Server Operators group can share folders on all Windows NT domain controllers; and members of the Power Users group can share folders on all Windows NT non-domain controllers, including Windows NT Workstation computers.

When a folder is shared, its *entire contents* (including all files and subfolders) are available to users who have the appropriate permissions to the share. Because all files and subfolders are accessible when a folder is shared, you should consider which groups and users need access to folders when you design your server's folder structure.

When sharing a folder, it's a good idea to assign it a share name that is easily recognized by users, and one that appropriately describes the resources contained in the folder. Otherwise, users can become frustrated trying to find the specific network resources they need.

Additionally, keep in mind when you assign a name to a shared folder that a long share name may *not* be readable by all client computers on your network. MS-DOS computers, for example, can only read share names up to eight characters (plus a three-character extension), and Windows 95/98 computers can only read share names up to 12 characters. Share names in Windows NT can be as long as 80 characters.

You can use either Windows NT Explorer or Server Manager to share folders.

You can use Windows NT Explorer to share folders only on the local computer; however, you can use Server Manager to share folders both locally and on remote computers.

Figure 7-1 shows the Sharing tab in the Data Properties dialog box. Note that the option button next to Shared As is selected. You can add a descriptive comment about the share in the Comment text box if you so choose. (This is an optional setting.) If you want to limit the number of users who can connect to this share simultaneously (because of licensing limitations and such) you can configure the User Limit section on the Sharing tab. The default User Limit setting is Maximum Allowed. A hand will appear under the folder you just shared, indicating that this is a shared folder.

You can use Server Manager to share a folder on a local or remote Windows NT computer that you have administrative permissions to. Using Server Manager, highlight the computer you want to create a share on and select Computer ⇨ Shared Directories.

The New Share dialog box is shown in Figure 7-2. Notice the various configuration options in the dialog box.

In the Share Name text box, you type in the name you want to assign to the new share. Then, in the Path text box, type in the full path to the share, in the form of `Drive_letter:\Folder\subfolder\...` For example, to share the CD-ROM drive on a remote Windows NT computer that uses E: as the drive letter, you would type E:\ in the Path text box.

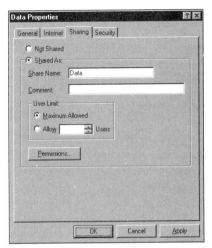

Figure 7-1 *Using Windows NT Explorer to share a folder*

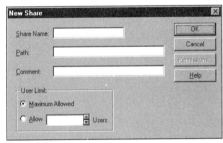

Figure 7-2 *Using Server Manager to share a folder*

You can enter a descriptive comment about the share in the Comment text box if you so choose. If you want to limit the number of users that can connect to this share simultaneously you can configure the User Limit section.

Shared Folder Permissions

Shared folder permissions control user access to shared folders. Shared folder permissions only apply when users connect to the folder over the network — they do not apply when users access the folder from the local computer.

 Shared folder permissions do not apply when users access the folder from the local computer. Shared folder permissions only apply if a user connects from over the network. To restrict access to files and folders for a local user, you must use NTFS security.

Shared folder permissions (commonly called *share permissions*) apply to the shared folder, its files, and subfolders (in other words, to the *entire* directory tree under the shared folder).

Share permissions are the only folder and file security available on a FAT partition (with the exception of file attributes), and control only over-the-network access to the share — local access is totally unrestricted on a FAT partition.

Table 7-2 lists and describes the Windows NT share permissions, from the most restrictive to the least restrictive.

TABLE 7-2 Windows NT Share Permissions	
Permission	**Description**
No Access	Permits a user to connect to a share only, but prevents a user from accessing the shared folder and its contents.
Read	Permits a user to view file and folder names. Permits a user to change current folder to a subfolder of the share. Permits a user to view data in files; and to run application files.
Change	Permits a user to perform all tasks included in the Read permission. Permits a user to create files and folders within the share; to edit data files and save changes; and to delete files and folders within the share.

Permission	Description
Full Control	Permits a user to perform all tasks included in the Change permission. Permits a user to change NTFS permissions and to take ownership of files and folders—this only applies to shares on NTFS partitions.

 Shared folder permissions are prime targets for exam questions. You need to know the four standard share permissions, and how they combine to create a user's effective permission.

Share permissions are assigned by adding a user or group to the permissions list for the share. From an administrative standpoint, it's much more efficient to add groups to the permissions list for a particular share than to add individual users. By default, the Everyone group is granted the Full Control permission to all newly created shared folders.

When assigning permissions to a share, you should consider assigning the most restrictive permission that still allows users to accomplish the tasks they need to perform. For example, on shares that contain applications, consider assigning the Read permission so that users can't accidentally delete application files.

You can assign share permissions by using Windows NT Explorer or Server Manager.

To assign share permissions by using Windows NT Explorer, open the *Folder_name* Properties dialog box, and click the Sharing tab. Then click the Permissions command button. The Access Through Share Permissions dialog box is shown in Figure 7-3. Notice that, by default, the Everyone group has Full Control. To add additional users, click the Add command button.

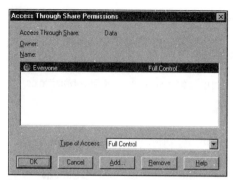

Figure 7-3 *Assigning share permissions*

The Add Users and Groups dialog box is shown in Figure 7-4. Notice that only group names from the WEST domain appear in the Names list box. If you want to add global groups and users from other trusted domains, click the arrow in the List Names From drop-down list box and select the domain you want.

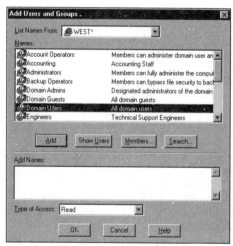

Figure 7-4 *Adding users and groups to the permissions list for the share*

Combining User and Group Permissions

It is not uncommon for a user to have permission to a share and to be a member of multiple groups that have different permissions to that share. When this occurs, the user and group permissions are cumulative, and the *least* restrictive permission is the user's effective permission. For example, a user has the Read permission to a share, and a group that the user is a member of has the Change permission to the share. The user's effective share permission is Change.

The exception to this rule is the No Access permission. *No Access always overrides all other share permissions.* If a user has the Full Control permission, but is a member of a group that has the No Access permission, the user's effective permission is No Access. *No Access always means no access.*

Multiple Access Rights Rule

When a user belongs to multiple groups with different permissions to a shared folder, the user and group permissions are cumulative. The exception is that the No Access permission overrides all other share permissions. If a user, or a group the user belongs to, has been assigned the No Access permission, the user's effective rights are No Access – period!

Administrative Shares

Every time you start Windows NT on a computer, NT automatically creates several hidden shares that only members of the Administrators group have permission to access. These shares are referred to as *administrative shares* because they are used by Administrators to perform administrative tasks.

The Windows NT administrative shares are: C$, D$, E$, and so on (one share for the root of each hard disk partition on the computer); and a share named Admin$, which corresponds to the folder in which NT is installed (<winntroot>). The $ at the end of each administrative share causes the share to be hidden from users when they browse the network.

Administrative shares make it possible for an Administrator to connect to any hard drive on a computer and access all of its files and folders, regardless of whether regular shares exist on that hard drive. In this way an Administrator can perform backup, restore, and other administrative functions on a Windows NT computer.

Any share can be configured as a hidden share by placing a $ at the end of its share name. However, hiding a share by appending a $ to the share name does *not* limit user access to the share. The hidden share retains its assigned share permissions. Only access to the hidden *administrative* shares is restricted, by default, to Administrators only.

POP QUIZ **True or False?**

1. The compress attribute is available on FAT and NTFS partitions.

2. Windows 95 computers can only see share names up to 12 characters long.

3. Only the Administrators group can create share folders.

4. No Access always overrides all other share permissions.

5. By default, the Everyone group is granted Read permission to all newly created shared folders.

Answers: *1. False 2. True 3. False 4. True 5. False*

NTFS Security

When files and folders are stored on an NTFS volume, NTFS permissions can be assigned to provide a greater level of security than share permissions, because:

- NTFS permissions, unlike share permissions, can be assigned to individual files as well as folders. This gives an administrator a much finer level of control over shared files and folders than is possible by using only share permissions.

- NTFS permissions apply to local users as well as to users who connect to a shared folder over the network. This fills the large security loophole left when files and folders on FAT partitions are secured only by share permissions.

The following sections discuss NTFS permissions, including how they are assigned to files and folders, how NTFS permissions are applied, and how NTFS and share permissions interact.

NTFS Permissions

NTFS permissions, which can only be assigned to files and folders on NTFS volumes, protect data from unauthorized access when users connect to the share locally or over the network.

The NTFS permissions that can be assigned, and how each permission applies to folders and files, are shown in Table 7-3.

TABLE 7-3 Windows NT NTFS Permissions

Permission	When applied to a folder, a user is able to. . .	When applied to a file, a user is able to. . .
Read (R)	View folder attributes, permissions, and owner; view names of files and subfolders.	View file attributes, permissions, owner, and file contents.
Write (W)	View folder attributes, permissions, and owner; change folder attributes; add files and subfolders.	View file attributes, permissions, and owner; change file attributes; change file contents.
Execute (X)	View folder attributes, permissions, and owner; change the current folder to a subfolder.	View file attributes, permissions, and owner; run the file if it is an executable program.
Delete (D)	Delete the folder.	Delete the file.

Continued

TABLE 7-3 *Continued*

Permission	When applied to a folder, a user is able to. . .	When applied to a file, a user is able to. . .
Change Permissions (P)	Assign NTFS permissions to the folder.	Assign NTFS permissions to the file.
Take Ownership (O)	Take ownership of the folder.	Take ownership of the file.

To make the assignment of NTFS permissions easier, Microsoft has created a set of standard directory (folder) permissions, and a set of standard file permissions. These *standard permissions* consist of the most commonly used combinations of NTFS permissions.

Standard permissions are used in most situations. Individual NTFS permissions are typically only used when a unique combination of permissions must be assigned. The individual NTFS permissions are sometimes referred to as *Special Access Directory permissions* and *Special Access File permissions*.

Table 7-4 shows the standard NTFS directory permissions. The permissions specified within the first set of parentheses following the permission name apply to the *folder*, and the permissions specified within the second set of parentheses following the permission name apply to *files* within the folder.

Table 7-5 shows the standard NTFS file permissions. NTFS file permissions apply only to the individual file they are assigned to. Other files in the same folder are *not* affected.

TABLE 7-4 Standard NTFS Directory (Folder) Permissions

Standard Permission	Description
No Access (None) (None)	Prevents access to the folder, and to any file in the folder. When the permission is initially assigned, the administrator can choose whether to apply the permission to existing files and subfolders.

Standard Permission	Description
List (RX) (Not Specified)	Assigns the Read and Execute permissions to the folder, but no permissions are assigned to any files in the folder.
Read (RX) (RX)	Assigns the Read and Execute permissions to the folder and to *new* files created in the folder. When the permission is initially assigned, the administrator can choose whether to apply the permission to all *existing* files and subfolders.
Add (WX) (Not Specified)	Assigns the Write and Execute permissions to the folder, but no permissions are assigned to any files in the folder.
Add & Read (RWX) (RX)	Assigns the Read, Write, and Execute permissions to the folder, and assigns the Read and Execute permissions to *new* files created in the folder. When the permission is initially assigned, the administrator can choose whether to apply the permission to all *existing* files and subfolders.
Change (RWXD) (RWXD)	Assigns the Read, Write, Execute, and Delete permissions to the folder and to *new* files created in the folder. When the permission is initially assigned, the administrator can choose whether to apply the permission to all *existing* files and subfolders.
Full Control (All) (All)	Assigns all NTFS permissions (Read, Write, Execute, Delete, Change Permissions, and Take Ownership) to the folder and to *new* files created in the folder. When the permission is initially assigned, the administrator can choose whether to apply the permission to all *existing* files and subfolders.

TABLE 7-5 Standard NTFS File Permissions

Standard File Permission	Description
No Access (None)	Prevents access to the file.
Read (RX)	Assigns the Read and Execute permissions to the file.
Change (RWXD)	Assigns the Read, Write, Execute, and Delete permissions to the file.
Full Control (All)	Assigns all NTFS permissions (Read, Write, Execute, Delete, Change Permissions, and Take Ownership) to the file.

Sometimes a user has a different set of NTFS permissions to a file than to the folder that contains the file. When the user wants to access a file, and the NTFS file and folder permissions conflict, the file permissions are applied. For example, if a user has the Change (RWXD) (RWXD) permission to the folder, and has the Read (RX) permission to the file, the user's effective permission to the file is Read (RX).

If a user has permission to access a file, but does *not* have permission to access the folder that contains the file, the user can access the file by typing the file's full path name (in an application, in the Run dialog box, or at the command prompt). The user can't see the file when browsing in Windows NT Explorer.

File permissions take precedence over folder permissions. You definitely need to know what happens when a user has conflicting file and folder permissions. You are very likely to see several scenarios like this on the Windows NT Server exam.

As with share permissions, it is not uncommon for a user to have one set of NTFS permissions to a file or folder, and to be a member of multiple groups that have different NTFS permissions to the file or folder. When this occurs, the user and group permissions are cumulative, and the *least* restrictive combination of permissions applies. The exception to this rule is the No Access permission. *No Access always overrides all other NTFS permissions.*

NTFS permissions are assigned by adding a user or group to the access control list (ACL) for the file or folder. From an administrative standpoint, it's much more efficient to add groups to the ACL for a particular file or folder than to add individual users. By default, the Everyone group is granted the Full Control (All) (All) NTFS permission to the root of all newly created NTFS volumes.

Assigning NTFS Permissions

A user can assign NTFS permissions to a file or folder only if one or more of the following criteria are met:

- The user is the owner of the file or folder.
- The user has the Change Permissions NTFS permission to the file or folder.
- The user has the Full Control NTFS permission to the file or folder. (The Full Control permission includes the Change Permissions NTFS permission.)

You can also assign individual (Special Access) NTFS file permissions (as opposed to the standard NTFS permissions). The Special Access dialog box is shown in Figure 7-5. Notice the individual NTFS permissions that can be assigned.

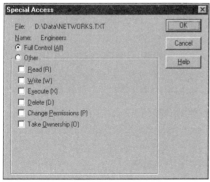

Figure 7-5 *Assigning individual (Special Access) NTFS permissions*

New, Moved, and Copied Files and Folders

When files are created in a folder on an NTFS volume, the new files inherit the NTFS permissions of the folder in which they are created. For example, if you create a new file in the Public folder, and the Public folder has the Change (RWXD) (RWXD) NTFS permission for the Everyone group, the new file inherits the Change (RWXD) permission for the Everyone group.

The permissions in the *second* set of parentheses following the NTFS folder permission name are the permissions that are assigned to the new *file*. So, if you create a new file in the Data folder, and the Data folder has the Add & Read (RWX) (RX) NTFS permission for the Users group, the file inherits the Read (RX) permission for the Users group.

When new subfolders are created on an NTFS volume, they inherit the NTFS permissions of the folder that contains them. For example, if you create a new subfolder in the Data folder, and the Data folder has the Add & Read (RWX) (RX) NTFS permission for the Everyone group, the new subfolder inherits the Add & Read (RWX) (RX) permission for the Everyone group.

When files or folders are moved or copied, their NTFS permissions often change. Normally, when files or folders are moved or copied, they inherit the NTFS permissions of the destination folder. The only exception to this rule is when files or folders are *moved* to a new folder on the *same* NTFS volume — in this case, the moved files or folders retain their original NTFS permissions.

Permission Inheritance

- When you create a file or folder on an NTFS volume, the file or folder inherits the permissions of the folder in which it was created.

- When you move or copy a file or folder to a different NTFS volume, the file or folder's permissions will be set to match the folder that contains it.
- When you move a file or folder within the same NTFS volume, the file or folder's permissions do not change.

The following examples illustrate how NTFS permissions are applied to moved or copied files:

Example 1: Moving a file to a folder on a different volume

You *move* the D:\Public\Readme.txt file (that has the Read (RX) NTFS permissions for the Everyone group) to the E:\Data folder (that has the Full Control (All) (All) NTFS permission for the Everyone group). When the file is moved to a folder on a different volume, it inherits the NTFS permissions from the E:\Data folder (the destination folder), so the moved file's permissions are now Full Control (All) for the Everyone group.

Example 2: Copying a file to a different folder on the same volume

You *copy* the D:\Data\Busplan.doc file (that has the Read (RX) NTFS permissions for the Managers group) to the D:\Public folder (that has the Change (RWXD) (RWXD) NTFS permissions for the Everyone group). When the file is copied, it inherits the NTFS permissions from the D:\Public folder (the destination folder), so the copied file's permissions are now Change (RWXD) for the Everyone group.

Example 3: Moving a file to a different folder on the same volume

You *move* the D:\Data\Busplan.doc file (that has the Read (RX) NTFS permissions for the Managers group) to the D:\Public folder (that has the Change (RWXD) (RWXD) NTFS permissions for the Everyone group). When the file is moved to a folder on the *same* NTFS volume, it retains its original NTFS permissions. In this case, the moved file's NTFS permissions are still Read (RX) for the Managers group.

Because FAT partitions can't support NTFS permissions, any files that you copy or move to a FAT partition lose all their NTFS permissions, along with the security that those permissions provided.

NTFS and Share Permission Interaction

When users access a share on an NTFS volume over the network, *both* NTFS and share permissions are used to determine the user's effective permission to the file or folder in the share. This means that if *either* the NTFS or the share permissions deny a user access, access is denied.

When NTFS and share permissions differ, the *most* restrictive permission becomes the user's effective permission to the file or folder in the share.

The following examples illustrate how NTFS and share permissions interact:

Example 1

A folder named Documents is shared on an NTFS volume. The Documents share has the Change share permission for the Everyone group, and the files and folders in the share all have the Full Control NTFS permission for the Everyone group. Users who access the Documents share over the network only have the Change permission to the files and folders, because Change is the most restrictive permission.

Example 2

A folder named Apps is shared on an NTFS volume. The Apps share has the Full Control share permission assigned to the Everyone group, and the files and folders in the share all have the Read NTFS permission for the Everyone group. Users who access the Apps share over the network the most restrictive permission.

Remember, share permissions only apply when users connect to a shared folder *over the network*. NTFS permissions are the only permissions that apply to users who log on locally to the computer that contains the share.

True or False?

1. File permissions take precedence over folder permissions.

2. A user can set permissions for a file if the user has the Change Permissions NTFS permission to the file.

3. When you move files between NTFS partitions, the file permissions stay the same.

4. A user can set permissions for a file only if the user is the owner of the file.

5. For remotely accessed resources on NTFS partitions, the effective permission is the more restrictive of the share and NTFS permissions.

Answers: *1. True 2. True 3. False 4. False 5. True*

Taking Ownership

The creator of a file or folder is its *owner* (except that when a member of the Administrators group creates a file or folder, the Administrators *group*, not the user, is the owner of the file or folder). The owner of a file or folder can always assign permissions to that file or folder. Only files and folders on NTFS partitions have owners.

Occasionally, you may need to change or assign permissions to a file or folder, but you do not have the Change Permissions NTFS permission (or the Full Control NTFS permission, which includes the Change Permissions NTFS permission) to the file or folder. Without being the owner of the file or folder or having the Change Permissions NTFS permission, the only way you can accomplish changing or assigning permissions to the file or folder is to *take ownership* of the file or folder.

Taking Ownership

A common situation where taking ownership becomes necessary is when a user (who created a folder and was its owner) leaves the company, and no one else has the Change Permissions NTFS permission (or the Full Control NTFS permission) to the folder. To change the permissions on the folder, the Administrator must first take ownership of it.

A user can take ownership of a file or folder only if at least one of the following criteria is met:

- The user is a member of the Administrators group.
- The user has the Take Ownership NTFS permission to the file or folder (or has the Full Control NTFS permission, which includes the Take Ownership permission).
- The user has the "Take ownership of files or other objects" user right.

Auditing

You can't be sure that your network is secure until you know that the permissions and other security measures you've put in place haven't been breached. Windows NT auditing makes it possible for you to determine whether unauthorized users have accessed or attempted to access sensitive data.

Windows NT auditing is *only* available on NTFS partitions. You can't audit files or folders that are located on FAT partitions.

Because auditing generates a large amount of data, it's important that you determine what is really necessary to audit. Not only does auditing data take up space in the Security Log, but it also takes administrative time to review the events in the log. In general, if you won't use the information obtained by auditing a given event, you probably shouldn't choose to audit it.

You can choose to audit both successful and unsuccessful (failure) events. For example, you can audit all successful attempts to access a particular program, or you can audit all unsuccessful attempts to access a file that contains confidential data. Success auditing is often performed to gather information about how resources, such as programs and printers, are used. Failure auditing is normally performed to determine whether unauthorized users are attempting to access restricted files or folders. Sometimes success and failure auditing are used simultaneously to determine if any unauthorized users have been successful in breaching the system's security.

When you choose to audit a sensitive resource to determine if your network security has been compromised, consider auditing the Everyone group's success and failure access to the resource. This way, you can track *all* attempts to access the resource, not just attempts made by Domain Users (in other words, the users that you know about).

Configuring Windows NT auditing for files and folders on NTFS partitions is a two-part process. First, the audit policy is configured in User Manager for Domains. Then, auditing is configured for each file and folder individually using Windows NT Explorer.

Only members of the Administrators group can configure the audit policy. Users with the "Manage auditing and Security Log" user right can establish file and folder auditing, and view and manage the Security Log in Event Viewer, but can't set audit policy.

Auditing is configured on an individual computer basis. If you want to audit an event that takes place on a domain controller, such as access to a particular folder, you need to set the audit policy for the domain and configure the folder for auditing on the domain controller. If you want to audit an event that takes place on a non-domain controller, such as access to a particular file, you need to set the audit policy on the non-domain controller and configure the particular file for auditing on the non-domain controller, as well.

In the Directory Auditing dialog box you can select the Success and/or Failure check boxes next to each NTFS permission you want to track for a resource. For example, if you want to know who has viewed or attempted to view a confidential file, you could select Success and Failure auditing for the Read permission.

If you are configuring auditing for a folder, you have the option of choosing to replace the existing auditing configuration on all files and/or subfolders with the settings you are configuring now. Select or deselect the check boxes next to Replace Auditing on Subdirectories and Replace Auditing on Existing Files as desired. Figure 7-6 shows the configured Directory Auditing dialog box for the D:\New Products Research Data folder. Notice that success and failure auditing for the Read permission is configured for the Everyone group.

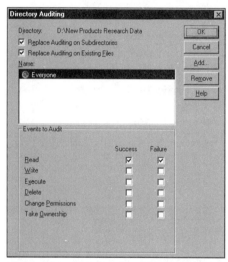

Figure 7-6 *Configuring folder auditing*

Troubleshooting Common Permission Problems

When a user can't access a resource (that he or she is supposed to be able to access), the administrator must determine why this is happening and correct the problem. Most resource access problems are caused by incorrectly configured permissions, conflicting permissions, or both.

Here are some recommended troubleshooting tips to help you to determine why a user can't access a shared network resource:

- **Look for conflicting share and NTFS permissions.**
  Determine which groups the user is a member of
  (including groups in other domains), and determine the
  user's effective share permissions and effective NTFS
  permissions to the resource.

- **Look for the No Access permission.** If the user, or any
  group of which the user is a member, has been assigned the
  No Access permission to the share or has been assigned the
  No Access NTFS permission to the resource, the user will
  not be able to access the resource.

- If you have just assigned the user permission to the
  resource, and the user can't access the resource, **try having
  the user log off and log on again**, so the user's access token
  will be updated.

Have You Mastered?

Now it's time to apply what you've learned in this chapter by testing your mastery of the material. These questions provide you with a means to determine if you are ready to move onto the next chapter or if you need to review the material again.

1. **You are managing a group of folders on a Windows NT Server computer. When you look at the attributes that are available for the files, you notice the Compress attribute is not shown. Why is the Compress attribute not shown?**

    ☐ A. You have insufficient permissions to configure the Compress attribute.
    ☐ B. The folders are on a FAT partition.
    ☐ C. The folders are on a NTFS partition.
    ☐ D. The folders are in a Windows NT stripe set.

The correct answer is **B**. The Compress attribute is available only on NTFS partitions, because only NTFS partitions have the ability to compress at the folder or file level. It does not matter if the files are stored on a volume that is part of a stripe set. For more information, see the "File and Folder Attributes" section.

2. You belong to three Windows NT groups, whose respective share permissions are Change, Read, and Full Control. What is your effective share permission?

    ☐ A. Change
    ☐ B. Read
    ☐ C. Full Control
    ☐ D. Special Access

The correct answer is C. User and group access permissions are cumulative, and the least restrictive access is your effective access permissions. So in this case your effective access permission for the share is Full Control. For more information, see the "Shared Folders" section.

3. You belong to three Windows NT groups, whose respective share permissions are No Access, Read, and Full Control. What is your effective share permission?

    ☐ A. No Access
    ☐ B. Read
    ☐ C. Full Control
    ☐ D. Special Access

The correct answer is A. This is the exception to the rule; even though user and group permissions are cumulative, if No Access is specified for the user or a group, the effective permission for the share is No Access. For more information, see the "Shared Folders" section.

4. You are the network administrator for a network consisting of Windows NT Server computers and Windows NT Workstation computers. You need to update a few files on the C: drive in one of the Windows NT Workstation computers. What can you do to access the hard drive of the Windows NT Workstation computer from your computer?

☐ A. Connect to the Windows NT Workstation computer's Admin$ share.

☐ B. Connect to the Windows NT Workstation computer's C$ share

☐ C. You cannot remotely access the hard drive of a Windows NT Workstation computer.

☐ D. Tell the user of the Windows NT Workstation computer to share the C: drive, as it is not shared by default.

The correct answer is **B**. By default, Windows NT automatically creates an administrative share for every hard drive partition in your computer. The administrative shares are named after their logical drive letter assignment and the $ sign is appended to hide the share from network browsers. For more information, see the "Administrative Shares" section.

5. **You are configuring the security settings and user group assignments for your Windows NT domain network. You want to allow users to create shared folders on their workstations, but you do not want them to be able to make changes to the Administrators local group. What groups can you place the users in?**

☐ A. Administrators

☐ B. Power Users

☐ C. Server Operators

☐ D. Users

The correct answer is **B**. The Administrators and Power Users groups allow users to create shared folders on a Windows NT Workstation. However, if the users are placed in the Administrators group, there would be nothing to prevent them from making changes to the group or even changing the Administrators password. The Users group has no permissions to add shared folders or printers on a Windows NT Workstation computer. For more information, see the "Shared Folders" section.

6. You are configuring the share permissions for a project folder on your Windows NT Server computer. You want to permit everyone in the Marketing department to have Read access to the folder. You want everyone in the Engineering department to have Full Control access to the folder. You configure the share permissions by granting the Marketing user group Read access and the Engineering user group Full Control. When users in the Engineering department attempt to make changes to the folder, they get an access denied message, but they are able to read the files in the folder. What is the most likely problem?

☐ A. The folder is on a FAT partition that has FAT permissions set as Read only.
☐ B. The users are only members of the Marketing user group.
☐ C. The users are members of both the Marketing and Engineering user groups.
☐ D. The folder is on an NTFS partition that has NTFS permissions set as Read only.

The correct answer is D. When NTFS file permissions and share permissions are different, the most restrictive access rights become the users' effective permissions. In this case, the NTFS permissions were set as Read only, so no matter what share permissions were granted, the file system would only allow read access. For more information, see the "NTFS and Share Permission Interaction" section.

7. You are moving a marketing ad campaign project folder from your Windows NT Workstation computer to a Windows NT Server computer. On your computer, the folder had NTFS partitions that allowed only the marketing department Full Control; the Everyone group was granted Read only access. The folder that will contain the project folder on the Windows NT Server computer has NTFS permissions set so that the Everyone

group has Change permission. What are the NTFS permissions for the folder after it has been moved?

☐ A. The permissions will stay the same. The marketing group will have Full Control and the Everyone group will have Read only access.

☐ B. The permissions will be set back to the default with the Everyone group having Full Control.

☐ C. The permissions will be set to match the new folder's permissions with the Everyone group having Change permission.

☐ D. The permissions will be set so that only the Administrators group has Full Control.

The correct answer is C. When files or folders are moved off of a NTFS partition to another partition or another computer, the files inherit the permissions of the new parent folder. If the files or folders are moved within the same partition, the file permissions will remain the same. For more information, see the "NTFS Security" section.

8. **You are the network administrator for your Windows NT domain network. One of company employees has left the company and went to work for a competitor. You have deleted the user's account to ensure that the employee will not be able to access the network. The employee's manager has requested that all of the employee's files be moved to the manager's personal folder for review. When you attempt to change the permissions for the files to allow the manager to work with the files, you are unable to set the permissions. What must you do in order to set the permissions on these files?**

☐ A. Use Windows Explorer and Take Ownership of the files and then change the permissions.

☐ B. Re-create the user account and change the permissions to allow the manager to work with the files.

☐ C. Move the files off of the NTFS partition and onto another one so that they are updated by the new partition permissions.

☐ D. Log on as a member of the Power Users group
and change the permissions for the files.

The correct answer is A. The only way that you can change the permissions for a file if you are not the owner/creator and do not have Change permission is to take ownership of the files. You must be logged in as a member of the Administrators local group to change the file permissions. When you delete an account and recreate it, it does not have the same security identifier and cannot be used to access files that had permissions assigned strictly for the original account. For more information, see the "Taking Ownership" section.

Practice Your Skills

Here is a chance to apply your practical hands-on experience and material from this chapter. These exercises are designed not only for you to apply the material in the book, but also for you to gain greater experience and exposure to the product. These exercises are a critical part of understanding the product and gaining valuable experience for using the product and passing the certification exam. For each of the following problems, consider the given facts and determine what you think are the possible causes of the problem and what course of action you might take to resolve the problem.

1. Managing shared folders

EXERCISE You are the network administrator for a Windows NT domain network. You have received a phone call from a user who says he is unable to share a folder on his Windows NT Workstation computer. You walk him through the steps, but he is still unable to share the folder. What is the most likely problem?

ANALYSIS The user is probably not a member of the Administrators or Power Users groups on his Windows NT Workstation computer. You either need to add him to one of these groups on his computer or you need to create the share while logged in with your administrative account.

2. Assigning share permissions

EXERCISE You are configuring the permissions for a shared folder on your network. You have assigned the Marketing and Sales user groups Change permissions for the share. You need to prevent the interns in the Marketing and Sales department from accessing the files in the shared folder. What can you do to prevent these few users from accessing the files?

ANALYSIS The No Access share permission overrides all other assigned permissions. So you can configure the share permissions and grant the user accounts for the interns the No Access permission.

3. Managing NTFS file and folder security

EXERCISE You are in the process of adding a new hard disk to your Windows NT Server computer. You want to move your project data files from the older, smaller hard disk to the new, larger hard disk. What is the largest problem you are likely to encounter after moving the files?

ANALYSIS Since the new hard disk will be in addition to the existing one, when the files are moved, all of the NTFS file permissions will be lost. When the files are placed on the new hard disk, the files will inherit the permission settings set on the new hard disk, or the folder containing the files. Before moving the files, document the NTFS file permission configuration and recreate the permissions after the files have been moved.

4. Taking ownership

EXERCISE You are updating your Windows NT Server computer. You have daily backups on the server, so you have created shared folders to allow people to save their files to your computer. You want to change the directory structure and update some of the files. When you try to open or access some of the files, you get an access denied message. When you try to change the permissions for the files, you are not permitted to. What should you do?

ANALYSIS You should take ownership of the files and change the file permissions to grant your account at least the Change permission. This will enable you to move the files and update the files as needed during your computer update.

Networking Protocols

In this chapter, you get your exam primer for TCP/IP and NWLink IPX/SPX Compatible Transport protocols. These are the two most common protocols in use today in Windows NT Server environments. You should be prepared to answer exam questions with an advanced level of knowledge in using these protocols. After a brief overview of TCP/IP, this chapter explores IP addressing, including how IP addresses are assigned. The chapter then describes NWLink IPX/SPX Compatible Transport, which provides protocol compatibility between Windows NT and NetWare computers. Finally, I present tips on troubleshooting common TCP/IP and connectivity problems.

Exam Material In This Chapter

Official Word

Based on Microsoft Objectives

Planning

- Choose a protocol for various situations. Protocols include:
  - TCP/IP
  - NWLink IPX/SPX Compatible Transport

Installation and Configuration

- Configure protocols and protocol bindings. Protocols include:
  - TCP/IP
  - NWLink IPX/SPX Compatible Transport

Inside Scoop

Based on Author's Experience

- You need to know how a TCP/IP address is define based on network and host IDs.
- You need to know the function of TCP/IP address properties such as the subnet mask and the default router.
- You should understand the requirements for assigning unique TCP/IP addresses and when a subnet mask is common to multiple computers.
- You should understand the benefits of using a DHCP server and how to manually assign TCP/IP addresses as well.
- You definitely need to understand how frame types and network numbers are used and assigned to network adapter cards.
- You should be prepared for exam questions on troubleshooting NWLink IPX/SPX Compatible Transport and TCP/IP protocol communication problems.

Are You Prepared?

Do you have what it takes? Try out these self-assessment questions to see if you have prepared for the material in this chapter or if you should review problem areas.

1. Your Internet Service Provider has assigned you a TCP/IP address to use to access the Internet from your corporate network. The address assigned to you is 10.10.222.200 and has a subnet mask of 255.255.0.0. What portion of the address is the network ID?

   - [ ] A. 10
   - [ ] B. 10.10
   - [ ] C. 10.10.222
   - [ ] D. 10.10.0.0

2. You are adding a Windows NT Server computer to a network that has NetWare 4.x server computers. Each of the servers is using a different frame type. How should you configure the frame type setting for the Windows NT Server network adapter?

   - [ ] A. Use auto frame type.
   - [ ] B. Add each frame type to the network adapter.
   - [ ] C. Choose one frame type and configure a default tree for Client Service for NetWare.
   - [ ] D. Add a network adapter card for each frame type and use auto frame type.

3. You are configuring your Windows NT Server computer, which has two network adapter cards. You install NWLink IPX/SPX Compatible Transport and need to configure the protocol to communicate with other servers on the network. What NWLink IPX/SPX Compatible Transport property must be configured in this server?

    ☐ A. Internal network number
    ☐ B. External network number
✓ ☐ C. Frame type
    ☐ D. Preferred Server

Answers:

1. B   *The subnet mask indicates which portion of a TCP/IP address is the network and host ID portions. In this scenario, the subnet mask of 255.255.0.0 shows that the first two octets are the network ID — 10.10. See the "IP Addressing" section.*

2. B   *A network adapter card can have more than one frame type configured, allowing it to work on networks with multiple frame types in use. See the "NWLink IPX/SPX Compatible Transport" section.*

3. A   *When more than one network adapter card is installed in a Windows NT Server running NWLink IPX/SPX Compatible Transport, each network adapter requires a unique Internal network number. See the "NWLink IPX/SPX Compatible Transport" section.*

Overview of TCP/IP

The *Transmission Control Protocol/Internet Protocol* (TCP/IP) is a widely used transport protocol that provides robust capabilities for Windows NT networking.

TCP/IP is a fast, routable enterprise protocol that is used on the Internet. TCP/IP is supported by many other operating systems, including Windows 95/98, Macintosh, UNIX, MS-DOS, and IBM mainframes. TCP/IP is typically the recommended protocol for large, heterogeneous networks.

A good place to begin a basic discussion of TCP/IP is with IP addressing — including subnet masks and default gateway addresses.

IP Addressing

An *IP address* is a 32-bit binary number, broken into four 8-bit sections (often called *octets*), that uniquely identifies a computer or other network device on a network that uses TCP/IP. IP addresses must be unique — *no two computers or other network devices on an internetwork should have the same IP address.*

 All TCP/IP devices on a network must have a unique address. This includes all of the client and server computers as well. This is an important item to remember for the exam and real life.

If two computers have the same IP address, one or both of the computers may be unable to communicate over the network. An IP address is *not* the same as a network adapter's hardware (or MAC) address.

Although an IP address is a 32-bit binary number, it is normally represented in a dotted decimal format. Each 8-bit octet is represented by a whole number between 0 and 255. The following numbers are sample IP addresses:

    192.168.59.5

    172.31.151.1

An IP address contains two important identifiers: a *network ID* and a *host ID*. One portion of each IP address identifies the network segment on which a computer (or other network device) is located. This portion is called the network ID. The length of the network ID within an IP address is variable and is specified by the subnet mask used in conjunction with the IP address. (Subnet masks are discussed in more detail in the next section.) The second portion of each IP address identifies the individual computer or network device. This portion is called the host ID.

To ensure that unique IP addresses are used, if you plan to connect your network to the Internet, you should contact your Internet Service Provider or InterNIC to obtain a range of valid IP addresses for your network.

All computers located on the same network segment have the same network ID. Each computer or other network device on a given network segment must have a unique host ID.

Subnet Masks

A *subnet mask* specifies which portion of an IP address represents the network ID and which portion represents the host ID. A subnet mask enables TCP/IP to determine whether network traffic destined for a given IP address should be transmitted on the local subnet, or whether it should be routed to a remote subnet.

A subnet mask should be the same for all computers and other network devices on a given network segment. When you take the exam, you need to remember that all of the devices on a physical network segment should use a common subnet mask.

A subnet mask is a 32-bit binary number, broken into four 8-bit sections (octets), that is normally represented in a dotted decimal format. Each 8-bit section is represented by a whole number between 0 and 255.

A common subnet mask is 255.255.255.0. This particular subnet mask specifies that TCP/IP will use the first three octets of an IP address as the network ID, and will use the last octet as the host ID.

Another common subnet mask is 255.255.0.0. This subnet mask specifies that TCP/IP will use the first two octets of an IP address as the network ID, and use the last two octets as the host ID. (Without getting into too much binary math, an octet number of 255 specifies the entire octet is part of the network ID; and an octet number of 0 specifies the entire octet is part of the host ID. Numbers between 0 and 255 specify that part of the octet corresponds to the network ID and the remaining part corresponds to the host ID.)

If subnet masks are incorrectly configured, network communications problems due to routing errors may occur. For example, TCP/IP may incorrectly determine that a computer on the local subnet is located on a remote subnet and attempt to route a packet to the remote subnet. In this instance, the computer on the local subnet would never receive the packet intended for it.

Default Gateway Addresses

A *default gateway address* specifies the IP address of a router on the local network segment. When a computer that uses TCP/IP determines that the computer it wants to communicate with is located on a remote sub-net, it sends all network messages intended for the remote computer to the default gateway address, instead of directly to the destination computer. The router on the local subnet specified by the default gateway address forwards the messages to the destination computer on the remote subnet, either directly or via other routers.

Watch out for scenarios where the client computer does not have a default router assigned. The default router will always be the router's network adapter on the local subnet.

If a computer's default gateway address does *not* specify a router on the local subnet, then that computer will be *unable* to communicate with computers or other network devices located on other network segments.

When a router is used to connect two network segments, it has two network cards and two IP addresses. Figure 8-1 illustrates how default gateway addresses are used to specify the IP address of a router on the local subnet.

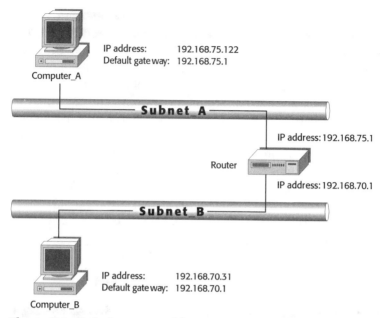

IP address: 192.168.75.122
Default gateway: 192.168.75.1
Computer_A

Subnet_A

IP address: 192.168.75.1

Router

IP address: 192.168.70.1

Subnet_B

IP address: 192.168.70.31
Default gateway: 192.168.70.1
Computer_B

Figure 8-1 *Default gateway addresses specify the local router*

Notice that in Figure 8-1, the default gateway address of Computer_A matches the IP address of its local router, and the default gateway address of Computer_B matches the IP address of its local router.

POP QUIZ True or False?

1. Each network adapter should have its own subnet mask address.

2. A TCP/IP address consists of a host ID address followed by a Network ID address.

3. The default router address should be the address of the router's network adapter on the local subnet.

4. Each network adapter should have a unique host ID address.

5. By default, a host uses the network adapter's MAC address as its TCP/IP address.

Answers: *1. False 2. False 3. True 4. True 5. False*

Assigning IP Addresses

IP addresses must be configured on each computer when TCP/IP is installed. You can assign an IP address to a Windows NT computer in one of two ways: by configuring a computer to obtain an IP address automatically from a DHCP server, or by manually specifying a computer's IP address configuration.

IP addresses are assigned to Windows NT computers in the Microsoft TCP/IP Properties dialog box. Instructions for accessing and configuring this dialog box are covered later in this chapter.

Assigning IP Addresses by Using a DHCP Server

The most convenient method for assigning IP addresses to multiple computers, in terms of administration time required, is to configure each of the computers to obtain its IP address from a *Dynamic Host Configuration Protocol* (DHCP) server.

This section discusses the advantages of using a DHCP server and how to configure a client computer to obtain its IP address from a DHCP server.

Using a DHCP server to assign IP addresses is the preferred because:

- You can manage IP addresses centrally, thus ensuring that addresses are valid and are not duplicated.

- A DHCP server reduces the amount of administration time required to manage and maintain IP addresses for each computer on the network.

- A DHCP server reduces the likelihood of human error when IP addresses are assigned because no need exists to enter an IP address manually on every individual computer.

- A DHCP server enables you to regain the use of an IP address no longer assigned to a host when the DHCP lease period for this IP address expires.

For the exam, make sure you understand the benefits of using a DHCP server. A DHCP server can be used to automatically assign and manage TCP/IP addresses for multiple subnets. Manually assigning and tracking these addresses is often too complex for many network environments.

Before you can assign an IP address to a Windows NT computer by using a DHCP server, you must first install and configure a DHCP server on your network. After a DHCP server is installed and configured, you can configure client computers to obtain their IP addresses from the DHCP server. Figure 8-2 shows the Microsoft TCP/IP Properties dialog box.

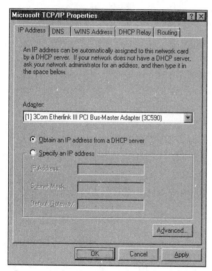

Figure 8-2 *Using a DHCP server to assign an IP address*

Assigning IP Addresses Manually

If you don't have a DHCP server, you must assign IP addresses manually. This method is both more time-consuming than using a DHCP server and more prone to error, because an IP address must be manually typed on each individual computer. Figure 8-3 shows a manually configured IP address for a Windows NT Server computer.

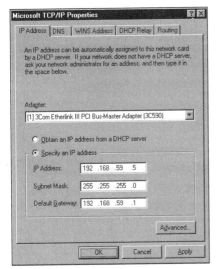

Figure 8-3 *Assigning an IP address manually*

NWLink IPX/SPX Compatible Transport

NWLink IPX/SPX Compatible Transport is a routable transport protocol typically used in a combined Windows NT and NetWare environment. NWLink IPX/SPX Compatible Transport is Microsoft's version of Novell's IPX/SPX protocol. (*IPX/SPX* is the protocol used on most Novell NetWare networks.) NWLink provides protocol compatibility between Windows NT and NetWare computers. In addition to its functionality in a NetWare environment, NWLink also fully supports Microsoft networking.

NWLink IPX/SPX Compatible Transport, which is included with Windows NT Server, must be installed on NT Server computers in order to enable them to communicate over the network with NetWare computers.

There are two important topics that need to be discussed before moving on to the installation of NWLink IPX/SPX Compatible Transport: frame types and network numbers. Because frame types and network numbers must be configured during installation, it's important to have a solid grasp of these basic network concepts.

Frame Types

Frame types (also called *frame formats*) are accepted, standardized structures for transmitting data packets over a network. All frame types include certain common components, such as source address, destination address, data field, and cyclic redundancy check — but the various frame types include different combinations of additional fields beyond the common components.

Windows NT and NWLink IPX/SPX Compatible Transport support nine different frame types, which are described in Table 8-1.

TABLE 8-1 NWLink IPX/SPX Compatible Transport Frame Types		
Frame Type	**Default/ Common Usage**	**Network Adapters That Support This Frame Type**
Ethernet 802.2	Default frame type for NetWare 3.12 and later NetWare versions on Ethernet networks.	Ethernet
Ethernet 802.3	Default frame type for NetWare 3.11 and earlier NetWare versions on Ethernet networks.	Ethernet
Ethernet II	Commonly associated with the TCP/IP protocol; not commonly used with NWLink IPX/SPX Compatible Transport.	Ethernet

Frame Type	Default/ Common Usage	Network Adapters That Support This Frame Type
Ethernet SNAP	Commonly associated with the AppleTalk protocol; not commonly used with NWLink IPX/SPX Compatible Transport.	Ethernet, FDDI
ARCNET	Default frame type for all versions of NetWare on ARCNET networks.	ARCNET
Token-Ring	Default frame type for all versions of NetWare on Token Ring networks.	Token Ring
Token-Ring SNAP	Commonly associated with the AppleTalk protocol; not commonly used with NWLink IPX/SPX Compatible Transport.	Token Ring
FDDI	Default frame type for NetWare 3.12 and later NetWare versions on FDDI networks.	FDDI
FDDI 802.3	Default frame type for NetWare 3.11 and earlier NetWare versions on FDDI networks.	FDDI

TEST TIP

If you do not know what frame type is being used, use the auto frame type. The auto frame type can be used in network environments where the default frame type on the NetWare servers is unknown. You are most likely to see this on the exam as a scenario where you are unable to access a NetWare server.

Before you select a frame type when installing and configuring NWLink IPX/SPX Compatible Transport, you should determine which frame type(s) are already in use on the network. You should select a frame type that matches the frame type already in use, or use the Windows NT auto frame type detection feature to automatically select a frame type. You can assign more than one frame type to an individual network adapter.

Frame type mismatching is a common cause of communications problems on networks that use NWLink IPX/SPX Compatible Transport.

Network Numbers

Network numbers are 32-bit binary numbers that uniquely identify an NWLink IPX/SPX Compatible Transport network segment for routing purposes. Because network numbers uniquely identify a network segment, they are used by IPX routers to forward data packets correctly from one network segment to another.

Network numbers are only assigned to Windows NT computers that use NWLink IPX/SPX Compatible Transport. Network numbers are assigned during the installation and configuration of NWLink IPX/SPX Compatible Transport.

Network numbers are commonly presented in an eight-digit hexadecimal format. (In a hexadecimal format, the numbers 0 through 9 and the letters A through F can be used.) Don't confuse a network number with a TCP/IP network ID or a computer's MAC (hardware) address.

There are two types of network numbers: *external network numbers* (network numbers that are assigned to network adapters) and *internal network numbers*. A Windows NT computer that uses NWLink IPX/SPX Compatible Transport can have one or more external network number(s) and an internal network number, as well.

When NWLink IPX/SPX Compatible Transport is used, an external network number is assigned to each network adapter installed in a computer. An external network number uniquely identifies the network segment to which the network adapter is connected. (If more than one frame type is assigned to a network adapter, then each frame type is assigned its own external network number.) Windows NT can automatically detect and use the external network number in use on a network segment. However, you can manually assign any unique eight-digit external network number to a network adapter during the configuration of NWLink IPX/SPX Compatible Transport. External network numbers are sometimes referred to simply as network numbers.

NWLink IPX/SPX Compatible Transport Networks

An external network number uniquely identifies the network segment to which the network adapter is connected. An internal network number must be assigned to a Windows NT computer that uses NWLink IPX/SPX Compatible Transport when more than one network adapter is installed in it.

If there is only one network adapter installed in a computer, Windows NT does not require you to assign an internal network number, although you can assign an internal network number if you want. An internal network number is an additional unique eight-digit network number that is used by the computer's operating system — an internal network number does *not* correspond to a specific network adapter installed in the computer. A Windows NT computer has only one internal network number, regardless of the number of network adapters installed in it.

Installing and Configuring NWLink IPX/SPX Compatible Transport

Installing and configuring NWLink IPX/SPX Compatible Transport is a fairly straightforward process. You should be prepared to enter the appropriate frame type(s) and network number(s) when prompted. If you have multiple adapters installed in your Windows NT computer, you will also have to assign an internal network number. Finally, only install this protocol at a time when you can shut down and restart the computer.

When installing and configuring NWLink IPX/SPX Compatible Transport, if there is more than one network adapter installed in your computer, an NWLink IPX/SPX warning dialog box appears, indicating that you need to configure your computer's internal network number, as shown in Figure 8-4. Figure 8-5 shows the NWLink IPX/SPX Properties dialog box.

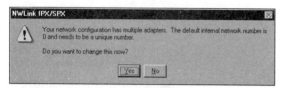

Figure 8-4 *Multiple network adapter warning*

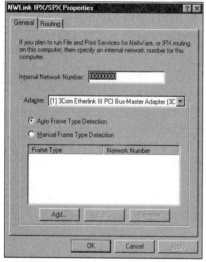

Figure 8-5 *Configuring the internal network number*

Notice that you can configure the internal network number and the frame type in this dialog box. The configurable options in this dialog box are:

- **Internal Network Number:** Change the Internal Network Number to a unique nonzero hexadecimal number up to eight digits long.

- **Auto Frame Type Detection:** If you want Windows NT to automatically detect and assign a frame type to a network adapter, select the option button next to Auto Frame Type Detection.

• **Manual Frame Type Detection:** If you want to manually assign a frame type to a network adapter, select the option button next to Manual Frame Type Detection, and click the Add command button. When you select Manual Frame Type Detection, the Manual Frame Detection dialog box appears, as shown in Figure 8-6. Note the Frame Type drop-down list box and the Network Number text box. Select the desired frame type from the Frame Type drop-down list box. Type in a unique nonzero hexadecimal number up to eight digits long in the Network Number text box. Click the Add command button. (Note: All computers on a single subnet should use the *same* network number.)

You can assign multiple frame types and network numbers to an individual network adapter. This is beneficial when your network contains multiple servers, which are running several different frame types. This way, a single network adapter can communicate with servers running different frame types.

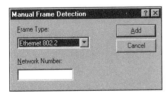

Figure 8-6 *Manually assigning a frame type and network number to a network adapter*

True or False?

1. NWLink IPX/SPX Compatible Transport does not fully support Microsoft networking.

2. A Windows NT computer can have more than one Internal IPX/SPX network number.

Continued

> **3.** A Windows NT Computer can only have one frame type per network adapter card.
>
> **4.** Each network card in a Windows NT computer running IPX/SPX should have its own network number.
>
> **Answers:** *1. False 2. False 3. False 4. True*

Troubleshooting Common TCP/IP Connectivity Problems

There are several common TCP/IP connectivity problems. Most TCP/IP connectivity problems are caused by incorrectly configured TCP/IP settings on the computer that has the problem.

TCP/IP connectivity problems commonly reported by users include:

- A user is unable to access a computer located on another subnet.
- A user is unable to access the Internet.
- A user is unable to access computers on both the local and remote subnets.
- TCP/IP fails to initialize on the user's computer.

When troubleshooting a TCP/IP connectivity problem, carefully check the TCP/IP settings on the computer experiencing the problem, including: IP address, subnet mask, and default gateway.

- **IP address:** Make sure the computer's IP address is *not* a duplicate of another IP address used on the network, and that it is an appropriate IP address for the local subnet (the network ID portion of the IP address must be the same for all computers on the local subnet).
- **Subnet mask:** Ensure the computer's subnet mask is the same subnet mask used by all computers and routers located on that subnet.

- **Default gateway:** Ensure the computer's default gateway address matches the IP address of a router on the local subnet.

Two command-line utilities exist that can help you when you're troubleshooting TCP/IP connectivity problems: `Ipconfig.exe` and `ping.exe`.

`Ipconfig.exe` displays the computer's current IP configuration settings, including IP address, subnet mask, and default gateway. To use `Ipconfig.exe`, select Start ➪ Programs ➪ Command Prompt. At the command prompt, type **ipconfig /all** and press Enter.

It is important to understand that the `ping` command can be used to determine if there are any communication failures or errors between two network computers. This is often the target of many TCP/IP troubleshooting questions.

`Ping.exe` verifies network communications between the local computer and any other computer specified on the network. To use `ping.exe`, select Start ➪ Programs ➪ Command Prompt. At the command prompt, type **ping *ip_address*** and press Enter. (The IP address entered is the IP address of the computer with which you are attempting to communicate.) If your computer is able to communicate with the remote computer specified, `ping.exe` will display four replies from the remote computer's IP address. The following is an example of a successful ping response:

```
Reply from 192.168.59.5: bytes=32 time<10ms TTL=128
Reply from 192.168.59.5: bytes=32 time<10ms TTL=128
Reply from 192.168.59.5: bytes=32 time<10ms TTL=128
Reply from 192.168.59.5: bytes=32 time<10ms TTL=128
```

If your computer is unable to communicate with the remote computer specified, `ping.exe` usually displays `Request timed out` four times.

You can ping your own computer's IP address to determine whether TCP/IP is correctly configured and initialized on your local computer. If TCP/IP is correctly configured on your local computer, `ping.exe` will display four replies from your local computer's IP address.

Have You Mastered?

Now it's time to apply what you've learned in this chapter by testing your mastery of the material. These questions provide you with a means to determine if you are ready to move on to the next chapter or if you need to review the material again.

1. **You are installing TCP/IP on a Windows NT Server computer. Which pieces of information must you have in order to configure TCP/IP to communicate with computers on the local subnet? (Choose two.)**

   ✓ ☐ A. TCP/IP host address
   ✓ ☐ B. Subnet mask
   ☐ C. Default router
   ☐ D. Frame Type
   ☐ E. Internal network number

   The correct answers are A and B. Because you only need to communicate with computers on the local subnet, you do not need a default router. Also, TCP/IP is not configured for a specific Frame type or internal network number as IPX/SPX is. For more information, see the "IP Addressing" section.

2. **You are installing three Windows NT Server computers onto a single subnet on your network. Your network consists of 30 subnets connected with routers. You install TCP/IP on each of the Windows NT Server computers. What TCP/IP configuration information will probably be the same on all of the computers? (Choose two.)**

☐ A. TCP/IP Address
☐ B. Subnet mask
☐ C. Default router
☐ D. Host name

The correct answers are B and C. Because the Windows NT Server computers are on the same subnet, they will most likely have the same subnet mask and default router defined for them, whereas the TCP/IP address and host name are unique to each computer, regardless of where it resides on a network. For more information, see the "IP Addressing" section.

3. You are troubleshooting a communications problem on a Windows NT Server computer. The computer can access other computers and devices on the local subnet, but is unable to access resources on other parts of the network and the Internet. What is the first thing you should verify?

☐ A. TCP/IP Address
☐ B. Subnet mask
☐ C. Default router
☐ D. Host name

The correct answer is C. If a computer is able to access resources on a local subnet and cannot communicate across subnets, the problem is likely to be an incorrect default router setting. Without a default router defined, the Server has no means to pass traffic to computers that reside on remote subnets. For more information, see the "IP Addressing" section.

4. Your Windows NT Workstation is configured to use a DHCP server to receive its TCP/IP configuration. You need to determine the IP address that the server has assigned to your computer. What can you do to view your IP address that was assigned to your computer?

☐ A. Use Network in the Control Panel to view the TCP/IP protocol configuration.
☐ B. Use the `ipconfig /all` command.
☐ C. Use the Internet Service Manager to view your TCP/IP configuration.
☐ D. Use the `ping /all` command.

The correct answer is **B**. The `ipconfig` command-line application can be used to display the current TCP/IP configuration for each network adapter in a computer. This application will show the TCP/IP address, subnet mask, and default gateway, among other things, for each adapter. Network in the Control Panel will not show the current TCP/IP assignments, it will only indicate that the computer is configured to use DHCP. For more information, see the "Troubleshooting Common TCP/IP Connectivity Problems" section.

5. **You are experiencing difficulty connecting to a TCP/IP host computer on a remote subnet on your network. Previously you have had no problems working with this remote host, but recently you are unable to reach the host. What can you do to determine if there is a communications problem between your Windows NT Server computer and the remote host?**

☐ A. Change your computer's subnet mask to match that of the remote host.
☐ B. Change your computer's default gateway to match that of the remote host.
☐ C. Use the `ipconfig` command.
☐ D. Use the `ping` command.

The correct answer is **D**. The `ping` command can be used in conjunction with the remote host name or TCP/IP address to determine if there is a communications failure. The ping command will trace the route to the remote host and report back if any errors are encountered or if the host was unreachable. The configuration settings on the Windows NT Server won't necessarily solve the problem, especially when the scenario stated that the two computers had been communicating previously. For more information, see the "Troubleshooting Common TCP/IP Connectivity Problems" section.

6. **You are installing Gateway Service for NetWare and the NWLink IPX/SPX Compatible Transport on your Windows NT Server computer. Your computer has one network adapter and you will be connecting to a NetWare 3.x server. What information must you have to configure these two components? (Choose two.)**

- ☐ A. An external network number
- ☐ B. An internal network number
- ☐ C. Frame type
- ☐ D. Default Context
- ☐ E. Default Tree
- ☐ F. Preferred Server

The correct answers are A and C. Because the computer only has one network adapter, you are required to only have an external network address. You also need the Frame type for the network segment the computer is connected to. For more information, see the "NWLink IPX/SPX Compatible Transport" section.

Practice Your Skills

Here is a chance to apply your practical hands-on experience and material from this chapter. These exercises are designed not only for you to apply the material in the book, but also for you to gain greater experience and exposure to the product. These exercises are a critical part of understanding the product and gaining valuable experience for using the product and passing the certification exam. For each of the following problems, consider the given facts and determine what you think are the possible causes of the problem and what course of action you might take to resolve the problem.

1. Using TCP/IP in large networks

EXERCISE You are designing a large enterprise-wide network. What makes TCP/IP such a good choice for large, routed networks supporting thousands of computers?

ANALYSIS The TCP/IP protocol is a high-speed routable protocol that scales to fit very large and complex networks. In addition to its ability to overcome network outages and downed links, TCP/IP is supported on more computing platforms than any other protocol. These factors, combined with the ability to provide services to clients over a single protocol, make TCP/IP the logical choice for today's complex enterprise networks.

2. Configuring TCP/IP properties

EXERCISE You are installing Windows NT Server computers on a network that contains several subnets connected with routers. When you configure the TCP/IP protocol, why is it important to know what the subnet mask should be for the Windows NT Servers computers?

ANALYSIS The subnet mask indicates to the Windows NT Server computer which portion of the host TCP/IP address is the network ID address and which is the host ID address. This not only allows the computer to know what its own host address is, but to know what the local subnet is, and which address are local to its subnet. When the computer determines that a destination address is not local, it forwards the traffic to the default router and indicates where it should be sent.

3. Using a DHCP server

EXERCISE You are in the process of deploying a large number of Windows NT Workstation computers. You will be using the NWLink IPX/SPX Compatible Transport and TCP/IP on the computers. What are some advantages of using a DHCP server to provide TCP/IP configuration to the clients rather than manually configuring the clients?

ANALYSIS The DHCP server can automate the process of delivering TCP/IP configuration settings to a client computer. Each time the computer starts, it checks in with a DHCP server and requests an address, or verifies the last address assigned to it, and retrieves configuration settings for default gateway, subnet mask, and so on. In addition, the DHCP server can specify the period of time that the configuration is valid for. This enables networks with thousands of client computers to share IP addresses, in that when a client is removed from a network, its DHCP lease expires and another computer can use the free TCP/IP address. However, if the lease has not expired, or the lease period is too long, the address will not be recycled to other computers.

4. Windows NT in a NetWare environment

EXERCISE You have just added a new Windows NT Server computer to your network. You have installed the Gateway Service for NetWare and the NWLink IPX/SPX Compatible Transport to the computer. You are able to see other Windows NT Server computers via IPX/SPX, but you cannot locate any NetWare 3.*x* servers. What is the most likely problem?

ANALYSIS Because you are able to see other computers using NWLink IPX/SPX Compatible Transport, the problem is probably that the wrong frame type was configured for the adapter. The NetWare servers are probably running a frame type other than what you have configured your adapter for. Check the NetWare server frame type and update the configuration on the Windows NT Server computer.

NetWare Coexistence and Migration

I n this chapter you continue your Windows NT Server exam preparation by examining how Windows NT Server can communicate with NetWare servers, and how a NetWare server contents can be migrated to a Windows NT Server computer. I begin with a look at the Gateway Service for NetWare and describe the requirements for establishing shared folders via the gateway. I then explore the use of the Migration Tool for NetWare and how it can be used to automate the migration process for a small network. The chapter wraps up with a look at performing trial migrations and troubleshooting common NetWare connectivity problems.

Exam Material In This Chapter

Based on Microsoft Objectives

Connectivity

- Configure Windows NT Server for interoperability with NetWare servers by using various tools. Tools include:
  - Gateway Service for NetWare
  - Migration Tool for NetWare

Troubleshooting

- Choose the appropriate course of action to take to resolve connectivity problems.

Based on Author's Experience

- You need to know the NetWare user account permission requirements when using the Gateway Service for NetWare.

- You should be familiar with the NetWare server requirements before performing a migration, such as the use of bindery emulation.

- You need to know what permissions you are required to have before using the Migration Tool for NetWare on a Windows NT Server computer.

- You need to know what must be configured on a Windows NT Server to be able to convert NetWare file and folder permissions during a migration.

- You should be prepared for questions about what types of information cannot be migrated, such as user passwords.

Are You Prepared?

Do you have what it takes? Try out these self-assessment questions to see if you have prepared for the material in this chapter or if you should review problem areas.

1. **You are installing Gateway Service for NetWare on your Windows NT Server computer. You add a NetWare account for the GSNW service to use to connect to the NetWare server. What NetWare group must this account belong to in order for GSNW to operate correctly?**

    - ☐ A. GSNW
    - ☐ B. NTGSNW
    - ☒ C. NTGATEWAY
    - ☐ D. GATEWAY

2. **You are preparing to migrate user accounts off of a NetWare 4.x server. You install Gateway Service for NetWare and NWLink IPX/SPX Compatible Transport on your Windows NT Server computer. How should the NetWare 4.x server be configured before you can migrate your user accounts?**

    - ☐ A. Bindery Emulation must be disabled.
    - ☐ B. Bindery Emulation must be enabled.
    - ☒ C. The Frame Type must be configured as 802.2
    - ☐ D. The Frame Type must be configured as 802.3

3. You are configuring a new shared folder using Gateway Service for NetWare. The NetWare file permissions for the gateway account is Read Only. You assign Full Control to the Everyone Windows NT user group. What are the effective access permissions when a member of the Everyone access the shared folder?

☐ A. Read only access
☐ B. Full Control access
☐ C. Special Access
☐ D. No Access

Answers:

1. C   *When configuring the NetWare user account for the Gateway Service for NetWare gateway service, the user account should have supervisor equivalent permissions and must be a member of a group called NTGATEWAY. This account does not exist by default. See the "Gateway Service for NetWare" section.*

2. B   *The NetWare to Windows NT Server migration utility does not support NDS access for migrations, so the server must be running bindery emulation. See the "Migration Tool for NetWare" section.*

3. A   *Like NTFS file permissions and shared permissions, when access permissions conflict, the most restrictive access permission is the effective permission for the user. Because the NetWare server only allowed Read only access, it didn't matter what the NT group access permissions were. See the "Gateway Service for NetWare" section.*

Windows NT in a NetWare Environment

Microsoft includes components with Windows NT Server that enable Windows NT Server computers to coexist with Novell NetWare servers and client computers on the same network.

In a nutshell, these features enable Windows NT Server computers to utilize the resources on NetWare servers in a heterogeneous networking environment. These components can be used for long-term integration in a mixed network operating system environment, or for the short-term during a migration from NetWare to Windows NT.

When you consider the large number of existing Novell NetWare networks, particularly when Windows NT was first released, it's not too surprising that Microsoft has developed and included these components with Windows NT. Solutions that enable both Windows NT and NetWare to be used on the same network were critical to Windows NT's wide acceptance in the network operating system arena.

Microsoft has addressed this challenge by developing Gateway Service for NetWare (GSNW), which increases the interoperability of Windows NT with NetWare.

Gateway Service for NetWare

Gateway Service for NetWare (GSNW) is a Windows NT Server service that, when installed and configured on a Windows NT Server computer, allows users to access resources (such as files, folders, and printers) on a NetWare server. GSNW enables access to resources on NetWare 4.*x* servers as well as NetWare 3.*x* servers. GSNW also enables users to run NetWare login scripts during the Windows NT logon process.

TEST TIP

Gateway Service for NetWare operates just like Client Services for NetWare, found on Windows NT Workstation computers. But GSNW adds the ability to share resources located on a NetWare server to client computers of the Windows NT Server computer.

In addition, GSNW enables the Windows NT Server computer to share resources (files, folders, and printers) located on a NetWare server transparently to client computers of the Windows NT Server computer. GSNW accomplishes this by converting the *Server Message Blocks* (SMBs) from the client computers of the Windows NT Server computer into *NetWare Core Protocol* (NCP) requests that are recognized by the NetWare server.

KNOW THIS

GSNW Features

GSNW does *not* enable a Windows NT Server computer to share its resources with NetWare client computers.

GSNW is included with Windows NT Server, and requires the use of NWLink IPX/SPX Compatible Transport.

Configuring Gateway Service for NetWare

You can either configure GSNW the first time you log on after installing GSNW, or you can configure GSNW at a later time by using the GSNW application in Control Panel.

When configuring GSNW, you should be prepared to enter either the name of a preferred NetWare 3.*x* server you want to use or your tree and context for a NetWare 4.*x* server.

Pay particular attention to the gateway configuration options, including the user account used to configure the gateway. The user account on the NetWare server *must* be a member of the NTGATEWAY group on the NetWare server, and the NTGATEWAY group *must* have the appropriate NetWare permissions to the share.

NetWare Account Requirements for GSNW

In order to share resources located on a NetWare server through GSNW, you must create a user account on the NetWare server and create a group called NTGATEWAY (this is the required name). The NetWare user account must be a member of the NTGATEWAY group.

The Gateway Service for NetWare dialog box is shown in Figure 9-1. Notice the various configuration options available.

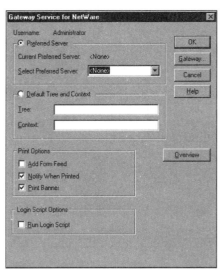

Figure 9-1 *Configuring Gateway Service for NetWare*

To configure GSNW, you must select from one of two primary options: Preferred Server, or Default Tree and Context. You can also select print, login script, and gateway options in this dialog box.

- **Preferred Server:** Specify a Preferred Server if you primarily access resources on NetWare 3.*x* servers. Then select the NetWare server of your choice from the Select Preferred Server drop-down list box.

- **Default Tree and Context:** Specify a Default Tree and Context if you primarily access resources on NetWare 4.*x* servers. Then enter the tree name and context that contain your NetWare 4.*x* user account in the Tree and Context text boxes.

- **Print Options:** If you print to a printer on a NetWare server, you can configure the Print Options section of the Gateway Service for NetWare dialog box. There are three options you can select:

  - **Add Form Feed:** Selecting this check box causes an additional form feed to be sent at the end of each print job. Deselect this check box if an additional blank page is printing at the end of each of your print jobs. By default, this check box is not selected.

  - **Notify When Printed:** Selecting this check box causes a pop-up message to appear on your screen after a print job is sent by the NetWare server to the print device. Clear this check box if you no longer want to receive these messages. This check box is selected by default.

  - **Print Banner:** Selecting this check box causes an additional sheet of paper that identifies the user that initiated the print job (called a banner page) to be printed at the beginning of each print job. If you want to save paper, deselect this check box. This check box is selected by default.

- **Login Script Options:** Selecting the check box next to Run Login Script in this section causes the NetWare login script to run during the Windows NT logon process.

- **Gateway:** You can configure the gateway if you want to share resources located on NetWare servers with clients of your Windows NT Server computer.

The Configure Gateway dialog box is used to configure the gateway properties for connecting to NetWare servers. The gateway can be configured using these options:

- **Enable Gateway:** Before you can share any resources located on a NetWare server with client computers of your Windows NT Server computer, the check box next to

Enable Gateway must be selected. (If you enable the gateway and you log in to the NetWare server, GSNW uses two user connections on the NetWare server: one for you, and one for the gateway. When using a five-user client license on the NetWare server, logging in and using the gateway leaves you only three connections.)

- **Gateway Account:** Enter a user account on the NetWare Server that you want to share resources from in the Gateway Account text box. If the user account is on a NetWare 4.*x* server, enter the complete account name, in the format: *.user_name.organizational_unit .organization_name.* This user account *must* be a member of a group on the NetWare server called NTGATEWAY. The gateway won't function correctly if the user account listed in this text box is not a member of this group. Also, the NTGATEWAY group must have the appropriate NetWare permissions to the resources that you want to share by using the gateway.

- **Password** and **Confirm Password:** Enter the password for the user account on the NetWare Server (that you entered in the Gateway Account text box) in the Password and Confirm Password text boxes.

Once the Gateway properties are configured, you can add new shares. These gateway shares are used to connect to the NetWare shared volumes. Each share requires that these options be configured:

- **Share Name:** Enter the name of the share, as you want it to appear to client computers of the Windows NT Server computer, in the Share Name text box.

- **Network Path:** Enter the complete UNC path to the NetWare folder that you are sharing in the Network Path text box.

- **Comment:** Enter the comment that will appear in the browse list of the client computers of the Windows NT Server computer.

- **Use Drive:** Enter the drive letter that GSNW will use to connect to the NetWare server. This drive letter can't already be in use on this computer.

- **User Limit:** You can specify either Unlimited or Allow *xx* Users. If you select Allow *xx* Users, you can enter the maximum number of concurrent users that will be allowed to access the share.

After you have configured each share, you will see the Share Permissions dialog box. You can configure Windows NT shared folder access permissions for the gateway share. The permissions you assign here are still limited to the permissions granted to the gateway account on the NetWare server. That is, the Windows NT share permissions can not be less restrictive than the NetWare shares.

 The most restrictive combination of NT share permissions and NetWare file and folder permissions applies. If the NetWare permissions are Read Only for the gateway account, all users will have effective permissions no greater than Read Only, even if the NT share permissions grant Full Control.

Accessing Resources on NetWare Servers

Resources on NetWare 3.*x* servers and NetWare 4.*x* servers are accessed by using two different types of universal naming convention (UNC) path names.

To access resources on NetWare 3.*x* servers from a Windows NT Server computer that is running GSNW, you can use standard UNC path names in the format:

```
\\server_name\share_name
```

For example, to connect to a volume named SYS on a NetWare 3.*x* server named NWSERVER, use the following UNC path name:

```
\\nwserver\sys
```

You can use these UNC path names when:

- Configuring the gateway by using the GSNW application in Control Panel
- Connecting to a printer by using the Add Printer Wizard
- Connecting to a shared folder in Windows NT Explorer

To access resources on NetWare 4.*x* servers from a Windows NT Server computer that is running GSNW, you can use UNC path names in the format:

```
\\tree_name\volume_name.organizational_unit.organization_
name\folder_name
```

For example, to connect to the `Public` folder in a volume named `NWSERVER_SYS` (on a NetWare 4.*x* server) in the Sales organizational unit in the Widgets organization in a tree named CORP, use the following UNC path name:

```
\\corp\nwserver_sys.sales.widgets\public
```

You can use these UNC path names when:

- Configuring the gateway by using the GSNW application in Control Panel
- Connecting to a printer by using the Add Printer Wizard
- Connecting to a shared folder in Windows NT Explorer

Migrating to Windows NT from NetWare

Microsoft supplies an administrative tool with Windows NT Server, called the *Migration Tool for NetWare*, that makes migrating to Windows NT from NetWare possible. The Migration Tool for NetWare can be used to migrate user accounts, group accounts, files, and folders from NetWare 2.*x*, 3.*x*, and 4.*x* servers to a Windows NT Server computer. You can choose to migrate only users, only files, only groups, or any combination of the three.

Migration Tool for NetWare

You don't have to install the Migration Tool for NetWare — it is automatically installed on a Windows NT Server computer during the installation process. However, before you can use the Migration Tool for NetWare, several prerequisites must be satisfied:

- NWLink IPX/SPX Compatible Transport must be installed and configured on the Windows NT Server computer.

- GSNW must be installed and configured on the Windows NT Server computer.

- The user who performs the migration must have Administrator privileges on the Windows NT Server computer, and must also have Supervisor privileges on the NetWare server(s).

- An NTFS partition must be configured on the Windows NT Server computer and must be specified as the destination volume if you want to retain file permissions on migrated files.

- If you are migrating from a NetWare 4.x server, the NetWare server must be configured for bindery emulation.

KNOW THIS Migration Tool for NetWare Requirements

Before you can migrate NetWare resources to Windows NT Server, you must first install NWLink IPX/SPX Compatible Transport and Gateway Services for NetWare. Additionally, you must have administrator privileges on the NT Server computer and Supervisor equivalent privileges on the NetWare server. You will also need a NTFS volume to retain NetWare file permissions and the NetWare server must be NetWare 3.x or running bindery emulation.

When planning a migration from NetWare to Windows NT, it's helpful to know exactly what can and can't be migrated. Table 9-1 lists this information.

TABLE 9-1 What Can and Can't Be Migrated

What Can Be Migrated	What Can't Be Migrated
User accounts and their properties	User account passwords
Group accounts and their properties	Print servers, print queues, and their configurations — all printing must be configured manually on the Windows NT Server computer *after* the migration is complete
Files and their permissions	Workgroup managers and user account managers
Folders (directories) and their permissions	Application-defined bindery objects
	Login scripts — NetWare login scripts don't run on client computers of Windows NT Server computers

Using the Migration Tool for NetWare

Using the Migration Tool for NetWare is fairly straightforward. When you start the Migration Tool for NetWare you are first asked to supply the source and destination server information.

The Migration Tool for NetWare dialog box is shown in Figure 9-2. Note that the NetWare Server and Windows NT Server list boxes display the source and destination servers.

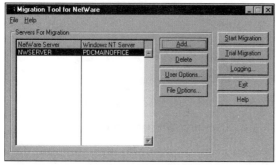

Figure 9-2 *Source and destination servers configured for migration*

 True or False?

1. Migration Tool for NetWare can migrate user passwords.

2. When using the Migration Tool for NetWare, the only user permission requirement is Supervisor privileges on the NetWare server.

3. You cannot connect to a printer using a UNC name.

4. You can configure Gateway Service for NetWare to alert you when your print job finishes.

5. Gateway Service for NetWare requires a NetWare user account that is a member of a NetWare group called NTGATEWAY.

Answers: *1. False 2. False 3. False 4. True 5. True*

Migrating user and group accounts

An important consideration is determining how duplicate user and group account names will be treated during the migration. If you are migrating more than one NetWare server, it is likely that users have accounts on more than one NetWare server. This is because each NetWare server maintains its own user account database, much like a stand-alone Windows NT Server computer.

An efficient way to deal with duplicate user and group account names is to create a mapping file. A *mapping file* specifies every source NetWare user and group account name that is being migrated, and specifies a corresponding user or group account name that will be created on the destination Windows NT Server computer during the migration for each specified NetWare user or group. A mapping file can also specify unique passwords for all user accounts being migrated.

To configure user and group account options in Migration Tool for NetWare, use the User Options command button in the Migration Tool for NetWare dialog box. The User and Group Options dialog box is shown in Figure 9-3. Notice the check boxes next to Transfer Users and Groups and Use Mappings in File.

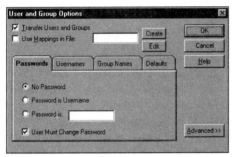

Figure 9-3 *Configuring options for migrating users and groups*

In the User and Group Options dialog box, you can configure these options:

- **Transfer Users and Groups:** Select the check box next to Transfer Users and Groups if you want to migrate user and group accounts from the NetWare server. Clear this check box if you don't want to migrate user and group accounts.

- **Use Mappings in File:** Select the check box next to Use Mappings in File if you want to use a mapping file to migrate user and group accounts. You don't need to select this check box if you are only migrating one NetWare server and you want to retain the same user and group account names on the NT Server computer that were used on the NetWare server.

- **Passwords tab:** Because NetWare user passwords can't be migrated, you can choose from one of three password options to apply to the migrated user accounts:
  - **No Password:** User accounts will be migrated without passwords.
  - **Password is Username:** User accounts are to have a password consisting of the user account name.
  - **Password is:** Specify one password that will be assigned to all user accounts that are migrated. If you select this option, type in the password you want to be assigned.
  - **User Must Change Password:** In addition to choosing from the three option buttons on the Passwords tab, you can select the check box next to User Must Change Password. When this check box is selected, users whose user accounts are migrated will have to change their passwords the first time they log on to the Windows NT Server computer.

You are likely to see questions on the exam relating to the password options available when migrating users from NetWare servers to Windows NT Server accounts. You need to know that the Migration Tool for NetWare cannot migrate user passwords from a NetWare server.

To configure user name options, use the Usernames tab in the User and Group Options dialog box. The Usernames tab is shown in Figure 9-4. The options available for handling user accounts are:

- **Log Error:** Selecting this option button causes an error to be logged to a log file when a duplicate user account is encountered during the migration process. Once a user account is migrated, each additional occurrence of an identical user account name will be logged to a log file but will not be migrated.
- **Ignore:** Selecting this option button causes duplicate user account names to be ignored during the migration process. Once a user account is migrated, each additional

occurrence of an identical user account name will be ignored.

- **Overwrite with new info:** Selecting this option button causes Windows NT to overwrite existing user account information with the account information from the duplicate user account(s) encountered during migration.

- **Add prefix:** Selecting this option button causes a prefix to be added to duplicate user account names encountered during the migration process.

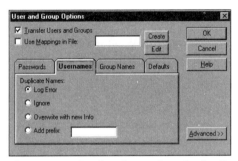

Figure 9-4 *Configuring options for duplicate user account names*

To configure group name options, use the Group Names tab in the User and Group Options dialog box. These options have the same effect as the identical options on the Usernames tab, except that they are applied to group accounts rather than to user accounts.

The last item to configure for User and Group Options is how to handle NetWare supervisors and users with supervisor equivalent permissions. The options available for the migration are:

- **Use Supervisor Defaults:** To migrate global NetWare account policy settings, such as password length and expiration, to the Windows NT Server account policy, select the check box next to Use Supervisor Defaults.

- **Add Supervisors to the Administrators Group:** NetWare Supervisor user accounts, and all NetWare user accounts with Supervisor equivalence, are to be added to the Administrators group on the Windows NT Server computer.

- **Migrate NetWare Specific Account Information:** All user account properties, such as group memberships, will be migrated to equivalent properties on the Windows NT Server computer.

Be on the look out for exam questions relating to how NetWare supervisor privileges can be handled when migrating user accounts to Windows NT Server accounts.

Migrating files and folders

When migrating files from a NetWare server to a Windows NT Server computer, the files must be migrated to an NTFS partition on the Windows NT Server computer for the file permissions to be retained.

NetWare file and folder permissions are *not* the same as Windows NT file and folder permissions. During migration, NetWare file and folder permissions are translated into Windows NT equivalent permissions.

File Migration Abilities

By default, certain files and folders on the NetWare server are *not* migrated. Hidden files, system files, and the contents of the \SYSTEM, \MAIL, \LOGIN, and \ETC directories are not migrated. You can override these defaults, however, by configuring the file options in the Migration Tool for NetWare.

To configure file migration options in Migration Tool for NetWare, use the File Options command button in the Migration Tool for NetWare dialog box. The File Options dialog box is shown in Figure 9-5. Note the check box next to Transfer Files.

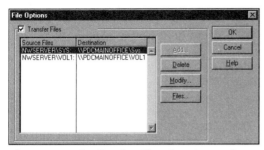

Figure 9-5 *Configuring file migration options*

Performing Trial Migrations

The Migration Tool for NetWare enables you to perform one or more trial migrations that simulate a migration without actually completing the migration process. The purpose of performing trial migrations is to test your migration configurations and to resolve any errors that occur *before* the actual migration is performed. The Migration Tool for NetWare can be configured so that errors that occur during a trial (or actual) migration are written to a log file, displayed on screen, or both. You can configure the following options:

- **Popup on errors:** The migration process will pause and display a message on the screen when an error occurs during the migration process.

- **Verbose User/Group Logging:** User and group migration errors will be written to the log file, in addition to recording a complete list of users and groups migrated.

- **Verbose File Logging:** File and folder migration errors will be written to the log file, in addition to recording a complete list of files migrated.

At the completion of the trial migration, the Transfer Completed dialog box appears, as shown in Figure 9-6. Notice the summary migration statistics presented.

Figure 9-6 *Trial migration completed*

If errors are displayed in the Totals section of the Transfer Completed dialog box, you can view the log files that contain the three logs created during the trial migration: Error.LOG, Summary.LOG, and LogFile.LOG.

True or False?

1. Migration Tool for NetWare requires a NTFS destination partition to migrate file permissions.

2. Migration Tool for NetWare can make NetWare supervisors members of a Windows NT Administrator group.

3. You cannot migrate group memberships using Migration Tool for NetWare.

4. Migration Tool for NetWare can migrate users and make their new passwords the same for everyone.

5. NetWare file permissions map directly to NTFS permissions.

Answers: *1. True 2. True 3. False 4. True 5. False*

Troubleshooting Common NetWare Connectivity Problems

There are several common NetWare connectivity problems. Most NetWare connectivity problems are caused by incorrectly configuring GSNW on the computer that is experiencing the problem. Most user-reported problems relate to an inability to connect a Windows NT computer to resources on NetWare servers.

Here are two of the most common configuration errors that cause NetWare connectivity problems and recommended solutions to these problems:

- If the gateway user account is not a member of the NTGATEWAY group on the NetWare server, make the gateway user account a member of the NTGATEWAY group on the NetWare server.

- If the gateway user account has permissions to access the resource on the NetWare server, but the NTGATEWAY group does not have these permissions, the NTGATEWAY group must have the appropriate permissions to access the shared resource on the NetWare server. Assign permissions to the NTGATEWAY group using the appropriate NetWare administration utility on the NetWare server. Remember that the most restrictive combination of gateway share permissions and NetWare file and folder permissions applies.

Have You Mastered?

Now it's time to apply what you've learned in this chapter by testing your mastery of the material. These questions provide you with a means to determine if you are ready to move on to the next chapter or if you need to review the material again.

1. **You are using the Migration Tool for NetWare to migrate user accounts and files from your NetWare 4.x server to your Windows NT Server computer. You have to configure the migration tool to migrate user accounts and files to your NT Server. After performing a trial migration, you examine the log files and notice that none of the files stored in the \MAIL were migrated. What should you do to enable files in the \MAIL directory to be migrated?**

   ☐ A. Create a \MAIL directory on the Windows NT Server volume first.

   ☐ B. Use the migration tool's file options to select the \MAIL directory to be copied.

   ☐ C. Grant your user account supervisor rights for the directory.

   ☐ D. Nothing, the \MAIL cannot be copied during a migration.

   The correct answer is **B**. By default, the \SYSTEM, \MAIL, \LOGIN, and \ETC directories are not copied during a migration. You can specify these directories or hidden/system files to be copied by using the file options button in the Migration Tool for NetWare. The migration process does not depend on having a directory structure on the destination NT volume, so you would not need to create a \MAIL directory beforehand. For more information, see the "Migrating files and folders" section.

2. **You are preparing to migrate your user accounts and files from a NetWare 3.x server using the Migration Tool for NetWare. You want to preserve file permissions during the migration of files from the NetWare server to your Windows NT Server. Before performing the migration, what should you do?**

   ☐ A. Grant the account you will be using to perform the migration Supervisor equivalent permissions.
   ☐ B. Configure the migration tool to copy the \PUBLIC directory.
   ☐ C. Do not configure any access permissions on the Windows NT Server destination volume.
   ☐ D. Configure the Windows NT Server destination volume as a NTFS partition.

The correct answer is **D**. The Migration Tool for NetWare can only preserve file permissions if it is able to configure them on the destination volume. Because only NTFS volumes support file permissions, you must configure the destination volume as a NTFS partition or all file permissions will be lost during the migration. If the destination volume already has access rights assigned, the migration tool will override the permissions to enable the NetWare file permissions to exist. For more information, see the "Migration Tool for NetWare" section.

3. **You are planning a migration from your NetWare 3.x servers to your Windows NT Servers using the Migration Tool for NetWare. Before you begin, which account permissions must your account have? (Choose two.)**

☐ A. Supervisor equivalent on the NetWare servers

☐ B. Account Operator permission on the NetWare servers

☐ C. Administrator permission on the Windows NT Servers

☐ D. Account Operator permission on the Windows NT Servers

The correct answers are **A** and **C**. Before beginning any migration using the Migration Tool for NetWare, the account that you will be logged in with on the Windows NT Server computer must have Supervisor equivalent access on the NetWare servers and Administrator permissions on the Windows NT Server computers. Account operator privilege is not sufficient to allow the Migration Tool for NetWare to function. For more information, see the "Migration Tool for NetWare" section.

4. **You are planning a migration from a NetWare 4.x server to a Windows NT Server computer. What must you install on the Windows NT Server computer before you can use the Migration Tool for NetWare? (Choose two.)**

☐ A. NWLink IPX/SPX Compatible Transport

☐ B. Gateway Service for NetWare

☐ C. Migration Tool for NetWare

☐ D. User Manager for Domains

The correct answers are **A** and **B**. The Migration Tool for NetWare requires that NWLink IPX/SPX Compatible Transport and Gateway Service for NetWare be installed. These components enable the migration tool to communicate with the target NetWare servers. The Migration Tool for NetWare is automatically installed during the Windows NT Server installation process, so you do not need to install it again. For more information, see the "Migration Tool for NetWare" section.

5. **You are attempting to connect to a shared folder on a NetWare 4.x server. The NetWare server is not running bindery emulation. You want to connect to the** Reports **folder in a volume named** Corp_Docs **that is in the Accounting organizational unit in the Financial organization in a tree named Justtogs. What UNC name should you use to connect to the shared folder?**

☐ A. \\Justtogs\Corp_Docs\Accounting\
    Financial\Reports

☐ B. \\Justtogs\Corp_Docs.Accounting\
    Financial\Reports

☐ C. \\Justtogs\Corp_Docs.Accounting.
    Financial\Reports

☐ D. \\Justtogs.Corp_Docs.Accounting.
    Financial\Reports

The correct answer is C. When connecting to resources using an NDS-based UNC name, the UNC format is \\tree_name\ volume_name.organizational_unit.organization_name\ folder_name. The others choices use the wrong syntax to reference the NDS resource and would not work. For more information, see the "Accessing Resources on NetWare Servers" section.

6. **You are installing Client Services for NetWare on a Windows NT Workstation computer and Gateway Service for NetWare on a Windows NT Server computer. What feature does Gateway Service for NetWare provide that Client Services for NetWare does not?**

☐ A. The ability to share Windows NT Server resources with NetWare clients.

☐ B. The ability to share resources located on a NetWare server with the Windows NT Server's client computers.

☐ C. The ability to override NetWare file access permissions by assigning NT access rights to the Gateway Service.

☐ D. The ability for the Windows NT Server to print to NetWare printer queues.

The correct answer is **B**. The main difference between the two products is that Gateway Service for NetWare enables Windows NT Server computers to share resources that physically reside on NetWare services. By resharing these resources, organizations can migrate users to Windows NT Server client computers and still have access to user data in its original place. Both CSNW and GSNW have the ability to print to NetWare printer queues. For more information, see the "Gateway Service for NetWare" section.

Practice Your Skills

Here is a chance to apply your practical hands-on experience and material from this chapter. These exercises are designed not only for you to apply the material in the book, but also for you to gain greater experience and exposure to the product. These exercises are a critical part of understanding the product and gaining valuable experience for using the product and passing the certification exam. For each of the following problems, consider the given facts and determine what you think are the possible causes of the problem and what course of action you might take to resolve the problem.

1. Gateway Service for NetWare

EXERCISE You are installing Gateway Service for NetWare on your Windows NT Server computer. You plan on using the gateway service to reshare NetWare volumes to users of your Windows NT Server computer. What are some considerations when configuring the gateway service on the Windows NT Server computer?

ANALYSIS The Gateway service will add an additional user connection to the NetWare server, so you must have a free client access license to enable the service to connect. This connection use is in addition to the user account logged into the server, which will also be using a server connection. You also need to determine how you will configure the share permissions and how they will interact with the permissions assigned on the NetWare volume.

2. NetWare migration

EXERCISE You are planning on using the Migration Tool for NetWare to migrate your user accounts from your ten NetWare 3.x servers to your Windows NT Server domain. Since you were not able to run NDS on your NetWare servers, what are some likely areas of problems during the migration?

ANALYSIS Because you need an account on each NetWare 3.x server you want to connect to, when user accounts are migrated from the servers to the NT Server domain, there will be duplicate account names. The best way to resolve this problem is by either defining account name prefixes or using a mapping file to determine which accounts will be migrated and which ones will not.

3. Migration Tool for NetWare logs

EXERCISE You are planning a trial NetWare migration using the Migration Tool for NetWare. You want to significantly increase the reliability of the trial run by logging as much information as possible. What can you do to increase the amount of information that is logged during the migration?

ANALYSIS The Migration Tool for NetWare allows you to enable verbose User, Group, and File logging. These options will increase the amount of information that is logged during the trial run. By referencing this information, you can take steps to reduce errors and resolve conflicts before committing to an actual migration. You can run multiple trial runs after making changes to determine if all the errors have been resolved.

Setting Up Remote Access Service

In this chapter, I will focus on using the Remote Access Service (RAS) to communicate with client and host computers over modems, serial ports, or Internet connections. Windows NT Server is often used as a central communications host using RAS, and it is important that you understand how to configure and use RAS to do well on the Windows NT Server exam. I begin with a look at connection protocols used by RAS and how they support common transport protocols. I then move on to explore how to configure transport protocols, encryption, and assigning dialin permissions. The chapter wraps up with a look at configuring Dial-Up Networking connections, PPTP security and troubleshooting common RAS problems. So let's continue.

Exam Material in This Chapter

Based on Microsoft Objectives

Connectivity

- Install and configure Remote Access Service (RAS). Configuration options include:
  - Configuring RAS communications
  - Configuring RAS protocols
  - Configuring RAS security
  - Configuring Dial-Up Networking clients

Troubleshooting

- Choose the appropriate course of action to take to resolve RAS problems.

Based on Author's Experience

- You need to know the abilities and restrictions for each of the Windows NT supported connection protocols, including which transport protocols are supported and their limitations.

- You definitely need to know what type of clients RAS supports and which types of hosts a Dial-Up Networking client can connect to.

- You need to know the process of assigning dialin permissions and using Call Back security. In addition, you also need to know what happens when you do not assign dialin permission.

- You should be prepared for a few questions about configuring and using PPTP on a Windows NT Server computer connected to the internet.

- You need to be familiar with how to configure the network protocol properties for RAS connections.

Are You Prepared?

Do you have what it takes? Try out these self-assessment questions to see if you have prepared for the material in this chapter or if you should review problem areas.

1. **You are configuring Remote Access Service on a Windows NT Server computer for your company. You want to use the highest level of security possible when users connect to the RAS server over the Internet. What should you do?**

   - ☐ A. Have the clients use a PPTP connection.
   - ☐ B. Have the clients use a SLIP connection.
   - ☐ C. Configure the RAS server to require encrypted passwords.
   - ☐ D. Use only the NWLink IPX/SPX Compatible Protocol for connections.

2. **You receive a phone call from a user who complains that whenever she dials into your RAS server, the server hangs up on her after she authenticates her user ID. What is the most likely problem?**

   - ☐ A. The server has PPTP filtering enabled.
   - ☐ B. Her account is configured to use Call Back security.
   - ☐ C. Her computer is using a protocol that is not supported by the RAS server.
   - ☐ D. Her Dial-Up Networking connection has a static IP address assigned that is not permitted by the RAS server.

3. You are installing Remote Access Server on your Windows NT Server computer. You want this server to be used by outside consultants to connect to the network and access your mail system. One of the consultants has called you because they are unable to connect to your computer from their UNIX system. What is the most likely problem?

☐ A. The server is configured for PPTP connections.
☐ B. The server does not have the TCP/IP protocol installed.
☑ C. The consultant's computer is using SLIP to connect to the server.
☐ D. The consultant's computer has a TCP/IP address that conflicts with an address on your corporate network.

Answers:

1. A   *The Point-to-Point Tunneling Protocol enables you to have a connection to your corporate RAS server while connected over the Internet. This enables you to leverage the global dispersion of ISPs and to use the infrastructure to provide a secure means of communications. See the "Connection Protocols" section.*

2. B   *If Call Back security is enabled for her account, the RAS server will hang up and call her computer back at a predetermined phone number, or if configured, at a number she specifies during authentication. See the "Remote Access Admin" section.*

3. C   *Microsoft Windows NT does not support using Windows NT as a SLIP host. SLIP is an older form of PPP and is very common among Unix systems. A Windows NT computer can dial in to a SLIP host, but not vice-versa. See the "Connection Protocols" section.*

RAS Overview

Remote Access Service (RAS) is a Windows NT service that enables dial-up network connections between a RAS server and a Dial-Up Networking client computer. RAS includes software components for both the RAS server and the Dial-Up Networking client in a single Windows NT service.

RAS enables users of remote computers to use the network as though they were directly connected to it. Once the dial-up connection is established, there is no difference in network functionality, except the speed of the link is often much slower than a direct connection to the LAN.

RAS is an important networking function in today's highly mobile workforce. With RAS and Dial-Up Networking, users can connect to their company's network from home, from a hotel room, or from a client's remote office.

Windows NT Server RAS can support up to 256 simultaneous dial-in connections.

Client computers that run MS-DOS, Windows 3.1*x*, Windows for Workgroups, Windows 95, and Windows NT can be configured as Dial-Up Networking or RAS client computers. These clients can all connect to a Windows NT RAS server.

RAS supports multiple connection types, connection protocols, and transport protocols. These features are discussed in the following sections.

Connection Protocols

RAS communications can be carried out over several connection protocols. These protocols provide the data-link connectivity for Dial-Up Networking in much the same way as Ethernet, ARCNET, or Token Ring provide the data-link connectivity on a local area network. Each of these protocols has different features and capabilities. The connection protocols commonly used by RAS include: Serial Line Internet Protocol (SLIP), Point-to-Point Protocol (PPP), Point-to-Point Multilink Protocol, and Point-to-Point Tunneling Protocol (PPTP). These protocols are discussed in the following sections.

Serial Line Internet Protocol

The *Serial Line Internet Protocol* (SLIP) is an older connection protocol, commonly associated with UNIX computers, that only supports one transport protocol — TCP/IP. SLIP connections don't support NWLink IPX/SPX Compatible Transport or NetBEUI.

The version of SLIP supported by Windows NT 4.0 requires a static IP address configuration at the client computer — dynamic IP addressing is not supported. Additionally, password encryption is not supported by this version of SLIP. A script file is usually required to automate the connection process when SLIP is used.

SLIP connections support only TCP/IP and require static IP addresses on the client computer.

Windows NT RAS can't be used as a SLIP server. Only the Dial-Up Networking portion of RAS (the client side) supports SLIP. This means that only dial-out SLIP connections are supported — such as when a Dial-Up Networking client computer dials out to connect to a UNIX SLIP server. (The Dial-Up Networking client computer, in this case, can be either a Windows NT Server or Windows NT Workstation computer that has RAS installed on it.)

Point-to-Point Protocol

Point-to-Point Protocol (PPP) is a newer connection protocol that was designed to overcome the limitations of SLIP. PPP is currently the industry standard remote connection protocol, and is recommended for use by Microsoft.

PPP is supported over both dial-in and dial-out connections. Windows NT computers that have RAS installed on them can function either as Dial-Up Networking clients or as RAS servers when using PPP.

PPP Connections

PPP connections support multiple transport protocols, including TCP/IP, NWLINK IPX/SPX Compatible Transport, and NetBEUI. Additionally, PPP supports dynamic server-based IP addressing (such as DHCP).

PPP supports password encryption, and the PPP connection process does not usually require a script file.

Point-to-Point Multilink Protocol

Point-to-Point Multilink Protocol is an extension of PPP. Point-to-Point Multilink Protocol combines the bandwidth from multiple physical connections into a single logical connection. This means that multiple modem, ISDN, or X.25 connections can be bundled together to form a single logical connection with a much higher bandwidth than a single connection can support.

Point-to-Point Multilink allows multiple connections to be bound together to provide a high aggregate bandwidth connection. The server must be configured to support this option.

In order to implement Point-to-Point Multilink Protocol, multiple modems and telephone lines (or multiple ISDN adapter cards and lines; or multiple X.25 adapters, PADs, and connections) are required at *both* the RAS server and at the Dial-Up Networking client locations. Also, both sides of the connection must be configured to use Point-to-Point Multilink Protocol.

Point-to-Point Tunneling Protocol

Point-to-Point Tunneling Protocol (PPTP) permits a virtual private encrypted connection between two computers over an existing TCP/IP network connection. The existing TCP/IP network connection can be over a LAN or over a Dial-Up Networking TCP/IP connection (including the Internet). All standard transport protocols are supported within the PPTP connection, including NWLink IPX/SPX Compatible Transport, NetBEUI, and TCP/IP.

A primary reason for choosing to use PPTP is that it supports the RAS encryption feature over standard, unencrypted TCP/IP networks, such as the Internet.

Transport Protocols Supported by RAS

All Windows NT standard transport protocols are supported by RAS. Client computers can connect to a RAS server by using:

- NetBEUI
- TCP/IP
- IPX — Including NWLink IPX/SPX Compatible Transport

The DLC protocol is *not* supported by RAS.

Client computers can use one or more of these transport protocols on a RAS connection. For example, a client computer that needs to access a NetWare server and a UNIX host via a RAS server can use both NWLink IPX/SPX Compatible Transport and TCP/IP during a single RAS session.

A RAS server acts as a router for client computers that use TCP/IP or IPX, enabling these clients to access other computers on the network via the RAS server's routing functionality. Access to NetBIOS-based resources (such as shared folders and printers, Lotus Notes servers, SQL Servers, and SNA Servers) and protocol-specific resources (such as NetWare servers and World Wide Web servers) is possible because of the RAS server's routing capability. The RAS server can only route protocols that are installed on the RAS server. For example, if a client computer has NWLink IPX/SPX Compatible Transport installed, but the RAS server doesn't, the client computer won't be able to access IPX-based resources, such as a NetWare server.

A RAS server acts as a NetBIOS gateway for client computers that use the NetBEUI protocol.

RAS NetBIOS Gateway

The *RAS NetBIOS gateway* is a function of the RAS server. The RAS NetBIOS gateway enables client computers that use NetBEUI to access shared resources on other servers located on the RAS server's local network. These other servers can use TCP/IP, NWLink IPX/SPX Compatible Transport, or NetBEUI. In a nutshell, the RAS NetBIOS gateway performs protocol translation for the remote NetBEUI client computer so it can access shared resources on the RAS server's local network.

Only NetBIOS-based services (such as shared folders and printers, Lotus Notes servers, SQL Servers, and SNA Servers) can be accessed by NetBEUI client computers via the RAS NetBIOS gateway. Protocol-specific services (such as NetWare servers and World Wide Web servers) can't be accessed by NetBEUI client computers via the RAS NetBIOS gateway.

Installing and Configuring RAS

Before installing RAS, you should install and configure all of the transport protocols you plan to use on the RAS server. Also, you should install and configure at least one connection device, such as a modem, ISDN adapter card, or X.25 adapter card in the Windows NT computer that you plan to install RAS on. Or, you can install the Point-to-Point Tunneling Protocol (PPTP).

The following sections explore the various steps involved in installing RAS, including configuring modems, ports, protocols, and encryption.

Modems and Ports

Configuring modems and ports is an integral part of the RAS installation and configuration process. Each RAS modem or port can be configured to either receive calls, make calls, or both. The three port usage options are:

- **Dial out only:** If you select the option button next to "Dial out only," the port will *only* be available for use by the Dial-Up Networking client. Selecting this option button for *all* ports effectively selects a client-only role for this computer. This computer won't be able to function as a RAS server if this option button is selected for all ports.

- **Receive calls only:** If you select the option button next to "Receive calls only," the port will *only* be available for use by the RAS server. Selecting this option button for *all* ports effectively selects a RAS server-only role for this computer. This computer won't be able to function as a Dial-Up Networking client if this option button is selected for all ports.

- **Dial out and Receive calls:** If you select the option button next to "Dial out and Receive calls," the port will be available for use by both the RAS server and the Dial-Up Networking client. This computer will be able to function both as a RAS server and as a Dial-Up Networking client.

 Each port is configured individually. If one port is configured to dial out only, another can be configured to receive calls only or to dial out and receive calls.

Configuring Protocols and Encryption

After configuring the port properties, the next part of the RAS installation/configuration process involves configuring protocols and encryption. The Network Configuration dialog box is shown in Figure 10-1. Notice the Dial out Protocols and Server Settings sections.

This is the primary RAS configuration dialog box. In this dialog box, select dial-out protocols (if you configured any ports for dial-out usage), configure dial-in protocols and RAS server settings (if you configured any ports for dial in-usage), select RAS encryption features, and enable the RAS server side of Point-to-Point Multilink Protocol connections, if desired.

Configuration options selected in the Network Configuration dialog box are global settings that apply to *all* ports. No individual port protocol or encryption settings are available.

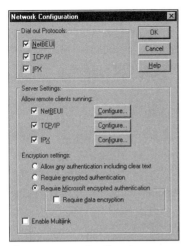

Figure 10-1 *Configuring protocols and security*

- **Dial out Protocols:** If you configured any ports for dial-out usage, you can select any or all of three dial-out protocols: NetBEUI, TCP/IP, and/or IPX (NWLink IPX/SPX Compatible Transport). If you *didn't* configure any ports for dial-out usage, these options are grayed out and not available.

- **Server Settings: Allow remote clients running:** If you configured any ports for dial-in (RAS server) usage, you can select any or all of three dial-in protocols: NetBEUI, TCP/IP, and/or IPX (NWLink IPX/SPX Compatible Transport). If you didn't configure any ports for dial-in usage, the Server Settings configuration section is not displayed.

- **Server Settings: Encryption settings:** Select one of the three possible password authentication encryption options:

  - **Allow any authentication including clear text:** The RAS server will authenticate user passwords in clear text or in any encryption format supported by the RAS server. Selecting this option button, in effect, enables the Dial-Up Networking client to determine the level of password encryption.

- **Require encrypted authentication:** Dial-Up Networking clients will be required to send encrypted user passwords in any encryption format supported by the RAS server. The RAS server won't authenticate user passwords that are sent in clear text.

- **Require Microsoft encrypted authentication:** Dial-Up Networking clients must send user passwords that are encrypted using Microsoft encrypted authentication. The RAS server won't authenticate user passwords sent in clear text or in any encryption format other than Microsoft encrypted authentication. This is the most secure password authentication option, and is selected by default. If the "Require Microsoft encrypted authentication" option button is selected, the "Require data encryption" check box is available.

- **Require data encryption:** The RAS server requires that all data sent to the RAS server from the Dial-Up Networking client be transmitted in an encrypted format. This check box is not selected by default. Currently, only Windows NT Dial-Up Networking clients support data encryption. If you want to use the RAS server to establish secure, private PPTP connections, ensure that you select the option button next to "Require Microsoft encrypted authentication" *and* the check box next to "Require data encryption."

- **Server Settings: Enable Multilink:** Enables the RAS server side of Point-to-Point Multilink Protocol connections. Selecting this check box enables the RAS server to support Multilink connections if requested to do so by the Dial-Up Networking client computer.

Multilink is not enabled by default, you must enable it before clients can request a Multilink connection. Look for a scenario where the client is unable to complete a Multilink session; it is most likely because Multilink is not enabled on the server.

Configuring NetBEUI

Once you have selected dial-out protocol(s) in the Server Settings section of the Network Configuration dialog box, you are ready to configure the protocols. If you selected NetBEUI as a dial-out protocol, it must be configured using one of these two options:

- **Entire network:** The RAS server's NetBIOS gateway will be enabled, and remote NetBEUI clients will be able to access shared resources on all servers on the RAS server's local network, even servers that use TCP/IP or NWLink IPX/SPX Compatible Transport.

- **This computer only:** The RAS server's NetBIOS gateway will be disabled, and remote NetBEUI clients will only be able to access shared resources located on the RAS server. This option is sometimes used in high-security environments to prevent unauthorized access to other computers on the corporate network.

Selections made in this dialog box apply to *all* Dial-Up Networking client computers that access the RAS server using NetBEUI. You either choose to allow all remote NetBEUI client computers to access the entire network, or you choose to allow all remote NetBEUI client computers to access *only* the RAS server.

Configuring TCP/IP

If you selected TCP/IP as a dial out protocol, it must be configured. The RAS Server TCP/IP Configuration dialog box is shown in Figure 10-2. Notice the options to configure IP address assignment for remote Dial-Up Networking clients. You can configure the TCP/IP properties for RAS clients using these options:

- **Entire network:** The RAS server will function as a router for Dial-Up Networking client computers, and remote TCP/IP clients will be able to access resources on all servers that use TCP/IP on the RAS server's local network.

- **This computer only:** The RAS server will not function as a router for Dial-Up Networking client computers, and remote TCP/IP clients will only be able to access resources located on the RAS server. This option is sometimes used in high-security environments to prevent unauthorized access to other computers on the corporate network.

- **Use DHCP to assign remote TCP/IP client addresses:** The RAS server will request an IP address for the remote TCP/IP client from the DHCP server on its local network when the remote TCP/IP client connects to the RAS server. This option should be selected if a DHCP server is available.

- **Use static address pool:** The RAS server will assign an IP address to the remote TCP/IP client from the range of IP addresses specified in the Begin and End text boxes.

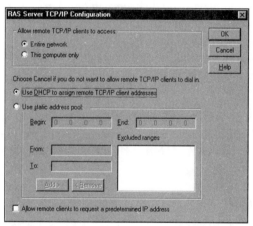

Figure 10-2 *Configuring RAS server TCP/IP options*

Configuring IPX

If you selected IPX (NWLink IPX/SPX Compatible Transport) as a dial-out protocol, it must be configured. The RAS Server IPX Configuration dialog box is shown in Figure 10-3. Notice the network number configuration options.

- **Entire network:** The RAS server will function as a router for Dial-Up Networking client computers, and remote IPX clients will be able to access resources on all servers that use IPX on the RAS server's local network.

- **This computer only:** The RAS server will not function as a router for Dial-Up Networking client computers, and remote IPX clients will only be able to access resources located on the RAS server. This option is sometimes used in high-security environments to prevent unauthorized access to other computers on the corporate network.

- **Allocate network numbers automatically:** The RAS server assigns a network number that is not currently in use to a remote IPX client computer when it connects to the RAS server.

- **Allocate network numbers:** The RAS server assigns a network number from the specified range of numbers listed in the From and To text boxes to a remote IPX client computer when it connects to the RAS server. You must specify a range of network numbers in the From and To text boxes if you select this option button.

Two additional check boxes are available in this section, regardless of the network number allocation method you selected:

- **Assign same network number to all IPX clients:** The RAS server assigns the same network number to all remote IPX client computers.

- **Allow remote clients to request IPX node number:** Select this option when remote IPX clients have been configured so that their Dial-Up Networking software requests a specific IPX node number from the RAS server.

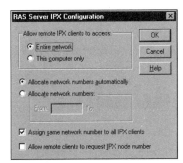

Figure 10-3 *Configuring RAS server IPX options*

If you enabled the IPX protocol for a dial-in port, you will need to configure the properties for routing the IPX protocol using one of these two options:

- Enable RIP if remote IPX clients will be accessing shared NetBIOS resources on servers (that use IPX) on the RAS server's local network. This causes RAS to automatically forward NetBIOS broadcasts from IPX clients.

- Do not enable RIP if remote IPX clients will only be accessing resources on the RAS server, or will only be accessing resources on NetWare servers on the RAS server's local network. This prevents the RAS server from automatically forwarding NetBIOS broadcasts from IPX clients.

POP QUIZ **True or False?**

1. You can configure individual port protocol or encryption settings.

2. RAS can only use a static pool of TCP/IP addresses for dial-in clients.

3. A RAS port can be configured for dial out or receive, but not both.

4. Multilink is not enabled by default when RAS is installed.

5. PPTP sessions require an existing TCP/IP connection to be available.

Answers: *1. False 2. False 3. False 4. True 5. True*

Remote Access Admin

Remote Access Admin is a Windows NT administrative tool that is primarily used to start and stop the Remote Access Service (RAS), to assign the dialin permission to users, and to configure a call back security level for each user. Remote Access Admin can also be used to view COM port status and statistics, to disconnect users from individual ports, and to remotely manage RAS on other Windows NT computers.

Remote Access Admin is available on all Windows NT computers that have RAS installed. In addition, because Remote Access Admin is a component of Client-based Network Administration Tools, it is also available on Windows NT Workstation computers that have these tools installed.

In addition to starting, stopping, or pausing RAS, Remote Access Admin is also used to manage the assignment of the dialin permission and to configure call back security.

Dialin Permission and Call Back Security

Before remote users can dial in and connect to a RAS server, they must be assigned the dialin permission. Until this permission is assigned to at least one user account, RAS connections and RAS functionality can't be established. The Remote Access Permissions dialog box is shown in Figure 10-4. Notice the Grant All command button.

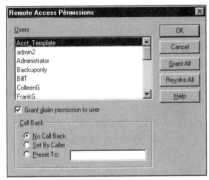

Figure 10-4 *Assigning the dialin permission and configuring call back security*

The dialin permission and call back security can also be configured by selecting the Dialin command button in the User Properties dialog box in User Manager for Domains.

Call back security is configured on an individual user basis in the Remote Access Permissions dialog box. Each user account can be configured with one of the following three options:

- **No Call Back:** The user can dial in to the RAS server, but the user can't request that the RAS server break the connection and call the user back. Selecting this option ensures that the user dialing in — not the server — is billed for any long-distance telephone charges. Selecting this option provides no security other than user account and password authentication.

- **Set By Caller:** The RAS server prompts the remote user for a telephone number to dial back. The RAS server then breaks the connection and dials the user back at the number specified by the remote user. This setting is typically used when remote employees must make a long-distance call to connect to the RAS server. Selecting this option button enables the company, rather than the remote employee, to incur the bulk of the long-distance telephone charges. There is no real security (other than user account and password authentication) provided when this option is selected, because the RAS server will dial back to *any* telephone number specified by a user, whether authorized or unauthorized.

- **Preset To:** Specifies a telephone number that the RAS server will always use to call back whenever this remote user dials in. This configuration provides the highest amount of call back security, because only a predetermined telephone number (such as an employee's home telephone number) will be used by the RAS server. Unauthorized remote users calling from a different location, even if they can provide a valid user name and password, won't be able to maintain a connection, because the RAS server will break the connection and call back only the prespecified number.

Preset To provides the best use of Call Back security, as the caller must be at a predefined location (phone number) before the connection will be allowed to complete. This prevents hackers from guessing a password and account name and gaining entry to your system, but it does prevent you from enabling callers to call from different locations, such as mobile users who travel a lot between hotels.

Dial-Up Networking Connections

Dial-Up Networking is the client/dial out component of RAS. The Dial-Up Networking accessory is installed during the RAS installation. Dial-Up Networking enables Windows NT computers to connect to dial-up servers, and to establish network connections through those servers. Dial-up servers include: Windows NT RAS servers; UNIX computers that are configured as SLIP or PPP servers; and any other computers, routers, or front-end processors that are configured as SLIP or PPP servers.

Before the Dial-Up Networking functionality on a Windows NT computer can be used, RAS must be installed and configured, and at least one of the computer's RAS ports must be configured for dial out usage. Additionally, you must create at least one phonebook entry that contains various dialing information and instructions. You can create phonebook entries using the Windows NT Dial-Up Networking accessory.

Compatible RAS Hosts

Windows NT can use Dial-Up Networking to access the following type of hosts.

- Windows NT RAS Servers.
- Hosts configured to support SLIP or PPP connections, such as routers, async servers, and UNIX hosts.

Configuring Server Properties

To configure server properties, including dial-up server type and network protocols, click the Server tab in the New Phonebook Entry dialog box. The Server tab is shown in Figure 10-5. You can configure the properties for connecting to the remote server using these options:

- **Dial-up server type:** Select the type of dial-up server you want to connect to from the "Dial-up server type" drop-down list box.

- **Network protocols:** Select the transport protocols that you want to use for this dial-up connection. Protocols available include TCP/IP, (NWLink) IPX/SPX Compatible (Transport), and NetBEUI. You can select more than one protocol.

- **TCP/IP Settings:** If you select TCP/IP, click the TCP/IP Settings command button to configure TCP/IP settings for this connection. You can configure TCP/IP properties such as accepting a server assigned IP address or specifying an IP address.

- **Enable software compression:** The Dial-Up Networking software will compress all data before it is transmitted to the RAS server. You should disable modem compression if you select this option.

- **Enable PPP LCP extensions:** Enable the newer PPP features. Deselect this check box only if you are unable to connect when it is selected.

Configuring Security Properties

To configure security, including password authentication and encryption options, use the Security tab in the New Phonebook Entry dialog box. The Security tab is shown in Figure 10-6. Notice that the authentication and encryption options are similar to the Server Settings that are configured for dial in connections during the installation of RAS.

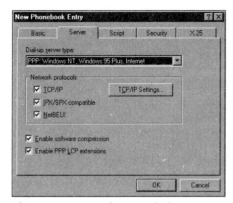

Figure 10-5 *Configuring dial-up server type and network protocols*

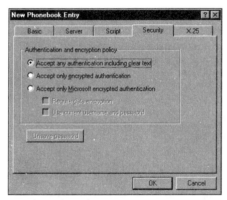

Figure 10-6 *Configuring password authentication and encryption options*

Options selected in this dialog box will be applied to the Dial-Up Networking client only, not to the RAS server.

- **Accept any authentication including clear text:** Dial-Up Networking will connect to a dial-up server using the lowest password authentication option accepted by the server. For example, if the dial-up server is configured to enable any authentication including clear text, and this option is selected, Dial-Up Networking transmits the password to the dial-up server by using clear text.

- **Accept only encrypted authentication:** Dial-Up Networking will only send an encrypted user authentication request to the server. The client may not be able to connect to a dial-up server that does not support some form of encrypted authentication.

- **Accept only Microsoft encrypted authentication:** Dial-Up Networking will not be able to establish a connection with a dial-up server unless that server supports Microsoft encrypted authentication. You must select this option if you want to use data encryption. If you select this option, two additional check boxes are available:

  - **Require data encryption:** The Dial-Up Networking client will encrypt all data sent over this connection. You should select this check box if you are configuring a PPTP connection.

  - **Use current username and password:** Dial-Up Networking will not prompt you for a user name or password when establishing a connection with the dial-up server.

PPTP Security

If your RAS server is connected to the Internet via a router and an ISP, and you want to permit only PPTP connections to your server, you can configure TCP/IP to only accept PPTP packets. To accomplish this, a TCP/IP PPTP option, called *PPTP filtering*, must be individually configured for each network adapter installed in the RAS server that has a routed connection to the Internet.

The Advanced IP Addressing dialog box is shown in Figure 10-7. Notice the check box next to Enable PPTP Filtering. Select the network adapter you want to configure from the Adapter drop-down list box.

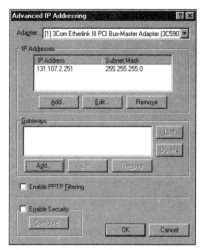

Figure 10-7 *Enabling PPTP filtering for a network adapter*

 True or False?

1. Windows NT can connect to a host configured for SLIP connections.

2. You can use the Remote Access Admin to stop a RAS service on another Windows NT Server.

3. A phonebook entry contains all of the configuration settings for a Dial-Up Networking connection.

4. You can only use one protocol for each Dial-Up Networking connection.

Answers: *1. True 2. True 3. True 4. False*

Troubleshooting Common RAS Problems

Most common RAS problems reported by users involve an inability to connect to a RAS server, a third-party SLIP server, or a front-end processor from a Dial-Up Networking client computer. Table 10-1 shows some common causes of RAS connection problems, and recommended solutions.

TABLE 10-1 Common Causes of RAS Problems and Recommended Solutions

Common Causes of RAS Problems	Recommended Solutions
Modem configuration or compatibility problem	If you suspect that your modem is the problem, first determine the type of modem to which you are attempting to connect; and then reconfigure your modem settings to the most compatible option, or as recommended by your ISP. If you are using an unsupported modem (for example, one that is not on the HCL), verify that your settings in the Modem.inf file are appropriate for your modem. If you have selected RAS software compression, ensure that your modem is not configured to compress data. If you are still unable to connect, you can configure your modem to record a log file of all attempted connections. To configure a modem log file, use the Modems application in Control Panel to access your modem's Properties dialog box. Select the Connection tab and then the Advanced Connection Settings dialog box.
Password authentication problem	If you suspect a password authentication problem, configure Dial-Up Networking to accept any authentication including clear text, and/or configure the RAS server to enable any authentication including clear text. (Note: Clear text passwords are usually required by SLIP servers.)

Common Causes of RAS Problems	Suggested/ Recommended Solutions
TCP/IP configuration problem	If you suspect a TCP/IP configuration problem, contact the manager of the dial-up server you are attempting to connect to and determine the dial-up server's TCP/IP configuration. Configure Dial-Up Networking so that the client's TCP/IP configuration settings match those of the dial-up server.
Dial-Up Networking configuration problem	Verify that you have chosen the appropriate dial-up server type (SLIP or PPP connection type) by contacting the manager of the dial-up server, if necessary.
Script problem	If you are using a script and your modem makes contact with the dial-up server, but you are *not* able to successfully complete a connection to the dial-up server, try editing your script file or try using a pop-up terminal window instead of the script file.

Have You Mastered?

Now it's time to apply what you've learned in this chapter by testing your mastery of the material. These questions provide you with a means to determine if you are ready to move on to the next chapter or if you need to review the material again.

1. **You are configuring your Windows NT computer to connect to a Windows NT RAS Server computer. Which protocols are supported over a PPP connection and will enable you to access computers at the RAS Server site? (Choose three.)**

   - ☐ A. TCP/IP
   - ☐ B. NetBEUI
   - ☐ C. DLC 16bit
   - ☐ D. DLC 32bit
   - ☐ E. NWLink IPX/SPX Compatible Transport
   - ☐ F. XNS/NB

   The correct answers are **A**, **B**, and **E**. Remote Access Server does not support DLC (in any flavor) or XNS/NB. Windows NT RAS servers do fully support TCP/IP, NetBEUI, and NWLink IPX/SPX Compatible Transport. For more information, see the "Connection Protocols" section.

2. **You are installing Remote Access Server on your Windows NT Server computer. You are going to let people in your office connect to the network using RAS on your computer. How many people can be connected to your computer simultaneously?**

☐ A. 1
☐ B. 5
☐ C. 256
☐ D. Unlimited

The correct answer is C. Remote Access Server on a Windows NT Server computer supports up to 256 simultaneous connections, whereas a Windows NT Workstation computer with RAS installed supports only one simultaneous connection. For more information, see the "RAS Overview" section.

3. **You are connecting to your corporate networking using Dial-Up Networking. You need to access HTTP and NetWare servers on the remote network using TCP/IP and NWLink IPX/SPX Compatible Transport. What Dial-Up Networking connection type must you use?**

☐ A. PPTP
☐ B. SLIP
☐ C. PPP
☐ D. ISDN

The correct answer is C. The Point-to-point protocol allows multiple protocols to be tunneled through the connection to the remote host. PPTP provides an encrypted connection over PPP and does not handle protocol specific issues, and SLIP can only use TCP/IP. For more information, see the "Connection Protocols" section.

4. **Because NetBEUI is a nonroutable protocol, how does Windows NT Remote Access Server treat PPP connections that are using NetBEUI?**

☐ A. The client computer is only permitted to access the RAS server.
☐ B. The RAS server will refuse connections made using NetBEUI.
☐ C. The RAS server provides a NetBIOS gateway.
☐ D. The RAS server translates the NetBEUI traffic into NWLink IPX/SPX Compatible Transport packets.

The correct answer is C. The Remote Access Server will automatically provide a gateway to NetBEUI users, enabling them to access the entire network through NetBIOS lookups. Unless the RAS server is configured to prohibit NetBEUI connections, the connection will not be refused. For more information, see the "RAS NetBIOS Gateway" section.

5. **You use Windows NT Dial-Up Networking to connect to your Internet Service Provider using PPP. When you connect, you are able to access Web servers at the ISP office, but you are unable to reach Web servers on the Internet. What configuration setting should you change?**

   ☐ A. Configure TCP/IP to use the default router on the remote network.
   ☐ B. Configure TCP/IP to disable PPP LCP extensions.
   ☐ C. Do not use a Multilink connection.
   ☐ D. Use TCP/IP instead of NWLink IPX/SPX Compatible Transport.

The correct answer is A. When you are able to connect to a RAS server and access hosts local to the RAS server, but are unable to reach other hosts, the problem is usually a TCP/IP default router configuration error. By using the default router on the remote network, the PPP connection will use the default router assigned by the RAS server. The use of LCP extensions or Multilink does not affect your ability to reach remote hosts once connected. For more information, see the "Configuring Protocols and Encryption" section.

6. **You are installing Remote Access Server on your Windows NT computer. Your computer has TCP/IP and NWLink IPX/SPX Compatible Transport installed. Users will access your RAS computer using Dial-Up Networking and TCP/IP or NWLink IPX/SPX Compatible Transport. How will RAS handle the TCP/IP and NWLink IPX/SPX Compatible Transport traffic?**

☐ A. RAS will act as a router for the protocols.
☐ B. RAS will act as a bridge for the protocols.
☐ C. RAS will act as a gateway for the protocols.
☐ D. RAS will act as a repeater for the protocols.

The correct answer is A. RAS will route the two protocols, making the Dial-Up Networking connection a virtual subnet. RAS will then route between its local subnet and the Dial-Up Networking subnet. If a connection uses the NetBEUI protocol, RAS will act as a NetBIOS gateway for that protocol. For more information, see the "Connection Protocols" section.

7. **You are installing Remote Access Server on your Window NT computer. You will be using a Window NT Workstation computer to dial into your Remote Access Server using PPP. Which security features should you implement to have the highest level of security available? (Choose two.)**

☐ A. Accept only Microsoft encrypted authentication.
☐ B. Accept any authentication including clear text.
☐ C. Accept only encrypted authentication.
☐ D. Require data encryption.
☐ E. Enable software compression.
☐ F. Enable PPP LCP extensions.

The correct answers are A and D. Because you will be using a Microsoft compatible platform to initiate a Dial-Up Networking connection, you can use a higher level of security than an open Remote Access Sever configuration. The use of Microsoft encrypted authentication provides the highest level of encrypted username and password authentication available. If you were using a non-Microsoft platform to make a PPP connection, this feature would most likely prevent a successful connection. For more information, see the "Installing and Configuring RAS" section.

8. **You are dialing in to your corporate Windows NT Server running RAS. After the modems connect, you receive an access denied message while authenticating with the RAS server. What should you do?**

☐ A. Use the User Manager for Domains to grant your account Dialin permission.

☐ B. Use the User Manager for Domains and remove any profile configurations.

☐ C. Use the Remote Access Admin to disable Call Back security for your user account.

☐ D. Use the Remote Access Admin to configure Call Back security as Set By Caller.

The correct answer is **A**. The most likely problem is that your account does not have dialin permission. You can use User Manager for Domains or Remote Access Admin to grant dialin permissions. Call Back security would not cause this problem, as it would either prompt you for a number to call you back at or hangup and dial a predefined phone number to reach you. For more information, see the "Remote Access Admin" section.

9. **You are the administrator of a Windows NT Server computer running Remote Access Service. Your company uses only PPTP connections for remote users to connect to server running RAS. You want to permit only PPTP connections to your server from the Internet. What should you do?**

☐ A. Configure the Remote Access Service not to use TCP/IP.

☐ B. Configure the Remote Access service to use only TCP/IP.

☐ C. Configure the TCP/IP protocol to enable PPTP filtering.

☐ D. Configure the TCP/IP protocol to enable Domain Suffix Search Ordering.

The correct answer is C. If you will only be using PPTP connections to a RAS server, you can enable PPTP filtering, which will prevent any connection types other than PPTP. Configuring the RAS server not to use TCP/IP will not prevent other connection types, as PPTP requires TCP/IP to be installed on the server. For more information, see the "PPTP Security" section.

Practice Your Skills

Here is a chance to apply your practical hands-on experience and material from this chapter. These exercises are designed not only for you to apply the material in the book, but also for you to gain greater experience and exposure to the product. These exercises are a critical part of understanding the product and gaining valuable experience for using the product and passing the certification exam. For each of the following problems, consider the given facts and determine what you think are the possible causes of the problem and what course of action you might take to resolve the problem.

1. Configuring Dial-Up Networking

EXERCISE You are configuring your Window NT Server to use Dial-Up Networking to connect to a remote host. The remote host support SLIP and PPP connections. What are the benefits of using PPP instead of SLIP?

ANALYSIS PPP connections support multiple transport protocols, including TCP/IP, NWLINK IPX/SPX Compatible Transport, and NetBEUI. In addition, PPP supports dynamic server-based IP addressing (such as DHCP). PPP supports password encryption, and the PPP connection process does not usually require a script file. SLIP connections can only use TCP/IP and usually require logon scripts to process the authentication.

2. Installing Remote Access Server

EXERCISE You are installing Remote Access Server on your Window NT Server. You plan to have users connect to your computer using PPP on a variety of platforms. What RAS options should you evaluate carefully to ensure that your Remote Access Server can support the largest variety of clients?

ANALYSIS Remote Access Server includes a number of features and options that may be unsupported on non-Microsoft platforms. Enabling Microsoft encrypted authentication may prevent non-Microsoft clients from properly authenticating themselves. In addition, the use of Call Back security is also supported on a limited set of clients. When you install Remote Access Server, the default settings for PPP generally provide the largest support for mixed-platforms environments.

3. Configuring RAS security features

EXERCISE You have installed Remote Access Server on your Windows NT Server. You are configuring the security features of Remote Access Server. What are some of the benefits of using Call Back security?

ANALYSIS The use of Call Back security can be leveraged in two separate ways. First, Call Back security can be configured with a preset phone number. The benefit of this type of configuration is that it reduces the opportunity for unauthorized access to the network, as even if a person got a username and password, unless they were at the proper phone number, they could not complete the connection. The second configuration is to permit the caller to specify a phone number for the server to use to call back. This enables you to shift the cost of remote access connection from the user to your Remote Access Server, usually with better phone rates.

4. Troubleshooting failed connections

EXERCISE You use Dial-Up Networking on your Window NT Server computer to access remote access servers using PPP. What are some basic troubleshooting steps you can take when PPP connections fail?

ANALYSIS The most common problem is incorrectly configured TCP/IP settings. Most hosts that support PPP will assign all of the TCP/IP settings required. Second, the use of PPP LCP extensions sometimes causes problems on older PPP hosts. By disabling these extensions, you may be able to resolve the problem. Third, the use of encrypted usernames and passwords often prove problematic when connecting to non-Microsoft PPP hosts.

5. Automating RAS connections

EXERCISE You are using Dial-Up Networking to connect to your Internet Service Provider. The ISP has a number of different clients dialing in to the same phone number. As a result, the ISP has implemented a menu to enable users to access different hosts and connect in various styles. What can you do to your Dial-Up Networking connection phonebook entry to simplify this process during logon?

ANALYSIS Dial-Up Networking provides the ability to script a pre- or post-logon process. To create the required script, log in to the ISP manually by configuring your Dial-Up Networking connection to pop up a terminal window so you can manually enter the information and wait for the system prompts. Then, using the phonebook entry dialog box, configure the Dial-Up Networking connection to use a script and edit the script to navigate the ISP menu.

Optimizing Performance

Getting a Windows NT Server installed and running on a computer is only a part of using Windows NT and passing the Windows NT Server exam. You must also be knowledgeable in tuning and optimizing Windows NT Server for optimal performance. In this chapter I introduce the Performance Monitor and explore how it can be used to view performance counters and resolve performance bottlenecks. I also take a look at the four Performance Monitor views, and discuss how to optimize common bottlenecks on a Windows NT Server computer.

Exam Material in This Chapter

Based on Microsoft Objectives

Monitoring and Optimization

- Monitor performance of various functions by using Performance Monitor. Functions include:
  - Processor
  - Memory
  - Disk
  - Network
- Identify performance bottlenecks

Based on Author's Experience

- You definitely need to know the common performance object and counters to view for a given scenario.
- You need to know which counters are not enabled by default, and what will happen if you view the counters before they are enabled.
- You should be familiar with the four Performance Monitor views and their most common uses.
- You should be prepared for questions about how to resolve common performance bottlenecks.

Are You Prepared?

Do you have what it takes? Try out these self-assessment questions to see if you have prepared for the material in this chapter or if you should review problem areas.

1. **You are experiencing long wait times when trying to access files on your Window NT Server computer. You suspect that an application may be writing to the hard disk excessively. What can you do to view the statistics of the hard disk using the Performance Monitor?**

   ☐ A. Use the Disk Administrator to enable the PhysicalDisk objects.

   ☐ B. Use the `diskperf.exe` utility to enable the PhysicalDisk objects.

   ☐ C. Nothing; the objects are enabled by default.

   ☐ D. Log on to the Window NT Server computer as member of the local Administrators group.

2. **You are using Performance Monitor to capture statistics that you will be archiving for future comparison and analysis. Which Performance Monitor view will enable you to capture statistics and store them for future retrieval?**

   ☐ A. Chart view

   ☐ B. Alert view

   ☐ C. Log view

   ☐ D. Report view

3. You have been receiving messages from users that their network performance seems to have slowed down in the last few days. You want to use Performance Monitor to alert you when the network segment performance for a select group of computers falls below specified level. What two things do you need to do in order to accomplish this? (Choose two.)

☐ A. Install the SNMP service on the computers.
☐ B. Install the Network Monitor Agent on the computers.
☐ C. Use the Report view in Performance Monitor.
☐ D. Use the Alert view in Performance Monitor.

Answers:

1. B   *Before Performance Monitor can access the statistics for PhysicalDisks, the objects must first be enabled using the* diskperf.exe *utility. The objects are installed by default, but because of a small increase in system utilization, the objects are not enabled by default. See the "Performance Monitor" section.*

2. C   *The Log view of Performance Monitor allows you to collect current system statistics and store them in a log file for future analysis in Performance Monitor or in other third-party applications capable of reading CSV files. See the "Gathering and Viewing Statistics" section.*

3. B and D
         Before you can access the Network Segment performance object, the Network Monitor Agent must be installed to capture the values used by the counters. Then by using the Alert view, you can establish a threshold where the computer will alert you to the current activity. See the "Performance Monitor" section.

Performance Monitor

Performance Monitor is a Windows NT tool that ships with Windows NT Server. You don't need to install Performance Monitor — it's installed automatically when you install Windows NT Server.

Performance Monitor can be used to:

- Identify performance problems and/or bottlenecks
- Determine current usage of system resources
- Track performance trends over time
- Predict future usage of system resources (capacity planning)
- Determine how system configuration changes affect system performance

Performance Monitor is often used when there's a problem to be resolved, but it can also be used for planning purposes.

Objects, Instances, and Counters

The system components that Performance Monitor can measure, such as processor, memory, and physical disk, are called *objects*. If a system has more than one of a particular object, such as multiple processors or multiple physical disks, there is said to be more than one *instance* of that object. Some objects, such as memory, do not have instances. This is because there can't be more than one of the particular object.

 Objects

Physical components of a computer, including hard disks, processors, and memory, are called *objects*. Each object has at least one measurement counter that tracks specific performance measurements.

Each instance of an object can be measured in different ways. Each possible measurement of an object is called a *counter*. For example, the PhysicalDisk object has multiple possible counters, including Disk Reads/sec (second), Disk Writes/sec, % Disk Time, % Disk Read Time, and % Disk Write Time. Each counter is selected individually. An object can be selected multiple times with a different counter for each selection, as shown in Figure 11-1. Notice the Performance Monitor report shows multiple counters selected for the PhysicalDisk object.

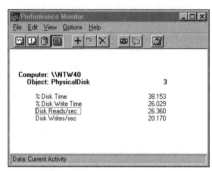

Figure 11-1 *Measuring multiple counters for a single object*

Not all Performance Monitor objects and counters are available when Windows NT is first installed. For example, the TCP (Transmission Control Protocol) object is not available until the *Simple Network Management Protocol* (SNMP) Service is installed, and the Network Segment object is not available until the Network Monitor Agent is installed. In addition, some objects and counters must be enabled before they can be effectively used in Performance Monitor.

The following sections explain how to add and enable certain Performance Monitor objects and counters.

TCP/IP Objects and Counters

By default, Performance Monitor does *not* make available TCP/IP objects and their counters, even when TCP/IP is installed and configured on the Windows NT computer.

The SNMP Service must be installed before you can monitor TCP/IP objects and counters in Performance Monitor. Until the counters are enabled, Performance Monitor will only show a zero value for all related counters.

Installing the SNMP Service adds four objects and their counters to Performance Monitor:

- IP (Internet Protocol)
- ICMP (Internet Control Message Protocol)
- TCP (Transmission Control Protocol)
- UDP (User Datagram Protocol)

These four objects and their counters are used by developers to optimize network use of applications, and by administrators of large networks to troubleshoot and optimize TCP/IP network traffic.

Network Segment Object and Counters

By default, the Network Segment object and its counters are *not* available in Performance Monitor. The Network Monitor Agent must be installed to make this object and its counters available.

The Network Monitor Agent must be installed to view the Network Segment objects and its counters.

The counters that are installed with the Network Segment object include:

- % Broadcast Frames
- % Network Utilization
- Total Bytes Received/second
- Total Frames Received/second

The Network Segment object has an instance for each network adapter installed in the Windows NT computer. You can monitor counters for each instance of the Network Segment object. In other words, you can monitor network traffic on each network segment that your Windows NT computer is connected to.

The Network Segment object and its counters are used by network administrators to determine network use on individual network segments. In addition, this object and its counters are often used for network capacity planning.

PhysicalDisk and LogicalDisk Objects and Counters

By default, the PhysicalDisk and LogicalDisk objects and their counters are installed, but *not* enabled. Although you can select these objects and their counters in Performance Monitor, until they are enabled, the counters will always display a value of zero.

KNOW THIS Disk Performance Counters

The Windows NT `Diskperf.exe` command-line utility is used to enable the PhysicalDisk and LogicalDisk objects and their counters. You must reboot the computer after running `Diskperf.exe` before these objects and their counters will be usable in Performance Monitor.

Table 11-1 shows how the `Diskperf.exe` command-line utility can be used to enable and disable the PhysicalDisk and LogicalDisk objects and their counters.

TABLE 11-1 The Windows NT Diskperf.exe Command

Diskperf.exe Command	Description
diskperf -y	Enables the PhysicalDisk and LogicalDisk objects and their counters.
diskperf -ye	Enables the PhysicalDisk and LogicalDisk objects and their counters for stripe sets and stripe sets with parity.
diskperf -n	Disables the PhysicalDisk and LogicalDisk objects and their counters.

True or False?

1. Each physical component is called a performance counter.
2. The PhysicalDisk counters are not enabled by default.
3. You must install SNMP before Performance Monitor can see actual TCP/IP counter values.
4. Performance objects must have more than one instance.
5. The Network Monitor Agent must be installed so that Performance Monitor can see actual Network Segment counter values.

Answers: *1. False 2. True 3. True 4. False 5. True*

Gathering and Viewing Statistics

Now that you have a basic understanding of the Performance Monitor objects and their counters, you're ready to use the Performance Monitor tool. In this section, you'll learn how to start Performance Monitor and how to use the "views" within Performance Monitor to gather and view statistics on a Windows NT computer's performance.

The Performance Monitor dialog box appears in Figure 11-2. Notice that no objects are monitored when Performance Monitor is first started.

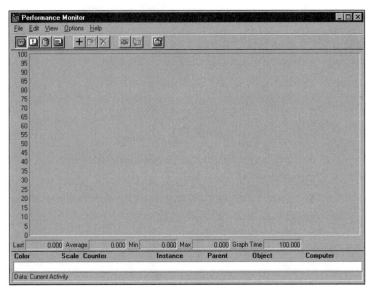

Figure 11-2 *Starting Performance Monitor*

There are four possible views in Performance Monitor: Chart, Alert, Report, and Log. By default, Performance Monitor starts in Chart view. The following sections explain how to use each of the four Performance Monitor views.

Chart View

The Performance Monitor Chart view displays activity in a graphical format. It can be used to view current performance activity, or to view archived performance activity from a Performance Monitor log file. (Log files are discussed later in this chapter.)

Chart view displays activity in a graphical format, and can be used to view current performance activity, or to view archived performance activity from a Performance Monitor log file.

Before you can view performance statistics in a Performance Monitor chart, you must first select one or more objects and their counters to be measured and displayed in a Chart view. To select objects and their counters to be displayed in a Performance Monitor chart, you need to access the Add to Chart dialog box. The Add to Chart dialog box is shown in Figure 11-3. Notice that you can select objects, counters, and instances in this dialog box.

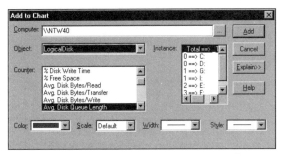

Figure 11-3 *Selecting objects, counters, and instances in the Add to Chart dialog box*

Figure 11-4 shows a Performance Monitor chart with several objects and counters selected. Notice the Last, Average, Min, Max, and Graph Time boxes toward the bottom of the chart.

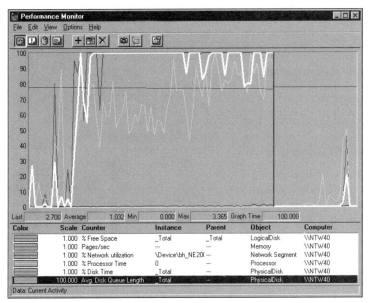

Figure 11-4 *Viewing a chart in Performance Monitor*

When you highlight any counter in the section at the bottom of the dialog box, that counter's statistics are displayed in the Last, Average, Min, Max, and Graph Time boxes directly below the chart. Table 11-2 explains the statistics displayed in each of these text boxes.

TABLE 11-2 Statistics Displayed in Performance Monitor Chart View

Statistic	Description
Last	Most recent measurement of the counter.
Average	Average of the counter's measurement over the period of time represented by the chart.
Min	Lowest (minimum) measurement of the counter during the period of time represented by the chart.
Max	Highest (maximum) measurement of the counter during the period of time represented by the chart.
Graph Time	Number of seconds represented by the entire chart. This is the total amount of time it takes Performance Monitor to graph from one side of the chart to the other.

Alert View

The Performance Monitor Alert view displays an alert when a monitored counter exceeds or drops below a specified value.

Performance Monitor has no preset alerts. Alerts must be created in Alert view by selecting one or more counters to be monitored, and by entering a threshold value for each counter. When this threshold value is exceeded or falls below a minimum level (depending on how the alert is configured), an alert is triggered.

Figure 11-5 shows a Performance Monitor alert. Notice the Alert Legend at the bottom of the dialog box. In this situation, I configured Performance Monitor to generate an alert when the amount of free space on my computer's hard disk dropped below thirty percent.

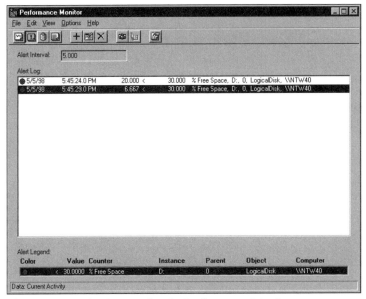

Figure 11-5 *Viewing an alert in Performance Monitor*

By default, Performance Monitor measures each specified counter in five-second intervals, and compares each measurement with the threshold value. If the threshold value is exceeded or falls below a minimum level (depending on how the alert is configured), Performance Monitor generates an alert. If the threshold value is consistently exceeded or consistently falls below a minimum level, an alert will be generated every five seconds.

Report View

The Performance Monitor Report view displays activity in a report format. It can be used to view current performance activity, or to view archived performance activity from a Performance Monitor log file. (Log files are discussed later in this chapter.) Figure 11-6 shows a Performance Monitor report with several objects and counters selected.

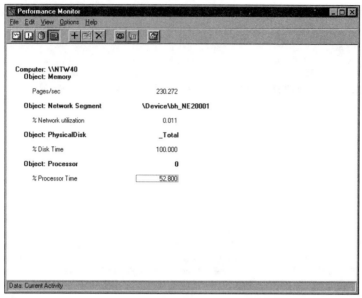

Figure 11-6 *Viewing a report in Performance Monitor*

The value displayed for each counter in the Report view represents an average of the last two Performance Monitor measurements for that counter. However, the value is not an average from the time Performance Monitor was started. Performance Monitor, by default, updates the report every five seconds.

Log View

The Performance Monitor Log view is used to save statistics gathered by Performance Monitor to a log file. The Performance Monitor log file can be viewed at a later time in Chart, Alert, or Report view. Figure 11-7 shows Performance Monitor in the process of collecting data for the log file. Notice the Status and File Size text boxes.

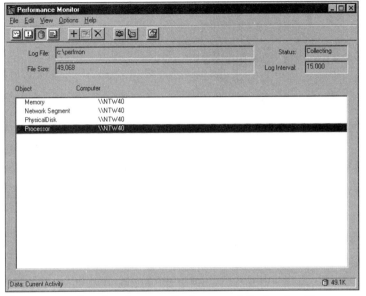

Figure 11-7 *Logging data to a Performance Monitor log file*

 True or False?

1. The Report view can use archived performance log files.

2. The Report view is a graphical display of performance counters.

3. The default refresh time for Performance monitor is every five seconds.

4. When you select an object in Log View, Performance Monitor automatically logs all of the object's counters.

5. Alert view displays an alert only when a counter exceeds a specified value.

Answers: *1. True 2. False 3. True 4. True 5. False*

Performance Optimization

Performance optimization is the process of modifying computer or network hardware and software configurations with the intent of speeding up computer or network response.

Performance optimization is performed for a couple of reasons:

- To get the most performance out of existing hardware
- In response to user or administrator observations of slow system performance

Performance optimization should be performed with a specific goal in mind. Your primary goal might be to provide the fastest possible file services to client computers. Or your goal might be to remedy slow system response by identifying the problem and implementing a solution. In short, your goal can be almost anything that focuses on improving efficiency and speed of system performance.

For most network administrators, performance optimization usually means resolving user reports of slow system performance. Determining the cause of the slow performance is referred to as *identifying a bottleneck.*

Identifying Bottlenecks

A *bottleneck* is the component in the system that is slowing system performance. In a networking environment, the bottleneck is the part of the system that is performing at peak capacity while other components in the system are not. In other words, if it weren't for the limiting component, the rest of the system could go faster.

When you are attempting to identify the bottleneck in your system, use Performance Monitor to measure performance of the computer's memory, processor, and disk. You can also use Performance Monitor to gather statistics about your network that may help you identify network bottlenecks.

The following tables contain Performance Monitor counters that may help you in identifying bottlenecks. Table 11-3 shows the counters you can use to monitor a Windows NT computer's memory.

TABLE 11-3 Performance Monitor Memory Counters

Object	Counter	Description and How to Interpret
Memory	Pages/sec	Measures the amount of 4KB memory pages that are read from or written to the paging file during a one-second time period. This counter is used to obtain an overall view of how memory is utilized by Windows NT. If the computer does not have enough memory, excessive paging will occur. A consistently high number for this counter (greater than 2 to 3) indicates that the current amount of RAM may be insufficient for the computer.
Paging File	% Usage	Measures the percentage of paging file utilization. A consistently high percentage for this counter (approaching 100%) may indicate that you should add RAM to the system or enlarge the paging file. Enlarging the paging file won't speed up the system – only adding RAM will do that.

Pages/sec and % Usage counters are likely to be used in scenarios where a Windows NT Server computer is experiencing slow performance and excessive disk access. Watch for exam questions that mention these traits and ask which performance objects/counters you should monitor.

Counters

It is very important that you review each of these high-lighted performance objects and counters. These counters are the most commonly used items, are they are extremely likely to show up on your exam.

Table 11-4 shows the counters you can use to monitor a Windows NT computer's processor.

TABLE 11-4 Performance Monitor Processor Counters

Object	Counter	Description and How to Interpret
Processor	% Processor Time	Measures the percentage of time that the processor is actively being used by processes other than the Idle process. This counter only measures one processor — if your system has multiple processors, use the System % Total Processor Time counter instead. A consistently high number for this counter (approaching 100%) may indicate that a faster processor (or an additional processor) may be required for adequate system performance. Check the memory counters *before* upgrading your processor — if the memory counters are consistently high, you might just need more RAM.
System	% Total Processor Time	Measures the percentage of time that *all* processors in the computer are actively being used by processes other than the Idle process. A consistently high number for this counter (approaching 100%) may indicate that faster processors (or an additional processor) may be required for adequate system performance. Check the memory counters *before* upgrading your processor(s) — if the memory counters are consistently high, you might just need more RAM.

% Processor Time and % Total Processor Time counters are likely to be used in scenarios where a Windows NT Server computer is experiencing slow performance and long wait times for system services. Watch for exam questions that mention these traits and ask which performance objects/counters you should monitor.

Table 11-5 shows the counters you can use to monitor a Windows NT computer's disk.

TABLE 11-5 Performance Monitor Disk Counters

Object	Counter	Description and How to Interpret
PhysicalDisk	Avg. Disk Queue Length	Measures the average number of disk reads and writes waiting to be performed. A consistently high number for this counter (greater than 2 to 3) may indicate that a faster hard disk or disk controller, or a different disk configuration (such as a stripe set) may be required for adequate system performance. Check the memory counters *before* upgrading your disk(s) — if the memory counters are consistently high, you might just need more RAM.
PhysicalDisk	% Disk Time	Measures the percentage of time that the disk is actually busy performing reads and writes. A consistently high number for this counter (approaching 100%) may indicate that a faster hard disk or disk controller, or a different disk configuration (such as a stripe set) may be required for adequate system performance. Check the memory counters *before* upgrading your disk(s) — if the memory counters are consistently high, you might just need more RAM.

Continued

TABLE 11-5 *Continued*

Object	Counter	Description and How to Interpret
LogicalDisk	% Free Space	Measures the percentage of unused disk space. A consistently high or gradually increasing number for this counter (approaching 100%) indicates that the computer does *not* have sufficient disk space available. An additional disk or a replacement disk that has more capacity may be required.

Avg. Disk Queue Length, % Disk Time, and % Free Space counters are likely to be used in scenarios where a Windows NT Server computer is experiencing slow hard disk performance and excessively long periods waiting for files to load. Watch for exam questions that mention these traits and ask which performance objects/counters you should monitor.

Table 11-6 shows a Performance Monitor counter you can use to monitor the network.

TABLE 11-6 Performance Monitor Network Counter

Object	Counter	Description and How to Interpret
Network Segment	% Network utilization	Measures the total network usage on a given network segment as a percentage of the maximum amount of network traffic possible on that segment. A consistently high number for this counter (approaching 100%) may indicate that there are too many computers or too much network traffic on that network segment. An additional network adapter may need to be installed in the computer, or a router may need to be installed on the network to further segment the network.

Optimizing Performance and Resolving Bottlenecks

Performance optimization involves getting the most speed out of your existing hardware and software combination. It can also involve adding or upgrading specific components to resolve bottlenecks.

You don't have to make a large number of configuration or Registry setting changes to optimize the performance of Windows NT. Windows NT is designed to automatically tune itself for providing the best performance it can with the hardware resources available in the computer. For example, Windows NT automatically adjusts the amount of memory assigned to cache, the amount of memory assigned to buffering network packets, and prioritizes processor allocation as needed.

However, the administrator can modify hardware and software configurations to optimize system performance and to resolve bottlenecks. You can add RAM, optimize paging files, optimize or upgrade disks, or upgrade or add a processor. Depending on your situation, implementing one or more of these options may improve your system's performance or resolve a bottleneck.

RAM

Perhaps the single most inexpensive and effective upgrade you can make to your Windows NT computer is to add additional RAM. I've never heard an administrator whine that he or she "just had too much RAM" in his or her computers. You can *never* have too much RAM.

Adding RAM can reduce how often the computer reads or writes virtual memory pages to or from the paging file on the hard disk. This is called *reducing paging*. Because paging uses both processor time and disk time, when paging is reduced, the performance of the processor and the disk can also be improved.

TEST TRAP Adding RAM often reduces or eliminates excessive paging. You can use this to your advantage when taking the Windows NT Server exam. Watch for scenarios where a Windows NT Server is experiencing excessive paging – the answer may be to add more RAM.

When RAM is added to the computer, Windows NT automatically increases the allocation of RAM made available to the disk cache. The disk cache temporarily stores requested files from the hard disk. Because the disk doesn't need to be accessed when a file is retrieved from the cache, files in the cache are more quickly available to users than files on the disk. Thus, increasing the size of the cache can improve disk performance because the number of disk accesses is reduced.

Paging Files

The best method for optimizing a paging file is adding more RAM. The more RAM in the computer, the less paging activity will occur. That said, there are a few additional things you can do to optimize paging file performance. If the Performance Monitor Paging File % Usage and Paging File % Usage Peak counters indicate that the paging file is being used a consistently high percentage of the time, you might consider trying one or more of the following:

- Configure the paging file so that its initial size and maximum size are equal. This prevents fragmentation of the paging file.
- Place the paging file on the physical disk in your system that has the least amount of activity.
- Place the paging file on a stripe set.
- Place multiple, smaller paging files on multiple physical disks in your system.
- Place the paging file on any other partition than the boot partition.

TEST TRAP Optimizing paging files is very likely to be on the exam, so check out the ways to improve access to the paging file.

Memory Dump File

If you have configured Windows NT to create a memory dump file (memory.dmp) when a stop error occurs, you *must* have a paging file on the boot partition that is at least as large as the amount of RAM in the computer. If the paging file isn't large enough or has been moved from the boot partition, a memory dump file won't be created.

Hard Disks

Optimizing disks is the process of speeding up hard disk response or adding to or replacing the existing disk(s). Consider optimizing disks when planning for a new Windows NT computer that will perform a specific task, such as CAD or graphics.

Consider optimizing or upgrading disks when you determine, through performance monitoring, that the Windows NT computer's disk is a bottleneck to system performance. Before you upgrade a disk(s), ensure that memory (RAM) is *not* the bottleneck in your system.

You can increase disk performance by doing the following:

- Defragmenting the hard disk(s) in your computer
- Upgrading to a faster disk controller or a faster hard disk(s)
- Configuring a stripe set across two or more disks

CPUs

When you determine, through performance monitoring, that the Windows NT computer's processor is a bottleneck to system performance, you should consider upgrading or adding a processor to the computer.

Before you upgrade or add a processor, ensure that memory (RAM) is *not* the bottleneck in your system.

The following are ways to improve processor performance, all of which involve replacing or adding hardware:

- Replacing the existing processor with a faster processor
- Replacing the existing motherboard and processor with a faster motherboard and processor
- Upgrading from a single processor system to a multiprocessor system

Have You Mastered?

Now it's time to apply what you've learned in this chapter by testing your mastery of the material. These questions provide you with a means to determine if you are ready to move on to the next chapter or if you need to review the material again.

1. **What does Performance Monitor call the physical components of a computer?**

   ☐ A. Objects
   ☐ B. Counters
   ☐ C. Instances
   ☐ D. Items

   The correct answer is **A**. Performance Monitor refers to physical components such as processors and hard disks as *objects*. Performance Monitor assigns each object at least one counter that measures specific performance activity for an object. An instance is each occurrence of an object, so if a computer had two processors, it would have two instances of the processor object. For more information, see the "Objects, Instances, and Counters" section.

2. **You want to measure the percentage of time that processes on a Windows NT computer actively use the processor. Which Performance Monitor object and counter should you use?**

   ☐ A. Object: Processor; Counter: %Processor Time
   ☐ B. Object: %Processor Time; Counter: Processor
   ☐ C. Object: Processor; Counter: %Privileged Time
   ☐ D. Object: %Privileged Time; Counter: Processor

The correct answer is **A**. The Performance Monitor refers to the processor as an object, and the individual reporting items as counters. This Object/Counter pair will show what percentage of the time is spent on processes running on the Window NT computer. For more information, see the "Identifying Bottlenecks" section.

3. **You are experiencing what appears to be slow network performance and long wait times on your Window NT computer. You want to monitor the local network segment performance to determine if that is where the problem lies. What should you do? (Choose two.)**

   ☐ A. Install the SNMP Service.
   ☐ B. Install the Network Monitor Agent.
   ☐ C. Use Performance Monitor to view the Network Segment object.
   ☐ D. Use Performance Monitor to view the Network Segment counter.

The correct answers are **B** and **C**. Before you can view network traffic performance activity, you must first install the Network Monitor Agent. Then you can use Performance Monitor to view the Network Segment object, which has several counters associated with it. For more information, see the "Objects, Instances, and Counters" section.

4. **You are having difficulty maintaining a TCP/IP connection with a host over the Internet. You suspect that your connection is being timed out, and you want to verify the problem. What should you do? (Choose two.)**

   ☐ A. Install the SNMP Service.
   ☐ B. Install the Network Monitor Agent.
   ☐ C. Use Performance Monitor to view the TCP and IP objects.
   ☐ D. Use Performance Monitor to view the Network Segment object.

The correct answers are A and C. Before the IP, TCP, ICMP, and UDP objects can be viewed with Performance Monitor, you must first install the SNMP service, which is responsible for creating the counter values. Once the SNMP service is installed, you can then use Performance Monitor to view the various TCP and IP object counters. For more information, see the "Objects, Instances, and Counters" section.

5. **You are experiencing slow disk performance on your Window NT Server computer. You suspect that either your computer is writing to the paging file too often, or there is a disk performance problem. When you start Performance Monitor, the PhysicalDisk counters are all zero. What should you do?**

   ☐ A. Log on to the Window NT Server computer as an administrator.

   ☐ B. Use `diskperf.exe` to enable the Performance Monitor objects.

   ☐ C. Use the Disk Administrator to enable the Performance Monitor objects.

   ☐ D. Install the PhysicalDisk Performance Monitor objects.

The correct answer is **B**. The PhysicalDisk related objects are installed by default, but are not enabled until the `diskperf.exe` utility is used. The objects are not enabled by default as they cause a slight decrease in system performance. The Disk Administrator cannot be used to enable the PhysicalDisk objects. For more information, see the "Objects, Instances, and Counters" section.

6. **You are using Performance Monitor on your Window NT Server computer. What three sources of performance data can you use in Performance Monitor when using the Report view? (Choose all that apply.)**

☐ A. Current activity on local Window NT Server computer
☐ B. Current activity on remote Window NT Server computer
☐ C. Windows NT Event Logs
☐ D. Windows NT modem logs
☐ E. Archived Performance Monitor data from a log file
☐ F. Archived Performance Monitor data that has been exported to a CSV file

The correct answers are **A, B,** and **E.** The view that you are using in Performance Monitor actually makes no difference; all of the views are capable of inputting from any of these sources, except Log view, which can only use current activity. Performance Monitor has no way of importing information from the Event log, modem logs, or from a CSV file. For more information, see the "Gathering and Viewing Statistics" section.

7. **You are preparing a monthly utilization report of your Windows NT computers on the network. You would like to use the Performance Monitor data in an Excel spreadsheet to graphically map the historical performance and merge the graphs with a monthly Word report template. Which Performance Monitor view should you use?**

☐ A. Report
☐ B. Log
☐ C. Chart
☐ D. Alert

The correct answer is **B.** The Log view stores only the performance counter values, and no extra text that may confuse the import process into applications such as Excel. The log file can be exported to a CSV file and then imported to Excel or any other application capable of reading CSV files. For more information, see the "Gathering and Viewing Statistics" section.

8. You are noticing an excessive amount of writing to the system paging file. You suspect that you have insufficient RAM in your Window NT Server computer. You want to obtain an overall view of how memory is being used on a particular Windows NT computer. Which Performance Monitor object and counter should you use?

   ☐ A. Object: Memory; Counter: Pages/sec
   ☐ B. Object: Pages/sec; Counter: Memory
   ☐ C. Object: Processor; Counter: Pages/sec
   ☐ D. Object: Pages/sec; Counter: Processor

The correct answer is A. The Performance Monitor object is Memory that has a counter called pages/sec, which shows the overall activity with the system RAM. It is important to remember which elements are objects and which are counters. The processor object does not track RAM activity such as pages/sec. For more information, see the "Optimizing Performance and Resolving Bottlenecks" section.

A

Practice Your Skills

Here is a chance to apply your practical hands-on experience and material from this chapter. These exercises are designed not only for you to apply the material in the book, but also for you to gain greater experience and exposure to the product. These exercises are a critical part of understanding the product and gaining valuable experience for using the product and passing the certification exam. For each of the following problems, consider the given facts and determine what you think are the possible causes of the problem and what course of action you might take to resolve the problem.

1. Viewing statistics on a remote computer

EXERCISE You received a call from a user of a Window NT Workstation computer on a remote network subnet. The user states that it is taking an extremely long time to connect to the corporate servers. You want to use Performance Monitor to view the statistics on the remote Window NT Workstation computer. What must you do?

ANALYSIS Before Performance Monitor can remotely view the Network Segment object, the Network Monitor Agent must be installed. This is the same procedure that is required if you were going to monitor the object locally. Other than administrative permission to the computer, there are no other configuration requirements.

2. Monitoring the system processor

EXERCISE You are using Performance Monitor to view the performance on a remote Window NT Server computer. You will be monitoring the utilization of the system processor as the user of the computer performs various tasks. What should you consider when choosing the Performance Monitor view you should use?

ANALYSIS Performance Monitor offers four different views of the activity. Since the scenario stated that you are basically watching the information interactively, you should probably use the Chart view as it provides quick graphical analysis of the system activity. The Report and Alert views are geared towards post-event monitoring and the Log view is good for evaluating the performance at a later time or in a third-party application.

3. Monitoring the amount of available disk space

EXERCISE You want to be alerted whenever a hard disk on one of your Windows NT Server computers has less than 250MB of free disk space left. What should you do in Performance Monitor to do this?

ANALYSIS By setting up an Alert view in Performance Monitor and specifying the 250MB threshold limit, Performance Monitor can notify you when this event occurs. You can specify a command-line program to run to notify you as well, which may be useful in dialing your beeper number and leaving a text message regarding the problem.

4. Using Performance Monitor views

EXERCISE You want to track the performance of your Windows NT Server computer. You decide to use Performance Monitor to gather the server statistics. What Performance Monitor view should you use to allow you to store and later examine the server statistics?

ANALYSIS By using the Log view within Performance Monitor, you can archive the performance data to be used as a baseline measurement on the performance of your computer. Whenever you make a change, you can create new log files and compare the performance before and after to determine how your network and servers are responding to recent changes. This information can be used to show a general trend in the health of your server.

Advanced
Troubleshooting

C hapter 12 explores a number of advanced Windows NT troubleshooting topics, beginning with a discussion of the Windows NT boot sequence and including a look at performing the Emergency Repair process. I also explain the Event Viewer, which can be used to determine why a service or driver failed during system startup. This chapter also provides valuable information on how to recover from a single or multiple disk failure, and explores how to manage Windows NT Server computers remotely from client computers by using Client-based Network Administration Tools.

Exam Material in This Chapter

Based on Microsoft Objectives

Troubleshooting

- Choose the appropriate course of action to take to resolve boot failures.

- Choose the appropriate course of action to take to resolve fault-tolerance failures. Fault-tolerance methods include:
  - Mirroring
  - Stripe set with parity

Managing Resources

- Administer remote servers from various types of client computers. Client computer types include:
  - Windows 95
  - Windows NT Workstation

Based on Author's Experience

- You need to be familiar with the boot sequence of Windows NT and how to troubleshoot common boot failures.

- You should know how to use the Event Viewer and how to determine the cause of a problem using information provided in the Event Viewer logs.

- You definitely need to know how to recover from a disk failure when using disk mirroring or a stripe set with parity.

- You should expect a few questions about using Client-based Network Administration Tools on a Windows NT Workstation or Windows 95 computer.

Are You Prepared?

Do you have what it takes? Try out these self-assessment questions to see if you have prepared for the material in this chapter or if you should review problem areas.

1. **You have installed a new Win32 application on your Windows NT Server computer. After rebooting the computer, you receive a "Missing Operating System" error. What should you do to repair this problem?**

   ☐ A. Start an Emergency Repair process and choose the Verify Windows NT system files option.

   ☐ B. Copy the `boot.ini` file from another Windows NT computer to the C: drive.

   ☐ C. You must reinstall Windows NT Workstation.

   ☐ D. Boot the computer using the Last Known Good control set.

2. **Your Windows NT Server computer has its boot disk in a mirrored set. The primary disk in the mirror fails and Windows NT Server is unable to boot the operating system. What should you do to boot Windows NT Server on this computer?**

   ☐ A. Boot the computer using the Emergency Repair Disk.

   ☐ B. Boot the computer using a fault tolerance boot disk.

   ☐ C. Boot the computer using the Windows NT Server installation CD-ROM.

   ☐ D. Change the drive cabling so the remaining good drive is the first drive on the cable.

3. You have just added a new hardware device to your Windows
   NT Server computer. When you reboot the server, you receive a
   blue screen. When you reboot again, you receive the same blue
   screen. What should you do?

   ☐ A. Start an Emergency Repair process and choose the
        Verify Windows NT system files option.
   ☐ B. Copy the boot.ini file from another Windows NT
        computer to the C: drive.
   ☐ C. You must reinstall Windows NT Workstation.
   ☐ D. Boot the computer using the Last Known Good
        control set.

Answers:

1. A   *If some of the core Windows NT boot files are missing,
        the best way to correct the problem is to start an
        Emergency Repair process using the original Windows
        NT setup disks and the Emergency Repair Disk that was
        created for the computer. You can then have the
        Windows NT system files checked and missing or
        corrupt files can be updated. See the "Troubleshooting
        the Boot Sequence" section.*

2. B   *When the boot partition for Windows NT is on a mirror
        set, and one of the disks fails, you will most likely need
        to boot using a fault tolerance boot disk. This disk will
        boot Windows NT Server from the remaining good
        drive. See the "Recovering from Disk Failures" section.*

3. D   *If, after making configuration changes, your Windows
        NT Server computer fails to successfully boot to the
        desktop, you can reboot and use the Last Known Good
        control set. This control set represents the last known
        bootable configuration of the server. You will probably
        need to reconfigure the server for the new device after
        booting. See the "Troubleshooting the Boot Sequence"
        section.*

Troubleshooting the Boot Sequence

The *boot sequence* refers to the process of starting Windows NT, including initializing all of its services and completing the logon process. There are several common problems that can occur during the boot sequence, and in order to successfully troubleshoot them, you need to have an understanding of the steps that occur during the boot sequence.

The following sections identify and explain the steps that occur during the boot sequence, list common boot sequence problems and recommended solutions, and discuss how to perform the Emergency Repair process, which is a solution to several common boot sequence problems.

Overview of the Boot Sequence

The Windows NT boot sequence consists of a sequential series of steps, beginning with powering on the computer and ending with completion of the logon process. Understanding the individual steps that make up the boot sequence will help you to troubleshoot problems that may occur during this process.

The boot sequence steps vary according to the hardware platform you are using. The boot sequence steps discussed in this section apply to the Intel platform only.

The Windows NT boot sequence (Intel platform) is as follows:

1. **Power On Self Test:** The *Power On Self Test* (POST) is performed by the computer's BIOS every time the computer is powered on to test for the existence of specific components, such as processor, RAM, and video adapter. If any errors are detected during this phase, an error message or onscreen diagnostic is typically displayed.

2. **Initial Startup:** In this step, the computer's BIOS attempts to locate a startup disk, such as a floppy disk, or the first hard disk in the computer. If the startup disk is the first hard disk, the BIOS reads the *Master Boot Record* from the startup disk, and the code in the Master Boot Record is run. The Master Boot Record then determines which partition is the active partition, and loads sector 0 (also called the partition boot sector) from the active partition into memory. Then the code contained in sector 0 is

run. This causes the `ntldr` file to be loaded into memory from the root folder of the active partition. `Ntldr` is then run. If the startup disk is a floppy disk, the code from sector 0 on the floppy disk is loaded into memory. Then the code contained in sector 0 is run. This causes `ntldr` to be loaded into memory from the root folder of the floppy disk. `Ntldr` is then run.

3. **Selecting an operating system:** `Ntldr` switches the processor into a 32-bit flat memory mode. `Ntldr` then initializes the appropriate minifile system (either FAT or NTFS) to enable `ntldr` to locate and load the `Boot.ini` file. `Ntldr` uses the `Boot.ini` file to create the *boot loader screen.*

A typical Window NT 4.0 boot loader screen appears as follows:

```
OS Loader V4.00
Please select the operating system to start:
        Windows NT Server Version 4.00
        Windows NT Server Version 4.00 [VGA mode]
        MS-DOS
Use  and  to move the highlight to your choice.
Press Enter to choose.
Seconds until highlighted choice will be started
automatically: 30
```

At this point, either the user selects an operating system from the boot loader menu, or the default operating system is automatically started after a specified number of seconds has elapsed.

If an operating system *other* than Windows NT is selected, the `Bootsect.dos` file is loaded into memory and run, and the appropriate operating system is started. (If an operating system other than Windows NT is selected, the remaining steps of the Windows NT boot sequence do not apply.) If Windows NT is selected, `ntldr` loads `Ntdetect.com` and executes it.

4. **Detecting hardware:** `Ntdetect.com` searches for computer ID, bus type (ISA, EISA, PCI, or MCA), video adapter, keyboard, serial and parallel ports, floppy disk(s), and pointing device (mouse). As it checks, the following is displayed on screen:

```
NTDETECT V4.0 Checking Hardware . . .
```

Ntdetect.com creates a list of the components it finds and passes this information to ntldr.

5. **Selecting hardware profile and loading the kernel:** Ntldr displays the following message:

```
OS Loader V4.0
Press spacebar now to invoke Hardware Profile/Last Known
Good menu.
```

Ntldr gives you approximately three to five seconds to press the spacebar. If you press the spacebar at this time, the Hardware Profile/Last Known Good menu is displayed as shown:

```
Hardware Profile/Configuration Recovery Menu
This menu enables you to select a hardware profile
to be used when Windows NT is started.
If your system is not starting correctly, then you may
switch to a previous system configuration, which may
overcome startup problems.
IMPORTANT: System configuration changes made since the
last successful startup will be discarded.
                Original Configuration
                Some other hardware profile
Use the up and down arrow keys to move the highlight
to the selection you want. Then press Enter.
To switch to the Last Known Good Configuration, press
'L'.
To Exit this menu and restart your computer, press F3.
Seconds until highlighted choice will be started
automatically: 5
```

If you press L while this screen is displayed, the Last Known Good control set will be used, and any configuration changes made during the last logon session will be discarded. If you don't press the spacebar and have only one hardware profile, the default hardware profile is loaded. If you don't press the spacebar and have more than one hardware profile, the Hardware Profile/Configuration Recovery Menu is displayed. Once you've selected a hardware profile, `ntldr` loads `Ntoskrnl.exe` and executes the Windows NT kernel.

TEST TIP The Last Known Good control set will use the registry set that was used during the last successful boot process. This allows you to revert back to a working set of system configuration files after making a change that could prevent a successful boot

6. Kernel initialization: When the kernel starts, a screen similar to the following is displayed:

```
Microsoft (R) Windows NT (TM) Version 4.0 (Build 1381)
1 System Processor (32 MB Memory)
```

This screen indicates that the kernel has successfully started.

7. Initializing device drivers: At this point, the kernel loads either the default control set or, if you selected the Last Known Good Configuration, it loads the Last Known Good control set. Then the kernel initializes all of the device drivers listed in the control set.

8. Initializing services: The kernel loads and starts the services listed in the control set being used.

9. Logon process: The Begin Logon dialog box is displayed, prompting the user to press Ctrl + Alt + Delete to log on. Then the user logs on, supplying an appropriate user name and password. Once a user has successfully logged on, the boot sequence is complete, and the control set currently in use is copied to the Last Known Good Configuration.

Troubleshooting Common Boot Sequence Problems

There are many common problems that can occur during the Windows NT boot sequence. Table 12-1 lists some of the most common problems, along with their possible causes and recommended solutions.

Using Event Viewer

Event Viewer is a Windows NT administrative tool that is used to view the System, Security, and Application Logs. These logs contain success, failure, and informational messages generated by the operating system, auditing, and applications.

The most common troubleshooting application of Event Viewer is determining why a service or device driver failed during system startup. After booting the computer, Windows NT notifies the user of such a failure by displaying a Service Control Manager warning dialog box. Figure 12-1 shows a typical Service Control Manager warning dialog box.

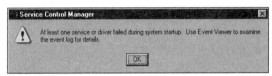

Figure 12-1 *Notification of service or driver failure during startup*

When a Service Control Manager warning is displayed, you can use the Event Viewer System Log to determine which service or driver failed, and to view a detailed description of the failure. This information will often help you to determine the cause of the failure and an appropriate solution. The Event Viewer System Log dialog box is shown in Figure 12-2. Notice the stop errors listed in the dialog box. A *stop error* in the System Log is identified by a red stop sign preceding the event on the left-hand side of the dialog box. A stop error indicates that the service or driver listed in the Source column was unable to initialize correctly during system startup.

Examining stop error event details is the key to troubleshooting failed services or drivers. When multiple stop errors are listed, it's usually best to start your troubleshooting by examining the *oldest* stop error in the list first. The oldest stop error is the *first* stop error that occurred during the boot process — it is also the last stop error on the System Log list. This stop error is probably the cause of all the later stop errors listed.

To view the stop error event detail, double-click the stop error in the System Log in Event Viewer. When you double-click the stop error, the Event Detail dialog box is displayed, as shown in Figure 12-3. Notice the description of the stop error in the Description text box.

TABLE 12-1 Troubleshooting the Windows NT Boot Sequence

Problem	Possible Cause	Recommended Solution
An error message is displayed during the POST.	This message most likely indicates a hardware failure.	Use the error message (or onscreen diagnostics) displayed to determine the offending hardware device. Repair, replace, or reconfigure the hardware device as necessary.
An error message, such as "Invalid partition table" or "Missing operating system" is displayed after the POST.	This type of error message often indicates that either sector 0 of the active partition is damaged, or that important operating system files (such as ntldr) are missing.	Perform the Emergency Repair process and select the inspect boot sector option during this process. If you suspect that there are missing files, also select the Verify Windows NT systems files options during the Emergency Repair process.
After you select MS-DOS from the boot loader menu, the following error is displayed: "I/O error accessing boot sector..."	This message indicates that ntldr can't find the Bootsect.dos file.	Restore this file from tape, or perform the Emergency Repair process, selecting the Inspect boot sector option during the process.

Problem	Possible Cause	Recommended Solution
During the boot sequence, NT displays a message indicating that it cannot find a specific file, such as Ntoskrnl.exe or ntldr.	There are two possible causes for this problem: the specified file is missing or corrupt, or the Boot.ini file does not specify the correct path to system files.	To restore a missing or corrupt file (except for the Boot.ini file), perform the Emergency Repair process, selecting the Verify Windows NT system files option during the process. If the Boot.ini file is missing perform the Emergency Repair process, selecting the Inspect startup environment option during the process, which will create a new Boot.ini file.
Your Windows NT computer crashes during a power outage. When you reboot the computer, a blue screen is displayed during the boot sequence.	The most likely cause of this problem is a corrupt file. Power outages can easily corrupt files on the hard disk.	Perform the Emergency Repair process, selecting the Inspect boot sector and Verify Windows NT system files options during the process.
You make several configuration changes and then reboot your Windows NT computer. A blue screen is displayed during the boot sequence.	The most likely cause of this problem is the configuration changes made during the last logon session.	Reboot the computer, and select the Last Known Good Configuration during the boot sequence. If this does not repair the problem, perform the Emergency Repair process, selecting the Inspect Registry files option during the process.
A STOP error (blue screen) is displayed during the device driver or service initialization steps of the boot sequence.	The most probable causes of this error are a corrupt Registry entry, a corrupt device driver, or a corrupt service file.	Perform the Emergency Repair process, selecting the Inspect Registry files and Verify Windows NT system files options during the process.

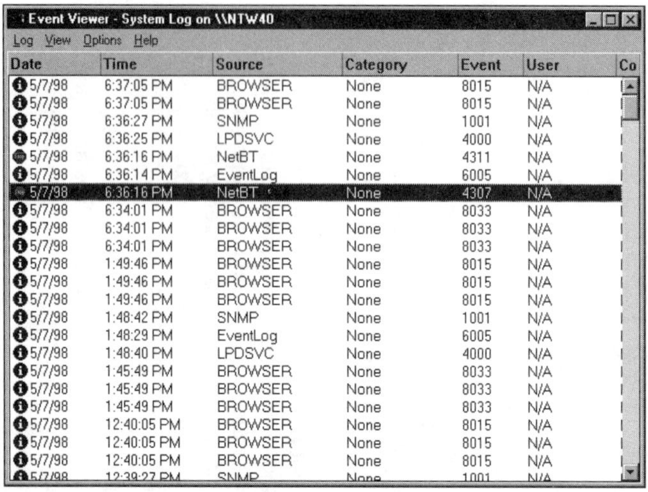

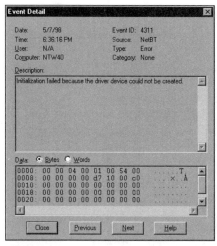

Figure 12-2 *Viewing the System Log in Event Viewer*

Figure 12-3 *Viewing the stop error event detail*

The stop error detailed in Figure 12-3 indicates that initialization of the NetBT service failed because the driver device could not be created.

Recovering from Disk Failures

So what do you do when it all comes crashing down — when the remote possibility of disk failure that you planned for, but never thought would actually happen, is a painful reality?

In some cases your disk configuration may enable you to continue operations (but without any fault tolerance) until you can replace the failed hard disk and restore your fault tolerance configuration.

In cases of stripe set, volume set, or multiple hard disk failure, you must repair the hardware and restore your data from tape to continue operations. If you don't have a tape backup in these situations, Windows NT will *not* be able to recover your data.

Disk Mirroring

Sometimes a disk that is part of a mirror set fails. To restore your fault tolerance disk configuration after one disk in a mirror set fails, you must use the Disk Administrator. If the failed mirror contains the boot partition, you may need to use your fault tolerance boot disk. In Disk

Administrator, you need to first break the mirror, and then commit the changes. Shut down the server and replace the failed mirror drive. Next, restart the computer and recreate the mirror set. It may take a while before disk activity stops, as the new mirror drive is receiving the mirror data information.

 When resolving a disk mirror problem, you must first break the mirror, replace the drive, and recreate the mirror set. You will definitely need to know this process when you take the Windows NT Server exam.

Stripe Sets with Parity

To recover from a *single* hard disk failure in a stripe set with parity, shut down the computer, replace the failed disk, and reboot the computer. Using the Disk Administrator, select any portion of the existing stripe set with parity and select the free space area on the new hard disk. Use the Disk Administrator's Regenerate command to rebuild the stripe set. A significant amount of disk activity will occur as the computer regenerates the data on the new hard disk. During the regeneration process, various messages are displayed at the bottom of the Disk Administrator dialog box, including: RECOVERABLE, REGENERATING, and HEALTHY. The process is complete when HEALTHY is displayed.

 When recovering from a single drive failure in a stripe set with parity, first replace the drive and then use the Disk Administrator to regenerate the stripe set.

Client-based Network Administration Tools

Client-based Network Administration Tools (often referred to as *Windows NT Server Tools*, particularly when used on a Windows 95 client computer) are a collection of Windows NT Server utilities that, when installed on a Windows 95 or Windows NT Workstation client computer, make it possible for a user at the client computer to remotely manage an NT Server computer on the network.

Client-based Network Administration Tools make remote administration of an NT Server computer practical and convenient for many administrators.

Because Client-based Network Administration Tools differ on Windows 95 and Windows NT Workstation computers, they are discussed separately in the following sections.

Windows NT Server Tools for Windows 95 Computers

The Windows NT Server Tools that can be installed on Windows 95 client computers are: *User Manager for Domains, Server Manager, Event Viewer*, and *security extensions for Windows Explorer* (to manage file and printer security on a remote Windows NT Server). These tools are Windows 95 versions of the same tools that ship with Windows NT Server and that are discussed throughout this book.

Table 12-2 shows the Windows NT Server Tools that can be installed on Windows 95 client computers and the basic functions that they enable an administrator to perform remotely from the client computer.

TABLE 12-2 Windows NT Server Tools for Windows 95 Client Computers

Windows NT Server Tool	Function
User Manager for Domains	Enables remote management of users, groups, domain security policy, and trust relationships on a Windows NT Server computer.
Server Manager	Enables remote management of shared folders, remote starting and stopping of services, remote management of Directory Replication, remote viewing of which users are accessing shared resources, and remote disconnection of users from shared resources on a Windows NT Server computer.
Event Viewer	Enables remote viewing, archiving, and management of the system, security, and application logs in Event Viewer on a Windows NT Server computer.
Security tab extensions for Windows Explorer	Adds a Security tab to the "file," "folder," or "printer" Properties dialog boxes (tabs that normally exist on NT Server but aren't present on Windows 95 computers). This feature enables remote management of file, folder, and printer security on a Windows NT Server computer.

Installing the Windows NT Server Tools does not allow you to remotely manage printers from a Windows 95 client computer.

Client-based Network Administration Tools for Windows NT Workstation Computers

The Client-based Network Administration Tools that can be installed on Windows NT Workstation computers are: User Manager for Domains, Server Manager, System Policy Editor, Remote Access Admin, DHCP Administrator, WINS Manager, and Remoteboot Manager. These tools are Windows NT Workstation versions of the same tools that ship with Windows NT Server, and that are discussed throughout this book.

Because Event Viewer and Windows NT Explorer are already installed on a Windows NT Workstation computer, they are not part of the Client-based Network Administration Tools add-on package.

Table 12-3 shows the Client-based Network Administration Tools that can be installed on Windows NT Workstation client computers and the basic functions that they enable an administrator to perform remotely from the client computer.

TABLE 12-3 Client-based Network Administration Tools for Windows NT Workstation Client Computers

Client-based Network Administration Tool	Function
User Manager for Domains	Enables remote management of users, groups, domain security policy, and trust relationships on a Windows NT Server computer.
Server Manager	Enables remote management of shared folders, remote starting and stopping of services, remote management of directory replication, remote viewing of which users are accessing shared resources, and remote disconnection of users from shared resources on a Windows NT Server computer.
System Policy Editor	Enables remote creation and editing of policy files on a Windows NT Server computer.

Continued

TABLE 12-3 *Continued*

Client-based Network Administration Tool	Function
Remote Access Admin	Enables remote configuration and management of the Remote Access Service (RAS) on a Windows NT Server computer.
DHCP Administrator	Enables remote configuration and management of the DHCP service on a Windows NT Server computer.
WINS Manager	Enables remote configuration and management of the WINS service on a Windows NT Server computer.
Remoteboot Manager	Enables remote configuration and management of the Remoteboot service on a Windows NT Server computer.

KNOW THIS Installation Differences

System Policy Editor, Remote Access Admin, DHCP Administrator, WINS Manager, and Remoteboot Manager are installed only on Windows NT client computers. You will not be able to remotely administer services that are managed by these components when using a Windows 95 client computer.

True or False?

1. When a disk fails in a Mirror set, you should first replace the drive before running Disk Administrator.

2. You cannot remotely manage printer queues from a Windows 95 computer with Windows NT Server Tools installed.

3. You cannot recover from a drive failure in a stripe set with parity.

4. The WINS Manager is only installed on Windows NT computers.

5. You may need to boot using a fault tolerance floppy disk if a mirror set containing the boot partition fails.

Answers: *1. False 2. True 3. False 4. True 5. True*

Have You Mastered?

Now it's time to apply what you've learned in this chapter by testing your mastery of the material. These questions provide you with a means to determine if you are ready to move on to the next chapter or if you need to review the material again.

1. **Your Windows NT computer crashes during a power outage. When you reboot the computer, a blue screen is displayed during the boot sequence. What should you do to resolve the boot problem?**

   ☐ A. Perform the Emergency Repair process, selecting the Inspect boot sector and Verify Windows NT system files options.

   ☐ B. Perform the Emergency Repair process to restore the Windows NT Registry.

   ☐ C. Run the Windows NT Diagnostics program.

   ☐ D. Reboot the computer, and select the Last Known Good Configuration during the boot sequence.

The correct answer is A. The most likely cause of this problem is a corrupt file. Power outages can easily corrupt files on the hard disk. Performing the Emergency Repair process, and selecting the Inspect boot sector and Verify Windows NT system files options, will probably resolve the missing or corrupted files. For more information, see the "Troubleshooting the Boot Sequence" section.

2. **You make several configuration changes and then reboot your Windows NT computer. A blue screen is displayed during the boot sequence. What should you do to resolve the boot failure?**

   ☐ A. Perform the Emergency Repair process, selecting the Inspect boot sector and Verify Windows NT system files options.

   ☐ B. Perform the Emergency Repair process to restore the Windows NT Registry.

   ☐ C. Run the Windows NT Diagnostics program.

   ☐ D. Reboot the computer, and select the Last Known Good Configuration during the boot sequence.

The correct answer is D. The most likely cause of this problem is the configuration changes made during the last logon session. The Last Known Good Configuration will contain the system settings that reflect the configuration of the computer before any recent changes were made that prevent the computer from booting. For more information, see the "Troubleshooting the Boot Sequence" section.

3. **You receive a Service Control Manager warning message that indicates that a service or device driver failed during system startup. Which Windows NT administrative tool should you use to obtain more information about the failure?**

   ☐ A. Windows NT Diagnostics application

   ☐ B. Windows NT Registry Editor

   ☐ C. Windows NT Event Viewer

   ☐ D. Windows NT System Log Viewer

The correct answer is C. The Windows NT Event Viewer is used to view the Windows NT logs that will indicate which system service failed during the startup or boot process. In addition, the logs may indicate errors from other services that are dependent on the failed service. For more information, see the "Using Event Viewer" section.

4. Your Windows NT Workstation computer indicated that a service failed to load or start during the boot process. When you use the Windows NT Event Viewer to view the system log, what Stop event should you look for first to troubleshoot the problem?

- ☐ A. The latest Stop event in the log.
- ☐ B. The oldest Stop event in the log.
- ☐ C. The latest Informational event in the log.
- ☐ D. The oldest Informational event in the log.

The correct answer is B. When troubleshooting system failures, by looking at the oldest Stop event, you can work your way forward through the progressive system errors. This will show you the history of the problem, and will probably show the original circumstances that caused the error. For more information, see the "Using Event Viewer" section.

5. Your Microsoft Windows NT Server computer has two drives configured as a mirrored set. One of the mirrored drives has failed. What should you do?

- ☐ A. Replace the drive and then break the mirror.
- ☐ B. Break the mirror and then replace the drive.
- ☐ C. Replace the drive and then use Disk Administrator to regenerate the mirror.
- ☐ D. Use Disk Administrator to regenerate the mirror and then replace the drive.

The correct answer is B. Before replacing a failed drive in a mirror set, you should first break the mirror using the Disk Administrator, and then replace the drive. Once the drive has been replaced, use Disk Administrator to recreate the mirror set. The regenerate process is used to restore failed stripe sets with parity. For more information, see the "Recovering from Disk Failures" section.

Practice Your Skills

Here is a chance to apply your practical hands-on experience and material from this chapter. These exercises are designed not only for you to apply the material in the book, but also for you to gain greater experience and exposure to the product. These exercises are a critical part of understanding the product and gaining valuable experience for using the product and passing the certification exam. For each of the following problems, consider the given facts and determine what you think are the possible causes of the problem and what course of action you might take to resolve the problem.

1. Recovering from failed drives

EXERCISE You are configuring your Windows NT Server computer to mirror its two hard drives. After creating the mirror set, what else should you do so that you will be able to recover from a failed drive in the mirror set?

ANALYSIS If a mirror set will contain the boot partition for a Windows NT Server computer, you should have a current emergency repair disk and a fault tolerance boot disk. The fault tolerance boot disk will allow you to boot Windows NT Server on the remaining good hard drive.

2. Installing Windows NT Server tools

EXERCISE You are preparing to install the Windows NT Server tools on your computer. Your computer dual-boots between Microsoft Windows 95 and Windows NT Workstation. What would be the advantage of installing the NT Server tools on the Windows NT Workstation OS rather than Windows 95?

ANALYSIS Although both platforms enable you to run the NT Server tools, several tools are available only on the Windows NT Workstation platform, such as the WINS and DNS managers. If you installed the NT Server tools in Windows 95, you would be unable to manage any of these services.

Practice Exam

1. You are installing Windows NT Server on a new computer. Your network contains a single Windows NT Server domain. You want to add the new Windows NT Server computer to the existing domain. You want the new computer to participate in domain authentication. What role should the computer take in the domain?

   ☐ A. Primary domain controller
   ☐ B. Backup domain controller
   ☐ C. Member server
   ☐ D. Stand-alone server

2. You are installing Windows NT Server on a new computer. The server will be placed on a network segment connected directly to the Internet. You will be using this server to host PPTP connections from remote corporate users. You want to allow only this type of connection from the Internet. What should you do?

   ☐ A. Configure the Remote Access Service not to use TCP/IP.
   ☐ B. Configure the Remote Access service to use only TCP/IP.
   ☐ C. Configure the TCP/IP protocol to enable PPTP filtering.
   ☐ D. Configure the TCP/IP protocol to enable Domain Suffix Search Ordering.

3. You are adding a new Windows NT Server computer to your
   network. Your network contains three Windows NT Server
   computers in a single domain. You do not want the new
   computer to participate in any domain directory services. You
   want to manage access to the server using users and groups
   stored on the local server. What role should this computer take
   in the domain?

   ☐ A. Primary Domain Controller
   ☐ B. Backup Domain Controller
   ☐ C. Member Server
   ☐ D. Stand-alone server

4. You are installing Windows NT Server onto a computer that is
   already running Windows NT Server. The computer has two IDE
   hard disks, each with a single NTFS partition. The existing
   installation is on the first disk, and your new install is on the
   second disk. What is the `boot.ini` ARC value for the new
   installation?

   ☐ A. `multi(0)disk(1)rdisk(0)partition`
          `(1)\WINNT="Windows NT Server Version`
          `4.00"`
   ☐ B. `multi(0)disk(2)rdisk(0)partition`
          `(1)\WINNT="Windows NT Server Version`
          `4.00"`
   ☐ C. `multi(0)disk(1)rdisk(2)partition`
          `(0)\WINNT="Windows NT Server Version`
          `4.00"`
   ☐ D. `multi(0)disk(2)rdisk(2)partition`
          `(0)\WINNT="Windows NT Server Version`
          `4.00"`

5. Which Dial-Up Networking connection protocol can only support
   the TCP/IP transport protocol?

   ☐ A. PPTP
   ☐ B. SLIP
   ☐ C. PPP
   ☐ D. ISDN

6. You are installing Windows NT Server on your computer. Which Windows NT Server fault tolerance method can you use for the boot partition?

    ☐ A. Stripe set
    ☐ B. Volume set
    ☐ C. Stripe set with parity
    ☐ D. Mirror set

7. You are configuring directory replication for your domain. What is the default incoming folder for directory replication on a Windows NT Server computer?

    ☐ A. `<winntroot>\system32\repl\import`
    ☐ B. `<winntroot>\system32\repl\export`
    ☐ C. `<winntroot>\import`
    ☐ D. `<winntroot>\export`

8. You have a test network consisting of four Windows NT Server computers running as domain controllers in a domain called TEST. You have completed your testing of the computers and want to place them in your production network domain called HQ. What must you do?

    ☐ A. Remove and reinstall Windows NT Server on all of the TEST servers and place them in the HQ domain.
    ☐ B. Change the domain configuration on the TEST PDC to HQ and then change the domain configuration on the TEST BDCs to HQ.
    ☐ C. Stop the server service on the TEST servers, change the domain configurations to HQ, and restart the server service.
    ☐ D. Configure the servers to be members of both the TEST domain and the HQ domain.

9. Your network consists of a single Windows NT Server domain. In the domain you have three Windows NT Server computers and 100 Windows NT Workstation computers. When the workstations join the domain, their local Administrators group automatically has a member added to it to enable the administrators for the domain to manage the workstations. What is added to the workstations' local Administrators group?

☐ A. The PDC's local Administrators group
☐ B. The local Administrators groups from all of the domain controllers
☐ C. The domain administrators global group
☐ D. The administrator account from the PDC

10. You are installing Windows NT Server on a new computer. You do not know if all the hardware is certified to run NT. What should you do to determine if you can install Windows NT Server on this computer?

☐ A. Run NTHQ before starting the install.
☐ B. Start the install with `Winnt32.exe`.
☐ C. Start the install with `Winnt.exe`.
☐ D. Remove all the network components in NT 3.51 before starting the install.

11. A Windows NT global group can contain which of the following group types? (Choose all that apply.)

☐ A. Local groups in other Windows NT domains
☐ B. Global groups from other Windows NT domains
☐ C. Local groups from computers in the same domain
☐ D. Global groups from the same domain

12. You are a consultant working at a client location that has a single stand-alone Windows NT Server computer. You have been asked to configure the server to audit file and printer access. When you configure the audit policies, you receive an access denied message. What is most likely the problem?

    ☐ A. Your account is not a member of the Server Operators local group.

    ☐ B. Your account is not a member of the Administrators local group.

    ☐ C. Your account is not a members of the Domain Admins global group.

    ☐ D. Stand-alone servers do not support auditing.

13. You want to create a Windows NT Server shared folder that maps to a shared volume on a NetWare server. What two Windows NT Server components must you install before you can create the shared folder? (Choose two.)

    ☐ A. Gateway Service for NetWare
    ☐ B. Client Service for NetWare
    ☐ C. NWLink IPX/SPX Compatible Transport
    ☐ D. TCP/IP

14. You are installing Windows NT Server on a new computer. Your network contains mostly Macintosh client computers and a few computers running Windows NT Workstation. You recently purchased a high-speed laser printer that you want to enable users on the network to print to. The printer did not come with any Macintosh printer drivers. What can you do?

    ☐ A. Nothing; Macintosh computers require a driver for each printer they use.

    ☐ B. Configure the Macintosh computers to access the printer using the default LaserWriter print driver.

    ☐ C. Have the Macintosh computers save the file to the printer spool directory to be printed automatically.

    ☐ D. Create the shared printer with an & at the beginning of the share name.

15. You are configuring an audit policy on your Windows NT Server computer. What can you do to view the audit events on your Windows NT Server computer?

    ☐ A. Use the Server Manager.

    ☐ B. Use the User Manager for Domains.

    ☐ C. Use the Performance Monitor.

    ☐ D. Use the Event Viewer.

16. **You want to monitor the performance of your local network segment connected to a Windows NT Server computer. What must you do to check the performance of the network segment?**

    ☐ A. Install the SNMP Service.

    ☐ B. Install the Network Monitor Agent.

    ☐ C. Change the network bindings.

    ☐ D. Use the Server Control Panel.

17. **You are a consultant working at a client location. You are creating a shared folder on a Windows NT Server computer. You grant everyone on the network Full Control to all the files in the share. You receive messages that people are unable to make changes to the files in the share. What is the most likely problem?**

    ☐ A. The users have not been authenticated by the server.

    ☐ B. The users do not belong to the Everyone global group.

    ☐ C. The Server service is not running on the server computer.

    ☐ D. The folder is on an NTFS partition that has NTFS permissions set as Read only.

18. **You are installing TCP/IP on a Windows NT Server computer. What configuration parameter indicates which portion of a TCP/IP address is the network address and which is the host address?**

    ☐ A. TCP/IP host address

    ☐ B. Subnet mask

    ☐ C. Default router

    ☐ D. Frame type

    ☐ E. Internal network number

19. You are unable to connect to a Windows NT Server computer using TCP/IP. You do not know if the server is online or has possibly failed. What can you do to determine if the server is still online?

    □ A. Use Windows Explorer.

    □ B. Use the `net config` command.

    □ C. Use the `ipconfig` command.

    □ D. Use the `ping` command.

20. Your network consists of 12 Windows NT Server computers and 300 Windows NT Workstation client computers. You have purchased a volume license agreement to license all of your Windows NT Workstation computers to access the Windows NT Server computers. You notice that the logs on the Windows NT Server computers show that you have exceeded the specified limit for client accesses, and clients are unable to connect to the servers. What should you do? (Choose two.)

    □ A. Configure the Windows NT Server computers to use per-seat licensing.

    □ B. Configure the license limit to be greater than 300.

    □ C. Configure the license limit to be between 12 and 200.

    □ D. Configure the Windows NT Workstation computers to use per-seat licensing.

    □ E. Configure the Windows NT Workstation computers to use per-seat licensing.

21. You are planning a NetWare server migration to Windows NT Server using the Migration Tool for NetWare. What must you do on the Windows NT Server computer to enable NetWare file permissions to be migrated?

☐ A. Create a `flag.perm` file in the destination volume on the Windows NT Server computer.

☐ B. Configure the Windows NT Server destination volume as a shared folder.

☐ C. Configure the Windows NT Server destination volume as a FAT partition.

☐ D. Configure the Windows NT Server destination volume as an NTFS partition.

---

22. **You are evaluating disk fault-tolerance schemes. You want to provide maximum protection against failure, regardless of the cost. In addition, you want to provide the fastest read times possible. What fault tolerance method should you use?**

☐ A. Stripe set

☐ B. Stripe set with parity

☐ C. Volume set

☐ D. Mirror set

---

23. **Your network consists of two Windows NT Server domains, each with three servers. Each domain has a PDC and two BDCs. One of the BDCs in domain A has completely failed. You want to move the BDC from domain B to domain A to replace the failed BDC. What must you do?**

☐ A. Use the Network Control Panel to change the domain name of the server.

☐ B. Change both the server's name and domain grouping.

☐ C. Create a computer account for the server in domain A, change the domain configuration on the server to domain A, and reboot the server.

☐ D. Remove and reinstall Windows NT Server and configure the domain setting as domain A.

24. You are the administrator of a Windows NT Server computer configured as a stand-alone server. You want to permit the backup operators to access the server only between the hours of 8 p.m. and 12 p.m. to perform backups on the server. What can you do?

☐ A. Configure the operators' accounts with logon hours restrictions.

☐ B. Configure the operators' accounts to be members of a group that has logon hours restrictions.

☐ C. Configure the operators' accounts with expiration settings.

☐ D. Nothing; you cannot restrict logon hours for accounts on a stand-alone server.

25. You are attempting to connect to a shared folder on a NetWare 4.x server. The NetWare server is running bindery emulation. You want to connect to the `Data` folder in a volume named `User_Docs` that is on a server named Peabody. What UNC name should you use to connect to the shared folder?

☐ A. `\\Peabody\Data.User_Docs`
☐ B. `\\Peabody.Data.User_Docs`
☐ C. `\\Peabody.Data\User_Docs`
☐ D. `\\Peabody\Data\User_Docs`

26. What is the maximum number of simultaneous Dial-Up Networking clients that a Windows NT Server computer can support?

☐ A. 1
☐ B. 5
☐ C. 256
☐ D. Unlimited

27. Which Dial-Up Networking connection protocol can provide secure communications channels over the Internet using an encrypted transmission packet?

☐ A. PPTP
☐ B. SLIP
☐ C. PPP
☐ D. ISDN

28. You are using a PPP connection to connect to a Windows NT Server computer running Remote Access Service. How does RAS handle your TCP/IP traffic once you are authenticated?

☐ A. RAS will act as a router for the protocol.
☐ B. RAS will act as a bridge for the protocol.
☐ C. RAS will act as a gateway for the protocol.
☐ D. RAS will act as a repeater for the protocol.

29. Your network consists of a single Windows NT Server domain. The accounting department has hired a group of temporary workers for the weekend. You want to ensure that the temps cannot access the network after their weekend project is completed. What should you do?

☐ A. Configure the accounts with logon hours restrictions.
☐ B. Configure the accounts with an expiration setting.
☐ C. Configure the accounts to be members of the Interactive special group.
☐ D. Configure the accounts to be members of a group that has an expiration setting.

30. Your Windows NT Server computer seems to be experiencing periods of slow responses to client requests. You suspect that the processor is overutilized. Which Performance Monitor object and counter should you use to verify your suspicions?

☐ A. Object: Processor; Counter: %Processor Time
☐ B. Object: %Processor Time; Counter: Processor
☐ C. Object: Processor; Counter: %Privileged Time
☐ D. Object: %Privileged Time; Counter: Processor

31. You have noticed that your Windows NT Server computer seems to be responding to TCP/IP requests very slowly. You want to check the performance of the protocol. What must you do?

    ☐ A. Install the SNMP Service.
    ☐ B. Install the Network Monitor Agent.
    ☐ C. Use the `diskperf` command.
    ☐ D. Use the `net view` command.

32. You are the administrator for a network that contains a Windows NT Server domain and two Windows NT Server computers. You want to enable two advanced users to manage the server in your absence, such as adding users, rebooting the server, and managing printers. You do not want them to be able to make changes to the administrator account. What group should you place them in?

    ☐ A. Administrators
    ☐ B. Power Users
    ☐ C. Server Operators
    ☐ D. None; this cannot be accomplished.

33. You are installing Windows NT Server on a new computer. If you want to create a Windows NT Server stripe set, what type of disk partitions must you use?

    ☐ A. Only partitions on IDE hard disks
    ☐ B. Only partitions on SCSI hard disks
    ☐ C. Partitions of equal size
    ☐ D. Partitions of unequal size

34. What must you do before you can see actual disk performance values in Performance Monitor?

☐ A. Log on to the Window NT Server computer as a member of the local administrators group.

☐ B. Use `diskperf.exe` to enable the Performance Monitor objects.

☐ C. Use the Disk Administrator to enable the disk statistics.

☐ D. Install the physicaldisk Performance Monitor objects.

---

35. You want to enable department managers to change the priority, scheduling, and status of their own print jobs. You do not want them to be able to delete other users' print jobs. Which Windows NT Server print permission should you grant them?

☐ A. Manage Documents permission

☐ B. Only Print permission

☐ C. Full Control

☐ D. Special permission

---

36. You are the administrator for a network that contains a Windows NT Server domain. You are attempting to resolve a problem with one Windows NT Server computer that is unable to access the Internet. The server can see and communicate with other Windows NT Server computers on the local network. What is the most likely problem?

☐ A. TCP/IP Address

☐ B. Subnet mask

☐ C. Default router

☐ D. Host name

---

37. You are planning on using system policies in your Windows NT Server domain. In which order are multiple group policies applied to a user account?

☐ A. The group with the lowest priority is applied first.

☐ B. The group with the lowest priority is applied last.

☐ C. The group policies are applied alphabetically.

☐ D. Only one group policy can be assigned to a single user.

38. You have a computer that is running Windows NT Server and is configured as a stand-alone server. You want this computer to join your domain on the network and participate as a Domain Controller. What can you do?

☐ A. Use the Network Control Panel on the computer to promote the server to a BDC.

☐ B. Use Server Manager for Domains to promote the server to PDC and demote the existing PDC to a BDC.

☐ C. Reinstall Windows NT Server on the computer and configure it as a BDC in the domain.

☐ D. You must use a new computer because once a computer has been configured as a stand-alone, it can never be used as a domain controller even if Windows NT is reinstalled.

39. Your Windows NT Server computer has been having difficulty running a new application on the computer. What can you use to view the log activity for the application?

☐ A. Windows NT Diagnostics application

☐ B. Windows NT Registry Editor

☐ C. Windows NT Event Viewer

☐ D. Windows NT System Log Viewer

40. You are working on a Windows NT Server computer and are about to perform maintenance on some of the files. You want to determine which files are currently being used on the computer. What can you do?

☐ A. Use the Event Viewer.
☐ B. Use the System Monitor.
☐ C. Use the User Manager for Domains.
☐ D. Use the Server Control Panel.

---

41. **You are installing Windows NT Server on a new computer that has 256MB of RAM. You want to configure the server so that it will create a memory dump when a system failure occurs. How should you configure the paging file on the server?**

☐ A. Configure a 256MB paging file on a partition other than the Windows NT boot partition.
☐ B. Configure a 256MB paging file on the Windows NT boot partition.
☐ C. Configure a 128MB paging file on a partition other than the Windows NT boot partition.
☐ D. Configure a 128MB paging file on the Windows NT boot partition.

---

42. **You are the administrator of a Windows NT Server computer. You are moving a directory that contains user data from one area of a partition to another area on the same partition. What are the NTFS permissions for the folders after they have been moved?**

☐ A. The permissions will stay the same.
☐ B. The permissions will be set back to the default, with the Everyone group having Full Control.
☐ C. The permissions will be set to match the new parent folder's permissions.
☐ D. The permissions will be set so that only the Administrators group has Full Control.

---

43. **You are the administrator of a Windows NT Server computer. The computer has four disks configured in two mirrored pairs. The first mirror contains the boot and system partitions. The second contains user data. When one of the disks in the first pair fails, what should you do first to resolve the problem?**

- [ ] A. Replace the drive and then break the mirror.
- [ ] B. Break the mirror and then replace the drive.
- [ ] C. Replace the drive and then use Disk Administrator to regenerate the mirror.
- [ ] D. Use Disk Administrator to regenerate the mirror and then replace the drive.

44. You are the administrator of a Windows NT Server computer. The computer has five hard drives. Two of the disks are configured as a mirrored pair and contain the boot and system partitions. The other three disks are configured as a stripe set with parity. When one of the stripe set disks fails, what should you do first to resolve the problem?

- [ ] A. Replace the drive and then use Disk Administrator to regenerate the stripe set.
- [ ] B. Use Disk Administrator to break the stripe set and then replace the drive.
- [ ] C. Replace the drive and then delete all of the remaining drives in the stripe set.
- [ ] D. Use Disk Administrator to create a stripe set with parity on the remaining drives and then replace the failed disk.

45. You are installing Windows NT Server onto a new computer. You log on using the default administrators account. You create a user account for yourself, log out, and log on as yourself. What user profile will you be given? (Choose two.)

- [ ] A. The default user profile
- [ ] B. The administrator user profile
- [ ] C. The all users profile
- [ ] D. The default admins user profile

46. You are the administrator of a Windows NT Server computer. The computer has four hard drives. One of the disks contains the boot and system partitions. The other three disks are configured as a stripe set. One of the stripe set disks has failed. What can you do?

☐ A. Replace the drive and then use the Disk Administrator to regenerate the stripe set.
☐ B. Use Disk Administrator to break the stripe set and then replace the drive.
☐ C. Replace the drive, recreate the stripe set, and restore or recreate the lost data.
☐ D. Use Disk Administrator to recreate the lost data using the parity information in the stripe set.

47. You are installing Remote Access Service on your Windows NT Server computer. What must you do before users will be able to connect to your server using Dial-Up Networking?

☐ A. Assign the users Log on as Service right.
☐ B. Grant the users Dialin permission.
☐ C. Place the users in the Server Operators group.
☐ D. Place the users in the Power Users group on their dialin computers.

48. You are configuring directory replication on your domain PDC. After directory replication begins to occur, you notice that the directories that you had created on the BDCs in the repl\import folder are gone. When you add the files and folders again, they disappear after the next directory replication. What must you do?

    ☐ A. Create a file called `delete.no` in the folders on the BDCs.

    ☐ B. Create a file called `flag.map` in the `repl\import` folder that contains the folder names.

    ☐ C. Give the replicator account read only access to the `repl\import` folder.

    ☐ D. Create the files and folders in the `repl\export` folder on the PDC.

49. Which Windows NT share permission overrides any other permission?

    ☐ A. No Access
    ☐ B. Read
    ☐ C. Full Control
    ☐ D. Special Access

50. You are planning a NetWare migration using the Migration Tool for NetWare. During the migration, which files are not migrated by default?

    ☐ A. Hidden files
    ☐ B. Files with Read only permission
    ☐ C. Files belonging to the NetWare supervisor account
    ☐ D. Files with Secret permission

Exam Key

1.	B	18.	B	35.	A
2.	C	19.	D	36.	C
3.	D	20.	A and B	37.	A
4.	B	21.	D	38.	C
5.	B	22.	D	39.	C
6.	D	23.	D	40.	D
7.	A	24.	D	41.	B
8.	A	25.	D	42.	A
9.	C	26.	C	43.	B
10.	A	27.	A	44.	B
11.	B and D	28.	A	45.	A and C
12.	B	29.	B	46.	C
13.	A and C	30.	A	47.	B
14.	B	31.	A	48.	D
15.	D	32.	C	49.	A
16.	B	33.	C	50.	A
17.	D	34.	B		

Exam Analysis

1. To participate in directory services and authentication in an existing domain, the server can only be configured as a Backup Domain Controller. A Member server does not participate in domain authentication, and you can only have one Primary Domain Controller in a domain. For more information, refer to Chapter 1.

---

2. If you will only be using PPTP connections to a RAS server, you can enable PPTP filtering, which will prevent any connection types other than PPTP. Configuring the RAS server to not use TCP/IP will not prevent other connection types, because PPTP requires TCP/IP to be installed on the server. For more information, refer to Chapter 10.

---

3. Stand-alone servers maintain their own security database and directory services. Stand-alone servers are often used for applications that require a higher level of security than running on a publicly accessible domain network. For more information, refer to Chapter 1.

---

4. The ARC syntax describes the rdisk value as the reference to the physical disk for BIOS detected hard disks. In this case, the new installation is on the second disk, so the `disk(2)` property points to the second IDE hard disk and uses the first partition, as indicated by the `partition(1)` entry. For more information, refer to Chapter 2.

5. The SLIP standard supports only a single transport protocol, which is TCP/IP. This implementation is less effective than PPP, which provides support for multiple simultaneous transport protocols and higher performance. Windows NT can use SLIP only as a client computer; RAS does not provide SLIP hosting abilities. For more information, refer to Chapter 10.

6. Windows NT cannot have the boot or system files as part of a volume or stripe set. A mirror set is the only form of fault tolerance that Windows NT can provide for the boot and system files. For more information, refer to Chapter 2.

7. The `import` subfolder in the `repl` folder is normally used when importing from other computers. Although you can choose any location you want to import files to, it is easier to manage if all the folder locations are consistent. For more information, refer to Chapter 3.

8. Once Windows NT Server has been configured as a domain controller, the server cannot join another domain; you must reinstall Windows NT Server on the computer. Once Windows NT Server is reinstalled, you can configure the domain properties to join the new domain as a domain controller. For more information, refer to Chapter 1.

9. When a Windows NT Workstation computer joins a domain, its local Administrators group has the domain admins global group added to it. This enables the domain administrators to manage Windows NT Workstation computers that are members of a domain. For more information, refer to Chapter 1.

10. Before performing an installation of Windows NT Server, you should check to ensure that your hardware is supported. If you cannot locate the information in the HCL, you can use NTHQ to determine if your hardware will support Windows NT Server. For more information, refer to Chapter 1.

11. Windows NT global groups can contain global groups from the local domain and global groups from trusted domains. They cannot contain local groups. For more information, refer to Chapter 4.

12. When configuring user rights, account policies, or auditing, you must be a member of the local administrators group. Because the server is stand-alone, it does not participate in a domain account database, so the domain admins global group cannot be used, as it is not accessible to the server. If your account were in the domain admins group and the server were a member server, then you would have access, because the domain admins are members of the local administrators group. For more information, refer to Chapter 4.

13. Creating a shared folder to access files and folders on a NetWare server requires Gateway Service for NetWare. GSNW relies on NWLink IPX/SPX Compatible Transport to communicate with the servers, so these two components must be installed. For more information, refer to Chapter 9.

14. When a Windows NT Server computer shares a printer and the server has Services for Macintosh installed, the client Macintosh computers can use the default LaserWriter print driver to access the shared printer. This is especially useful when the printer manufacturer doesn't supply a Macintosh client print driver. For more information, refer to Chapter 6.

15. Once audit policy and audit rules have been defined, you can view audit events by using the Event Viewer and looking at the Security log. For more information, refer to Chapter 7.

16. The Network Monitor Agent service must be installed before Windows NT Server will begin to track network segment statistics. Once these statistics are gathered, you can use Performance Monitor to view them. For more information, refer to Chapter 11.

17. When NTFS file permissions and share permissions are different, the most restrictive access permissions become the users' effective permissions. When you set the share permissions as Full Control, the NTFS permissions must have been configured as Read only, so users were not allowed to modify the files. For more information, refer to Chapter 7.

18. The TCP/IP subnet mask indicates how the IP address is divided into network and host ID address space. Using a mathematical process, you can determine the network address and host address when using a subnetted IP address. For more information, refer to Chapter 8.

19. The `ping` command is very useful to determine the status of a TCP/IP host. Because the `ping` command sends a very simple low-level packet to the host, the host is often able to respond even if it is extremely busy or has failed at a higher level. If the ping is successful, you should try a test that queries a higher level of the operating system. For more information, refer to Chapter 8.

20. Because you already have a volume license, your servers must be configured to enable your users to connect. Using the license manager, you should establish a per-seat license mode that will enable the clients to connect to all of your servers and be in compliance with your license agreement. For more information, refer to Chapter 3.

21. The Migration Tool for NetWare can migrate file permissions only if it is able to set them on the destination partition. Because Windows NT Server only supports file permissions on NTFS partitions, you must have one to migrate file permissions. For more information, refer to Chapter 9.

22. A mirrored set offers the best fault tolerance performance in most implementations, but has the highest cost per MB for fault tolerance. If read access is extremely important from a fault tolerant disk set, a mirrored pair is the best option. This is often the case with high-performance databases, where read times are paramount. For more information, refer to Chapter 2.

23. Once Windows NT Server has been configured as a domain controller, you must reinstall Windows NT before you can place the server in another domain. This prevents unauthorized access to the SAM database stored on domain controllers. For more information, refer to Chapter 1.

24. Windows NT Servers that are not configured as domain controllers do not have the ability to configure Account, Hours, or Logon To settings. The server would need to be configured as a domain controller before these settings would be available to use. For more information, refer to Chapter 4.

25. To connect to a NetWare resource that is running bindery emulation, the format is the same as for Windows NT resources, the UNC is \\Peabody\Data\User_Docs. For more information, refer to Chapter 9.

26. Windows NT Server can support up to a maximum of 256 remote clients connecting to Remote Access Service. The actual numbers will depend on available hardware, communication channels, and performance characteristics. For more information, refer to Chapter 10.

27. Point to Point Tunneling Protocol (PPTP) provides an encrypted communications channel across an unsecured network such as the Internet. Using this protocol., remote users can dial in to Internet service providers and communicate with their corporate office over a secured channel. For more information, refer to Chapter 10.

28. Remote Access Service will route all TCP/IP traffic from remote client computers. This allows the clients to act just as they would if they were directly connected to the network. For more information, refer to Chapter 10.

29. Because the temps will be working over the weekend, you can establish an expiration setting for their accounts so that on Monday morning they will be prevented from logging in to the network. For more information, refer to Chapter 4.

30. The Processor object contains the %Processor Time counter, which will indicate how much time is being spent serving software requests, or the total amount of available time the processor is busy. For more information, refer to Chapter 11.

31. You must install the SNMP service before Performance Monitor will show actual TCP/IP objects values. Otherwise, you will only see zero count values for all the TCP/IP associated counters. For more information, refer to Chapter 11.

32. To enable these users to perform the server management, you should add them to the Server Operators group. This will enable them to fulfill most requests, and will prevent them from making administrator-level changes and possibly locking you out. For more information, refer to Chapter 4.

33. A stripe set uses two or more partitions of equal size to create the stripe set. The partitions can be of any supported size, and can be on any supported hard disk type. For more information, refer to Chapter 2.

34. The physicaldisk related objects are installed by default, but are not enabled until the `diskperf.exe` utility is used. The objects are not enabled by default as they cause a slight decrease in system performance. The Disk Administrator cannot be used to enable the PhysicalDisk objects. For more information, refer to Chapter 2.

35. You should grant the managers the Manage Documents permission, which will allow them to make advanced changes to their print jobs. They will not be able to make changes to other users' print jobs without the Full Control permission. For more information, refer to Chapter 6.

36. If a computer is able to access resources on a local subnet but cannot communicate across subnets, the problem is likely to be an incorrect default router setting. Without a default router defined, the computer has no means to pass traffic to computers that reside on remote subnets. For more information, refer to Chapter 8.

37. Group policies are applied so that the group with the lowest priority is applied first. This allows more important groups with a higher priority to override the options of a lower-priority group. For more information, refer to Chapter 5.

38. A stand-alone or Member server cannot be promoted to a domain controller. You must first reinstall Windows NT Server and then configure the server to participate in another domain. For more information, refer to Chapter 1.

39. Most Windows NT Server-compatible 32-bit applications are configured to write application log events to the Windows NT Server application log. You can use the Event Viewer to view the application log and determine what the problem with the application is. For more information, refer to Chapter 12.

40. The Server Control Panel provides a list of all connected users and a list of files that are currently open. Using these two lists, you should be able to determine if your update will affect any of these files, or if you will need users to disconnect during the update. For more information, refer to Chapter 3.

41. By placing a paging file on the boot partition that is at least as large as the RAM in the server, Windows NT Server will use the paging file to create a memory dump when a critical system error occurs. Using this memory dump, Microsoft can often determine the cause of the error to prevent it from happening again. For more information, refer to Chapter 3.

42. Because the files are staying on the same disk partition, all the NTFS file permissions will be retained. If the files were moved to a different partition, the permissions would be lost and the files would inherit the permissions of the new parent folder. For more information, refer to Chapter 7.

43. To begin the recovery process of a failed mirrored pair, you must first break the mirror using Disk Administrator. Then replace the failed disk and use Disk Administrator to recreate the mirrored pair. For more information, refer to Chapter 2.

44. To recover from a failed disk in a stripe set with parity, first replace the failed disks and then use Disk Administrator to regenerate the stripe set. Because your stripe set has parity information, the new disk will automatically be restored with the data that was on the old disk before it failed. This prevents you from having to restore data using a tape restore process. For more information, refer to Chapter 2.

45. When you log on for the first time, you will be given the default user profile and the all users profile. The all users profile is given even to users that have their own profile — including roaming profiles. For more information, refer to Chapter 5.

46. Because the stripe set does not have parity information, you must replace the failed disk and then use a tape restore process to restore the data to all of the disks. All of the data that was in the stripe set is now inaccessible, including the data on the remaining drives. For more information, refer to Chapter 2.

47. Before users will be permitted to connect to your RAS server, they must be granted Dialin permission. Once Dialin permission is granted, they can authenticate themselves using their network usernames and passwords and will be permitted to connect. For more information, refer to Chapter 10.

48. When the directory replication process occurs, the export server file and folder structure is mirrored to all of the import servers. If the BDC import servers have files or folders that are not present on the export server, they will be removed during the replication process. For more information, refer to Chapter 3.

49. The No Access permission is the trump card permission — it overrides any other permissions granted to a user or group. For more information, refer to Chapter 7.

50. By default, hidden files are not migrated when using the Migration Tool for NetWare. You can configure the tool to migrate the hidden files, however. For more information, refer to Chapter 9.

Exam Revealed

1. You are the network administrator of a network that contains a Windows NT Server domain. You want to create a new domain, and you want to use the BDC computer in the existing domain as the PDC for the new domain. What should you do?

    A.   Change the domain settings for the BDC.

    B.   Promote the BDC to a PDC and place it in the new domain.

    C.   Reinstall Windows NT Server on the computer and configure it as the PDC for the new domain.

    D.   You must use a new computer, as the BDC can not be used in the new domain.

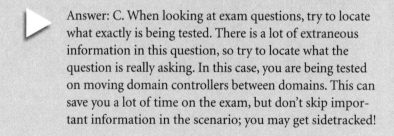

Answer: C. When looking at exam questions, try to locate what exactly is being tested. There is a lot of extraneous information in this question, so try to locate what the question is really asking. In this case, you are being tested on moving domain controllers between domains. This can save you a lot of time on the exam, but don't skip important information in the scenario; you may get sidetracked!

MCSE NT SERVER 4.0 ACE IT!

2. **You are configuring a mirror set on your Windows NT Server computer. You configure NT Server to mirror disk 1 and disk 2. You create a fault tolerant boot disk and edit the** `boot.ini` **file. You want to change the ARC for the** `boot.ini` **file on the floppy disk so that you can boot the server if disk 1 fails. How should you configure the ARC?**

A. `multi(0)disk(1)rdisk(0)partition(1)\WINNT="Windows NT Server Version 4.00"`

B. `multi(0)disk(2)rdisk(0)partition(1)\WINNT="Windows NT Server Version 4.00"`

C. `multi(0)disk(0)rdisk(1)partition(1)\WINNT="Windows NT Server Version 4.00"`

D. `multi(0)disk(0)rdisk(2)partition(1)\WINNT="Windows NT Server Version 4.00"`

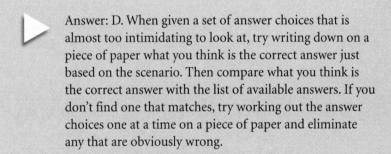

Answer: D. When given a set of answer choices that is almost too intimidating to look at, try writing down on a piece of paper what you think is the correct answer just based on the scenario. Then compare what you think is the correct answer with the list of available answers. If you don't find one that matches, try working out the answer choices one at a time on a piece of paper and eliminate any that are obviously wrong.

3. **You are configuring the hard disks in your Windows NT Server computer. You want to protect the boot and system files on drive C: in case of a hard disk failure. Which NT fault tolerance method can be used on this disk?**

    A.   Stripe set
    B.   Volume set
    C.   Stripe set with parity
    D.   Mirror set

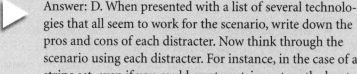

Answer: D. When presented with a list of several technologies that all seem to work for the scenario, write down the pros and cons of each distracter. Now think through the scenario using each distracter. For instance, in the case of a stripe set, even if you could create a stripe set on the boot partition, you would not be able to recover, because all of the hard drives in a stripe set would contain useless information if one of the drives failed. So you really wouldn't be able to recover using this technology.

4. **You are configuring your Windows NT 4.0 Server computer. You have two network adapters, one connected to your corporate network and the other connected to the Internet. What can you do to prevent people from accessing your shared folders over the Internet?**

    A.   Change the network access order, so Microsoft Networks is last.
    B.   Place the computer in a workgroup rather than an NT domain.
    C.   Disable the server service on the network adapter connected to the Internet.
    D.   Disable the NetBEUI protocol on the network adapter connected to the Internet.

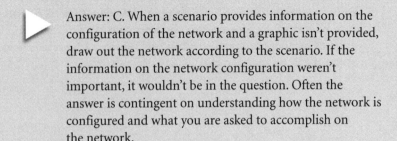

Answer: C. When a scenario provides information on the configuration of the network and a graphic isn't provided, draw out the network according to the scenario. If the information on the network configuration weren't important, it wouldn't be in the question. Often the answer is contingent on understanding how the network is configured and what you are asked to accomplish on the network.

5. You are working on your Windows NT Server and you notice that someone appears to be accessing sensitive files on the server. You want to disconnect only the user accessing the sensitive files. What should you do?

A. Change the network access order.

B. Disable the Server service on the network adapter interface.

C. Disable the Workstation service on the network adapter interface.

D. Use the Server icon in Control Panel to view the user connection and disconnect it.

Anwser: D. Watch out for questions that put constraints on the desired results. In this case, the scenario only wants a specific user disconnected, but if you skipped that portion of the scenario, you could choose the wrong answer.

6. You are logging in to a new Windows NT Server computer named ServerA. You do not belong to any special groups and you have never logged in to this computer before. ServerA has a computer policy included in the main system policy file. What profiles and policies will be assigned? (Choose 3.)

A. Default Computer policy
B. ServerA Computer policy
C. Default User profile
D. All Users profile
E. All Users policy

Answers : B, C, and D. When preparing to answer a question, first determine how many answers the questions is looking for. In this case the question is looking for three answers; if you only select two correct answers, you will not receive any credit for the question. Don't overlook this information as you could miss several questions by not picking enough answers.

---

7. **You are the network administrator for a network that contains a Windows NT Server domain. You have created a shared printer that connects to a Postscript print device. You want the Macintosh users to be able to access the shared printer on the Windows NT Server. What should you do?**

A. Configure the Macintosh computers to have user logons validated by the NT Server domain.
B. Configure the Macintosh computers to access the printer using the default LaserWriter print driver.
C. Install the print device's AppleTalk print driver on the Macintosh computers.
D. Install the print device's AppleTalk print driver on the Windows NT Server computer.

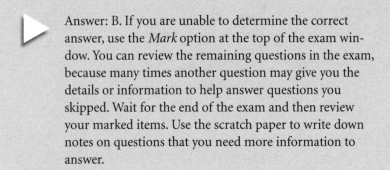

Answer: B. If you are unable to determine the correct answer, use the *Mark* option at the top of the exam window. You can review the remaining questions in the exam, because many times another question may give you the details or information to help answer questions you skipped. Wait for the end of the exam and then review your marked items. Use the scratch paper to write down notes on questions that you need more information to answer.

8. **You are moving a marketing ad compaign project folder from your Windows NT Workstation computer to a Windows NT Server computer. On your computer, the folder had NTFS partitions that granted only the marketing department Full Control; the Everyone group was granted Read only access. The folder that will contain the project folder on the Windows NT Server computer has NTFS permissions that grant the Everyone group Change permissions.** What are the NTFS permissions for the folder after it has been moved?

    A.   The permissions will stay the same; the marketing group will have Full Control and the Everyone group will have Read only access.

    B.   The permissions will be set back to the default with the Everyone group having Full Control.

    C.   The permissions will be set to match the new folder's permissions with the Everyone group having Change permissions.

    D.   The permissions will be set so that only the Administrators group has Full Control.

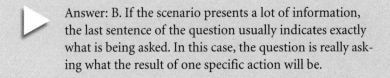

Answer: B. If the scenario presents a lot of information, the last sentence of the question usually indicates exactly what is being asked. In this case, the question is really asking what the result of one specific action will be.

9. **Your Microsoft Windows NT Server computer has two drives configured as a mirrored set. One of the mirrored drives has failed. What should you do first?**

A. Replace the drive and then break the mirror.

B. Break the mirror and then replace the drive.

C. Replace the drive and then use Disk Administrator to regenerate the mirror.

D. Use Disk Administrator to regenerate the mirror and then replace the drive.

Answer: B. Watch out for questions that use distracters based on similar technologies, but are absolutely incorrect answers. The regenerate process is for stripe sets with parity, not for mirrored sets. If you weren't clear on the two different methods, you could get confused and choose the wrong answer.

---

10. **You are experiencing slow disk performance on your Window NT Server computer. You suspect that either your computer is writing to the pageing file too often, or there is a disk performance problem. When you start Performance Monitor, you are unable to see values for the physicaldisk object counters. What should you do?**

A. Log onto the Window NT Server computer as an administrator.

B. Use `diskperf.exe` to enable the Performance Monitor objects.

C. Use the Disk Administrator to enable the Performance Monitor objects.

D. Install the PhysicalDisk Performance Monitor objects.

Answer: D. Look for questions where the scenario includes wording that may indicate the correct answer. In this case the scenario describes that the computer is having slow *disk performance*. This same wording appears in only three of the answers, so you have already eliminated a distracter.

Glossary

A

access control list (ACL) The ACL is a list that contains user and group security identifiers (SIDs), with the associated privileges of each user and group. Each object, such as a file or folder, has an access control list associated with it. *See also* security identifier (SID).

account policy The account policy is the set of rules indicating how passwords and account lockout are managed in Windows NT. Account policy is managed by using the Account Policy dialog box in User Manager for Domains.

active partition The active partition is a primary partition on the first hard disk in a computer that has been marked active by a partitioning program, such as `Fdisk` or Disk Manager. A computer loads its operating system from the active partition.

answer files (`Unattend.txt`) Answer files are text files that contain stylized responses to the queries posed by the Windows NT setup program during installation. You can use an answer file, in conjunction with a network installation startup disk, to fully automate the installation of Windows NT on a single computer (in other words, perform an unattended installation). The default name for an answer file is `Unattend.txt`, but you can use any file name you want for your answer files.

AppleTalk   AppleTalk is a routable network protocol developed by Apple Computer, Inc. This protocol is associated with Macintosh computers.

application programming interface (API)   An API is a set of operating system functions that can be called by an application running on the computer. Windows NT supports the Win32, Win16, POSIX, MS-DOS, and OS/2 1.*x* APIs.

archive bit   The archive bit is a file attribute that indicates that the file or folder has been modified since the last backup. The archive bit is applied by the operating system when a file or folder is saved or created, and is commonly removed by backup programs after the file or folder has been backed up. This file attribute is not normally changed by the administrator.

auditing   Auditing is a Windows NT feature that enables you to collect and view security-related information concerning the success and failure of specified events, such as file access, printer access, logon and logoff, and security policy changes. File auditing is only available on NTFS partitions. File and printer auditing require that auditing of File and Object Access be selected in the Audit Policy dialog box.

authentication   Authentication is the verification of a user account name and password by Windows NT. Authentication can be performed by the local Windows NT computer or by a Windows NT Server domain controller.

B

Backup   *See* Windows NT Backup.

backup browser A backup browser is a computer that maintains a backup copy of the browse list. The backup browser receives the browse list from the master browser, and then makes the browse list available to any computer that requests it. All computers on the network, when they request a copy of the browse list, do so from a backup browser. A backup browser updates its browse list by requesting an update from the master browser every twelve minutes. There can be more than one backup browser on each subnet. Any Windows NT Server, Windows NT Workstation, Windows 95, or Windows for Workgroups computer can perform the role of the backup browser. *See also* Computer Browser service and master browser.

backup domain controller (BDC) A BDC is a Windows NT Server computer that is configured to maintain a backup copy of the domain Directory Services database (SAM). The BDC receives updates to the Directory Services database from the primary domain controller (PDC) via a process called synchronization. *See also* primary domain controller and synchronization.

binary tree A binary tree is the type of search used by the NTFS file system to quickly locate files and folders on an NTFS partition. A binary tree search is much faster than a sequential read or search. *See also* sequential read.

bindings Bindings are associations between a network service and a protocol, or between a protocol and a network adapter.

BIOS BIOS stands for *Basic Input/Output System*. The BIOS is a program that is stored in ROM (read-only memory) on a computer's motherboard. The BIOS contains instructions for performing the Power On Self Test (POST).

blue screen A blue screen is displayed by Windows NT when it encounters a STOP error that it cannot recover from. A blue screen contains information about the type of error that occurred, a list of loaded drivers, and a processor stack dump.

boot loader Boot loader is a program that is used to load a computer's operating system. In Windows NT, the boot loader is a program called ntldr, and it creates a menu (the boot loader menu) by parsing the contents of the Boot.ini file. Once the user selects an operating system from this menu (or the default time period expires), ntldr begins the process of starting the selected (or default) operating system.

boot partition The boot partition is the partition that contains the Windows NT system files. The boot partition contains the folder that Windows NT is installed in.

boot sequence The Windows NT boot sequence consists of a series of steps, beginning with powering on the computer and ending with completion of the logon process. The boot sequence steps vary according to the hardware platform you are using.

bottleneck A bottleneck is the component in the system that is slowing system performance. In a networking environment, the bottleneck is the part of the system that is performing at peak capacity while other components in the system are not working at peak capacity. In other words, if it weren't for the limiting component, the rest of the system could go faster.

browsing Browsing is the process of viewing a list of computers and their available shared resources, or viewing a list of files and folders on a local or network-connected drive.

built-in groups Built-in groups are the default groups created by the operating system during a Windows NT installation. Different groups are created on Windows NT domain controllers than are created on non-domain controllers.

C

C2 secure environment C2 is a designation in a range of security levels identified in the computer security specifications developed by the National Computer Security Center. If installed and configured correctly, Windows NT meets the C2 level of security.

cache Cache is a section of memory used to temporarily store files from the hard disk.

capacity planning Capacity planning is the process of determining current usage of server and/or network resources, as well as tracking usage over time, in order to predict future usage and the additional hardware that will be required to meet the projected levels of use.

CDFS CDFS stands for *Compact Disc Filing System*. CDFS supports access to compact discs, and is only used on CD-ROM devices.

client A client is a computer that is capable of accessing resources on other computers (servers) across a network. Some computers are configured with both client and server software. *See also* server.

Client-based Network Administration Tools Client-based Network Administration Tools are a collection of Windows NT Server utilities that, when installed on a Windows NT Workstation client computer, make it possible for a user at the client computer to remotely manage an NT Server computer on the network. Client-based Network Administration Tools are sometimes called Windows NT Server Tools, particularly when referring to these tools as installed or run on a Windows 95 client computer. *See also* Windows NT Server Tools.

MCSE NT SERVER 4.0 ACE IT!

complete trust domain model The complete trust domain model is a decentralized domain model that consists of two or more domains that contain both user accounts and shared resources. In the complete trust domain model, a two-way trust relationship must be established between each and every domain. Because of the excessive number of trusts required for this model, the complete trust domain model is not often implemented. See also trust relationship and two-way trust.

Computer Browser service The Computer Browser service is the Windows NT service is responsible for the process of building a list of available network servers, called a browse list. The Computer Browser service is also responsible for determining the role a computer will play in the browser hierarchy: domain master browser, master browser, backup browser, or potential browser. *See also* backup browser, domain master browser, master browser, and potential browser.

computer name A computer name is a unique name, up to fifteen characters in length, that is used to identify a particular computer on the network. No two computers on the same internetwork should have the same computer name.

computer policy A computer policy is a collection of Registry settings created in System Policy Editor that specify a local computer's configuration. A computer policy enforces the specified configuration on all users of a particular Windows NT (or Windows 95) computer.

Control Panel Control Panel is a group of mini-applications that are used to configure a Windows NT computer.

Default Computer policy The Default Computer policy is a computer policy that applies to all computers that don't have an individual computer policy. *See also* computer policy.

default gateway A default gateway is a TCP/IP configuration setting that specifies the IP address of the router on the local network segment.

Default User policy The Default User policy is a user policy that applies to all users that don't have an individual user policy. *See also* user policy.

Default User profile The `Default User` profile is a user profile folder created during the Windows NT installation process. The settings in the `Default User` profile are applied, by default, to new user profiles as they are created. The `Default User` profile can be modified by using the Registry Editors or by using Windows NT Explorer. *See also* user profile.

demand paging Demand paging is a process used by the Windows NT Virtual Memory Manager that involves reading pages of memory from the paging file into RAM, and writing pages of memory from RAM into the paging file as required by the operating system. *See also* paging file.

desktop The desktop is the screen that is displayed after Windows NT 4.0 boots and you log on. The desktop replaces the Program Manager interface from earlier versions of Windows and Windows NT.

DHCP DHCP stands for *Dynamic Host Configuration Protocol*. This protocol is used to dynamically assign IP addresses to client computers on a network.

DHCP Relay Agent The DHCP Relay Agent is a Windows NT Server service that forwards client computers' DHCP requests to a DHCP server on another subnet. *See also* DHCP.

Dial-Up Networking Dial-Up Networking is a Windows NT service that enables a computer to use its modem to make a network connection over a telephone line to another computer. Dial-Up Networking is installed during the installation of the Remote Access Service (RAS) on a Windows NT computer. *See also* Remote Access Service (RAS).

directory A directory is a folder. In Windows NT terminology, the terms *directory* and *folder* are synonymous. The two terms are used interchangeably throughout Windows NT documentation and the Windows NT user interface.

directory replication Directory replication was designed to copy logon scripts from a central location, usually the PDC, to all domain controllers, thus enabling all users to execute their own logon scripts no matter which domain controller validates their logon. Replication involves copying subfolders and their files from the source folder on the source server to the destination folder on all Windows NT computers on the network that are configured as replication destinations. *See also* Directory Replicator service.

Directory Replicator service The Directory Replicator service is a Windows NT service that copies (replicates) files from a source Windows NT computer to a destination Windows NT computer. *See also* directory replication.

Directory Services *See* Windows NT Directory Services.

Directory Services database *See* Security Accounts Manager (SAM) database.

disk duplexing Disk duplexing is a fault tolerance method that involves duplication of a partition from one hard disk onto a second hard disk. In disk duplexing, each hard disk must be on a different hard disk controller.

disk mirroring Disk mirroring is a fault tolerance method that involves duplication of a partition from one hard disk onto a second hard disk. In disk mirroring, each hard disk can be on the same or a different hard disk controller.

DNS *See* Microsoft DNS Server.

domain A domain is a logical grouping of networked computers in which one or more of the computers has shared resources, such as a shared folder or a shared printer, and in which all of the computers share a common central domain Directory Services database that contains user account and security information.

domain controller A domain controller is a Windows NT Server computer that maintains a copy of the domain Directory Services database (also called the SAM). *See also* backup domain controller, primary domain controller, and Security Accounts Manager (SAM) database.

domain master browser The domain master browser is a computer that maintains a list of available network servers located on all subnets in the domain. In addition, the domain master browser maintains a list of available workgroups and domains on the internetwork. The domain master browser is the primary domain controller. *See also* Computer Browser service.

domain name A domain name is a unique name, up to fifteen characters in length, assigned to identify the domain on the network. A domain name must be different than all other domain names, workgroup names, and computer names on the network.

Dr. Watson for Windows NT Dr. Watson is a Windows NT tool that is used to debug application errors.

dual boot Dual boot refers to the capability of a computer to permit a user to select from more than one operating system during the boot process. (Only one operating system can be selected and run at a time.)

dynamic routing In dynamic routing, a router automatically builds and updates its routing table. In a dynamic routing environment, administrators don't have to manually configure the routing table on each individual router. As changes are made to the network, dynamic routers automatically adjust their routing tables to reflect these changes. Periodically, each dynamic router on the network broadcasts packets containing the contents of its routing table. Dynamic routers that receive these packets add the routing table information received to their own routing tables. In this way, dynamic routers are able to recognize other routers as they are added to and removed from the network.

Emergency Repair Disk The Emergency Repair Disk is a floppy disk created during (or after) the Windows NT installation process that is used to repair Windows NT when its configuration files have been damaged or corrupted.

enhanced metafile (EMF) An enhanced metafile is an intermediate print job format that can be created very quickly by the graphic device driver interface. Using an EMF enables Windows NT to process the print job in the background while the foreground process continues.

Event Log service The Event Log service is a Windows NT service that writes operating system, application, and security events to log files. These log files can be viewed by an administrator using Event Viewer. *See also* Event Viewer.

Event Viewer Event Viewer is a Windows NT administrative tool that enables an administrator to view and/or archive the System, Application, and Security Logs.

exabyte An exabyte is a billion gigabytes (1,152,921,504,606,846,976 bytes).

Executive Services (Windows NT Executive) Executive Services is the entire set of services that make up the kernel mode of the Windows NT operating system.

extended partition An extended partition is a disk partition that can be subdivided into one or more logical drives. An extended partition can't be the active partition. *See also* active partition.

fault tolerance Fault tolerance refers to the ability of a computer or operating system to continue operations when a severe error or failure occurs, such as the loss of a hard disk or a power outage.

file allocation table (FAT) file system FAT is a type of file system that is used by several operating systems, including Windows NT. Windows NT does not support security or auditing on FAT partitions. The maximum size of a FAT partition is 4GB.

file attributes File attributes are markers assigned to files that describe properties of the file and limit access to the file. File attributes include: Archive, Compress, Hidden, Read-only, and System.

file system A file system is an overall architecture for naming, storing, and retrieving files on a disk.

folder A folder is a directory. In Windows NT terminology, the terms *directory* and *folder* are synonymous. The two terms are used interchangeably throughout Windows NT documentation and the Windows NT user interface.

frame type A frame type (also called a *frame format*) is an accepted, standardized structure for transmitting data packets over a network.

fully qualified domain name (FQDN) An FQDN is a fancy term for the way computers are named and referenced on the Internet. The format for an FQDN is:
`server_name.domain_name.root_domain_ name.` For example, a server named `wolf` in the `alancarter` domain in the `com` root domain has a fully qualified domain name of `wolf.alancarter.com`. Fully qualified domain names always use lowercase characters.

G

gateway A gateway is a computer that performs protocol or data format translation between two computers that use different protocols or data formats.

Gateway Service for NetWare (GSNW) Gateway Service for NetWare (GSNW) is a Windows NT Server service that, when installed and configured on a Windows NT Server computer, provides all of the functionality of Client Service for NetWare (CSNW). Additionally, GSNW enables the Windows NT Server computer to transparently share resources (files, folders, and printers) located on a NetWare server to client computers of the Windows NT Server computer. GSNW accomplishes this by converting the Server Message Blocks (SMBs) from the client computers of the Windows NT Server computer into NetWare Core Protocol (NCP) requests that are recognized by the NetWare server.

gigabyte (GB) A gigabyte is 1,024 megabytes (MB), or 1,073,741,824 bytes.

global group A global group is a Windows NT Server group that can only be created in the domain Directory Services database. Global groups are primarily used to organize users that perform similar tasks or have similar network access requirements. In a typical Windows NT configuration, user accounts are placed in a global group, the global group is made a member of one or more local groups, and each local group is assigned permissions to a network resource. The advantage of using global groups is ease of administration — the network administrator can manage large numbers of users by placing them in global groups. Global groups are only available in Windows NT Server domains — they are not available in workgroups or on a stand-alone server. *See also* local group.

Graphics Device Interface (GDI) The GDI is a specific Windows NT device driver that manages low-level display and print data. The GDI used to be part of user mode in Windows NT 3.51, but is now part of the kernel mode (Executive Services) in Windows NT 4.0.

group dependencies Group dependencies are groups of services or drivers that must be running before a given service (or driver) can start.

group policy A group policy is a policy that applies to a group of users. Group policies apply to all users that are members of a group (that has a group policy), and that do not have individual user policies.

Hardware Compatibility List (HCL) The HCL is a list of hardware that is supported by Windows NT. The HCL is shipped with Windows NT. You can access the latest version of the HCL at `www.microsoft.com/hwtest/hcl`.

hertz (Hz) Hz is a unit of frequency measurement equivalent to one cycle per second.

hive A hive is a group of Windows NT Registry keys and values that are stored in a single file. *See also* key, Registry, and value.

host A host is a computer that is connected to a TCP/IP network, such as the Internet.

HPFS HPFS stands for *high performance file system*. This is the file system used by OS/2. Windows NT used to support HPFS, but HPFS support was dropped for NT version 4.0.

I

Internet Information Server (IIS) Internet Information Server is a Microsoft Windows NT Server service that provides World Wide Web (WWW), File Transfer Protocol (FTP), and Gopher publishing services.

internetwork An internetwork consists of multiple network segments connected by routers and/or WAN links.

interrupt (IRQ) An interrupt (or interrupt request) is a unique number between two and fifteen that is assigned to a hardware peripheral in a computer. No two devices in the computer should have the same interrupt, unless the devices are capable of sharing an interrupt, and are correctly configured to do so.

intranetwork An intranetwork is a TCP/IP internetwork that is not connected to the Internet. For example, a company's multi-city internetwork can be called an intranetwork as long as it is not connected to the Internet. *See also* internetwork.

kernel A kernel is the core component of an operating system.

kernel mode Kernel mode refers to a highly privileged mode of operation in Windows NT. "Highly privileged" means that all code that runs in kernel mode can access the hardware directly, and can access any memory address. A program that runs in kernel mode is always resident in memory — it can't be written to a paging file. *See also* user mode.

key A key is a component of the Registry that is similar to a folder in a file system. A key can contain other keys and value entries. *See also* Registry and value.

kilobyte (KB) A kilobyte is 1,024 bytes.

line printer daemon (LPD) LPD is the print server software used in TCP/IP printing. LPD is supported by many operating systems, including Windows NT and UNIX.

local group A local group is a Windows NT group that can be created in the domain Directory Services database on a domain controller or in the SAM on any non-domain controller. Local groups are primarily used to control access to resources. In a typical Windows NT configuration, a local group is assigned permissions to a specific resource, such as a shared folder or a shared printer. Individual user accounts and global groups are then made members of this local group. The result is that all members of the local group then have permissions to the resource. Using local groups simplifies the administration of network resources, because permissions can be assigned once, to a local group, instead of separately to each user account. *See also* global group.

local print provider A local print provider is a Windows NT kernel mode driver that manages printing for all print devices managed by the local computer.

LocalTalk LocalTalk is a specification for the type of network cabling, connectors, and adapters developed by Apple Computer, Inc. for use with Macintosh computers.

logging on Logging on is the process of supplying a user name and password, and having that user name and password authenticated by a Windows NT computer. A user is said to "log on" to a Windows NT computer.

logical drive A logical drive is a disk partition (or multiple partitions) that has been formatted with a file system and assigned a drive letter.

logon hours Logon hours are the assigned hours that a user can log on to a Windows NT Server domain controller. The logon hours configuration only affects the user's ability to access the domain controller — it does not affect a user's ability to log on to a Windows NT Workstation computer or to a non-domain controller.

logon script A logon script is a batch file that is run when a user logs on. All MS-DOS 5.0 (and earlier versions) batch commands can be used in logon scripts.

M

mandatory user profile   A mandatory user profile is a user profile that, when assigned to a user, can't be modified by the user. A user can make changes to desktop and work environment settings during a single logon session, but these changes are not saved to the mandatory profile when the user logs off. Each time the user logs on, the user's desktop and work environment settings revert to those contained in the mandatory user profile. A mandatory user profile is created by renaming the user's `ntuser.dat` file to `ntuser.man`. *See also* user profile.

master browser   A master browser is the computer on the subnet that builds and maintains the browse list for that subnet. The master browser distributes this browse list to backup browsers on the subnet and to the domain master browser. *See also* backup browser, Computer Browser service, and domain master browser.

Maximum Password Age   The Maximum Password Age is the maximum number of days a user may use the same password.

megabyte (MB)   A megabyte is 1,024 kilobytes, or 1,048,576 bytes.

member server   A member server is a Windows NT Server computer that is not installed as a domain controller, and that has joined a Windows NT Server domain.

memory dump   The term memory dump refers to the process of Windows NT copying the contents of RAM into a file (the `memory.dmp` file) when a STOP error or blue screen occurs.

Microsoft DNS Server   Microsoft DNS Server is a Windows NT Server service. This service is a TCP/IP-based name resolution service. It is used to resolve a host name or an FQDN to its associated IP address.

Migration Tool for NetWare Migration Tool for NetWare is a Windows NT Server administrative tool that makes it possible for an administrator to migrate a NetWare server's user accounts and files to a Windows NT Server computer. Migration Tool for NetWare requires that Gateway Service for NetWare and NWLink IPX/SPX Compatible Transport be installed in the Windows NT Server computer. *See also* Gateway Service for NetWare and NWLink IPX/SPX Compatible Transport.

million bits per second (Mbps) Mbps is a measurement of data transmission speed that is used to describe WAN links and other network connections.

Minimum Password Age The Minimum Password Age is the minimum number of days a user must keep the same password.

Minimum Password Length Minimum Password Length specifies the minimum number of characters required in a user's password.

MS-DOS MS-DOS is a computer operating system developed by Microsoft. MS-DOS stands for *Microsoft Disk Operating System.*

multihomed A computer is said to be multihomed when it has more than one network adapter installed in it.

multiple master domain model The multiple master domain model consists of two or more master domains that contain user accounts, and any number of resource domains that contain shared resources. In this model, a two-way trust is used between each of the master domains, and a one-way trust is used from each resource domain to each and every master domain. *See also* trust relationship, one-way trust, and two-way trust.

multiprocessing Multiprocessing refers to the capability of an operating system to use more than one processor in a single computer simultaneously.

N

NetBEUI NetBEUI is a nonroutable protocol designed for use on small networks. NetBEUI is included in Windows NT 4.0 primarily for backward compatibility with older Microsoft networking products.

network access order The network access order specifies which protocol or service Windows NT will use first when it attempts to access another computer on the network.

network adapter A network adapter is an adapter card in a computer that enables the computer to connect to a network.

Network Client Administrator Network Client Administrator is a Windows NT Server tool you can use to create an installation disk set to install network clients or services on client computers. You can also use Network Client Administrator to create a network installation startup disk. A network installation startup disk, when run on a computer that needs to be set up (the target computer), causes the target computer to automatically connect to the server and start an interactive installation/setup routine.

network device driver A network device driver is a Windows NT kernel mode driver that is designed to enable Windows NT to use a network adapter to communicate on the network.

Network Monitor Network Monitor is a Windows NT Server administrative tool that allows you to capture, view, and analyze network traffic (packets).

network number Network numbers are 32-bit binary numbers that uniquely identify an NWLink IPX/SPX Compatible Transport network segment for routing purposes. Because network numbers uniquely identify a network segment, they are used by IPX routers to correctly forward data packets from one network segment to another.

non-browser A non-browser is a computer that is not capable of maintaining a browse list either because it was configured not to do so, or because the operating system on this computer is incapable of maintaining a browse list. *See also* Computer Browser service.

NT Hardware Qualifier (NTHQ) The NT Hardware Qualifier (NTHQ) is a utility that ships with Windows NT. NTHQ examines and identifies a computer's hardware configuration, including the hardware settings used by each adapter.

NTFS *See* Windows NT file system.

NTFS permissions NTFS permissions are permissions assigned to individual files and folders on an NTFS partition that are used to control access to these files and folders. NTFS permissions apply to local users as well as to users who connect to a shared folder over-the-network. If the NTFS permissions are more restrictive than share permissions, the NTFS permissions will be applied. *See also* share permissions.

NWLink IPX/SPX Compatible Transport NWLink IPX/SPX Compatible Transport is a routable transport protocol typically used in a combined Windows NT and NetWare environment. NWLink IPX/SPX Compatible Transport is Microsoft's version of Novell's IPX/SPX protocol. (IPX/SPX is the protocol used on most Novell NetWare networks.) NWLink provides protocol compatibility between Windows NT and NetWare computers. In addition to its functionality in a NetWare environment, NWLink also fully supports Microsoft networking.

ODBC ODBC stands for *Open Database Connectivity*. ODBC is a software specification that enables ODBC-enabled applications (such as Microsoft Excel) to connect to databases (such as Microsoft SQL Server and Microsoft Access). The ODBC application in Control Panel is used to install and remove ODBC drivers for various types of databases. In addition, this application is used to configure ODBC data sources.

OEM subfolder The OEM subfolder is used to store source files that are used to install applications, components, or files that do not ship with Windows NT. This subfolder is used during an automated setup of Windows NT.

one-way trust When a single trust relationship exists between two domains, it is called a one-way trust. Both domains must be configured by an administrator in order to establish a trust relationship. Trusts are configured in Windows NT by using User Manager for Domains. The trusted domain should be configured first, and then the trusting domain. *See also* trust relationship, trusted domain, and trusting domain.

packet A packet is a group of bytes sent over the network as a block of data.

paging file A paging file (sometimes called a page file or a swap file) is a file used as a computer's virtual memory. Pages of memory that are not currently in use can be written to a paging file to make room for data currently needed by the processor. *See also* virtual memory.

partition A partition is a portion of a hard disk that can be formatted with a file system, or combined with other partitions to form a larger logical drive. *See also* logical drive.

pass-through authentication Pass-through authentication is a process in which one Windows NT computer passes a user name and password on to another Windows NT computer for validation. Pass-through authentication makes it possible for a user to log on to a Windows NT computer by using a user account from a Windows NT Server domain.

Password Uniqueness Password Uniqueness specifies how many different passwords a user must use before a previous password can be reused.

Performance Monitor Performance Monitor is a Windows NT tool that is used to gather statistics on the current performance of a Windows NT computer. Performance Monitor statistics can be displayed in a Chart, Alert, or Report view; or can be saved to a log file for later viewing.

permissions Permissions control access to resources, such as shares, files, folders, and printers on a Windows NT computer.

Plug and Play Plug and Play is a specification that makes it possible for hardware devices to be recognized and configured automatically by the operating system without user intervention.

Point-to-Point Multilink Protocol Point-to-Point Multilink Protocol is an extension of the Point-to-Point Protocol. Point-to-Point Multilink Protocol combines the bandwidth from multiple physical connections into a single logical connection. This means that multiple modem, ISDN, or X.25 connections can be bundled together to form a single logical connection with a much higher bandwidth than a single connection can support. *See also* Point-to-Point Protocol.

Point-to-Point Protocol (PPP) Point-to-Point Protocol (PPP) is a newer connection protocol that was designed to overcome the limitations of the Serial Line Internet Protocol (SLIP). PPP is currently the industry standard remote connection protocol, and is recommended for use by Microsoft. PPP connections support multiple transport protocols, including: TCP/IP, NWLink IPX/SPX Compatible Transport, and NetBEUI. Additionally, PPP supports dynamic server-based IP addressing (such as DHCP). PPP supports password encryption, and the PPP connection process does not usually require a script file. *See also* Serial Line Internet Protocol (SLIP).

Point-to-Point Tunneling Protocol (PPTP) Point-to-Point Tunneling Protocol (PPTP) permits a virtual private encrypted connection between two computers over an existing TCP/IP network connection. The existing TCP/IP network connection can be over a local area network or over a Dial-Up Networking TCP/IP connection (including the Internet). All standard transport protocols are supported within the Point-to-Point Tunneling Protocol connection, including NWLink IPX/SPX Compatible Transport, NetBEUI, and TCP/IP. A primary reason for choosing to use PPTP is that it supports the RAS encryption feature over standard, unencrypted TCP/IP networks, such as the Internet.

POSIX *Portable Operating System Interface for Computing Environments* (POSIX) was developed as a set of accepted standards for writing applications for use on various UNIX computers. POSIX environment applications consist of applications developed to meet the POSIX standards. These applications are sometimes referred to as POSIX-compliant applications. Windows NT provides support for POSIX-compliant applications via the POSIX subsystem. Windows NT supports the POSIX subsystem on all hardware platforms supported by Windows NT. To fully support POSIX-compliant applications, at least one NTFS partition is required on the Windows NT computer. POSIX applications are source compatible across all supported hardware platforms. This means that POSIX applications must be recompiled for each hardware platform in order to be run on that platform.

potential browser A potential browser is a computer that does not currently maintain or distribute a browse list, but is capable of doing so. A potential browser can become a backup browser at the direction of the master browser. *See also* backup browser, Computer Browser service, and master browser.

preemptive multitasking In preemptive multitasking, the operating system allocates processor time among applications. Because Windows NT, not the application, allocates processor time among multiple applications, one application can be preempted by the operating system, and another application enabled to run. When multiple applications are alternately paused and then allocated processor time, they appear to run simultaneously to the user.

primary domain controller (PDC) A PDC is a Windows NT Server computer that is configured to maintain the primary copy of the domain Directory Services database (also called the SAM). The PDC sends Directory Services database updates to backup domain controllers (BDCs) via a process called synchronization. *See also* backup domain controller, Security Accounts Manager (SAM) database, and synchronization.

primary partition A primary partition is a disk partition that can be configured as the active partition. A primary partition can only be formatted as a single logical drive. *See also* active partition.

print device In Windows NT, the term print device refers to the physical device that produces printed output — this is what most people refer to as a printer.

print device driver A print device driver is a Windows NT kernel mode driver that formats print jobs into a RAW format. (The RAW format is ready to print, and no further processing is required.) A print device driver can also convert EMF formatted print jobs into a RAW format. *See also* enhanced metafile (EMF).

print job A print job is all of the data and commands needed to print a document.

print monitor A print monitor is a software component that runs in kernel mode. A print monitor sends ready-to-print print jobs to a print device, either locally or across the network. Print monitors are also called port monitors.

print processor A print processor is a kernel mode driver that manages printer device drivers and the process of converting print jobs from one format into another.

print queue In Windows NT terminology, a print queue is a list of print jobs for a specific printer that are waiting to be sent to a print device. The print queue is maintained by the Windows NT Spooler service. *See also* Spooler service.

print server A print server is a software program on a computer that manages print jobs and print devices. The Windows NT Spooler service functions as a print server. The term print server is also used to refer to a computer used primarily to manage multiple print devices and their print jobs. *See also* Spooler service.

printer In Windows NT, the term printer does not represent a physical device that produces printed output. Rather, a printer is the software interface between the Windows NT operating system and the device that produces the printed output. In other operating systems, what Windows NT calls a printer is often referred to as a print queue.

printer pool When a printer has multiple ports (and multiple print devices) assigned to it, this is called a printer pool. Users print to a single printer, and the printer load-balances its print jobs between the print devices assigned to it.

RAM *Random access memory*, or RAM, is the physical memory installed in a computer.

Rdisk.exe `Rdisk.exe` is a Windows NT utility that is used to update the Emergency Repair Disk. Using `Rdisk /s` causes this utility to back up the `SAM` and `Security` hives in the Registry. (If the `/s` switch is not used, the `SAM` and `Security` hives in the Registry are not backed up.) *See also* Emergency Repair Disk.

refresh Refresh means to update the display with current information.

Registry The Windows NT Registry is a database that contains all of the information required to correctly configure an individual Windows NT computer, its user accounts, and applications. Registries are unique to each computer — you shouldn't use the Registry from one computer on another computer. The Registry is organized in a tree structure consisting of five subtrees, and their keys and value entries. *See also* key and value.

Registry editors Registry editors are tools that enable you to search and modify the Windows NT Registry. There are two primary tools for editing the Windows NT Registry: the Windows NT Registry Editor (`regedt32.exe`), and the Windows 95 Registry Editor (`regedit.exe`). In addition, you can use the Windows NT System Policy Editor (`poledit.exe`) to modify a limited number of settings in the Registry. However, you can't use System Policy Editor to search the Registry.

Remote Access Admin Remote Access Admin is a Windows NT administrative tool that is primarily used to start and stop the Remote Access Service (RAS), to assign the dialin permission to users, and to configure a call back security level for each user. Remote Access Admin can also be used to view COM port status and statistics, to disconnect users from individual ports, and to remotely manage RAS on other Windows NT computers.

Remote Access Service (RAS) Remote Access Service (RAS) is a Windows NT service that enables dial-up network connections between a RAS server and a Dial-Up Networking client computer. RAS includes software components for both the RAS server and the Dial-Up Networking client in a single Windows NT service. RAS enables users of remote computers to use the network as though they were directly connected to it. Once the dial-up connection is established, there is no difference in network functionality, except that the speed of the link is often much slower than a direct connection to the LAN.

RIP *Routing Information Protocol* (RIP) is the software that enables routers to dynamically update their routing tables. Windows NT ships with two versions of RIP: RIP for Internet Protocol, and RIP for NWLink IPX/SPX Compatible Transport. *See also* dynamic routing, RIP for Internet Protocol, and RIP for NWLink IPX/SPX Compatible Transport.

RIP for Internet Protocol RIP for Internet Protocol is a Windows NT service that enables Windows NT to dynamically update its routing tables when it is configured as a TCP/IP router. *See also* dynamic routing and RIP.

RIP for NWLink IPX/SPX Compatible Transport RIP for NWLink IPX/SPX Compatible Transport is a Windows NT service that enables Windows NT to dynamically update its routing tables when it is configured as an IPX router. *See also* dynamic routing and RIP.

roaming user profiles Roaming user profiles are user profiles that are stored on a server. Because these profiles are stored on a server instead of a local computer, they are available to users regardless of which Windows NT computer on the network they log on to. The benefit of using roaming user profiles is that users retain their own customized desktop and work environment settings even though they may use several different Windows NT computers.

router A router is a network device that uses protocol-specific addressing information to forward packets from a source computer on one network segment across one or more routers to a destination computer on another network segment.

routing Routing is the process of forwarding packets from a source computer on one network segment across one or more routers to a destination computer on another network segment by using protocol-specific addressing information. Devices that perform routing are called routers.

S

SAP Agent The *Service Advertising Protocol* (SAP) Agent is a Windows NT service that advertises a Windows NT computer's services (such as SQL Server and SNA Server) to NetWare client computers. The SAP Agent requires the use of NWLink IPX/SPX Compatible Transport. The SAP Agent should be installed when NetWare client computers will access services on a Windows NT computer.

SCSI SCSI stands for *Small Computer System Interface.* SCSI is a hardware specification for cables, adapter cards, and the devices that they manage, such as: hard disks, CD-ROMs, and scanners.

Security Accounts Manager (SAM) database The SAM is a Windows NT Registry hive that is used to store all user account, group account, and security policy information for a Windows NT computer or a Windows NT domain. On a domain controller, the SAM is also referred to as the domain Directory Services database.

security identifier (SID) A security identifier (SID) is a unique number assigned to a user account, group account, or computer account in the Security Accounts Manager (SAM) database. *See also* Security Accounts Manager (SAM) database.

Security Log The Security Log is a file that is managed by the Windows NT Event Log service. All auditing of security events is written to the Security Log. An Administrator can view the Security Log by using Event Viewer.

segment In network terminology, a segment refers to a network subnet that is not subdivided by a bridge or a router. The term segment can also be used as a verb, describing the process of dividing the network into multiple subnets by using a bridge or a router.

sequential read A sequential read is a read performed (normally by the operating system) from the beginning of a file straight through to the end of the file. No random access to different parts of the file can occur during a sequential read.

Serial Line Internet Protocol (SLIP) The Serial Line Internet Protocol (SLIP) is an older connection protocol, commonly associated with UNIX computers, that only supports one transport protocol — TCP/IP. SLIP connections don't support NWLink IPX/SPX Compatible Transport or NetBEUI. The version of SLIP supported by Windows NT 4.0 requires a static IP address configuration at the client computer — dynamic IP addressing is not supported. In addition, password encryption is not supported by this version of SLIP. A script file is usually required to automate the connection process when SLIP is used.

server A server is a computer on a network that is capable of sharing resources with other computers on the network. Many computers are configured as both clients and servers, meaning that they can access resources located on other computers across the network, and they can share their resources with other computers on the network. *See also* client.

Server Manager Server Manager is a Windows NT Server administrative tool that enables remote management of shared folders, remote starting and stopping of services, remote management of Directory Replication, remote viewing to determine which users are currently accessing shared resources, and remote disconnection of users from shared resources on a Windows NT Server computer.

Server service The Server service is a Windows NT service that enables Windows NT computers to share their resources with other computers on the network.

service dependencies Service dependencies are services and drivers that must be running before a particular service (or driver) can start.

Services for Macintosh Services for Macintosh is a Windows NT Server service that enables Macintosh client computers to connect to Macintosh-accessible volumes on a Windows NT Server computer, enables Macintosh client computers to access shared printers on a Windows NT Server computer, enables a Windows NT Server computer to connect to network-connected print devices that support the AppleTalk protocol, and enables a Windows NT Server computer to function as an AppleTalk router.

Setup Manager Setup Manager is a Windows NT tool that is used to create an answer file (`Unattend.txt`) for use in automating the installation of Windows NT. *See also* answer files.

share name A share name is a name that uniquely identifies a shared resource on a Windows NT computer, such as a shared folder or printer.

share permissions Share permissions control access to shared resources, such as shared folders and shared printers on a Windows NT computer. Share permissions only apply to users who access a shared resource over the network.

shared folder A shared folder is a folder on a Windows NT computer that can be accessed by other computers on the network because the folder has been configured to be shared and has been assigned a share name.

single domain model The single domain model consists of one domain, and does not use trust relationships. All user accounts and shared resources are contained within one domain.

single master domain model The single master domain model consists of one master domain that contains all user accounts, and one or more resource domains that contain shared resources. This domain model uses one-way trusts from each resource domain to the master domain. *See also* trust relationship and one-way trust.

SNMP SNMP stands for *Simple Network Management Protocol.* The Windows NT SNMP service, once installed on a Windows NT computer, gathers TCP/IP statistics on the local computer and transmits those statistics to any SNMP management station on the network that is correctly configured to receive them. In addition, installing the SNMP service enables various TCP/IP counters within Windows NT Performance Monitor.

special groups Special groups are groups created by Windows NT during installation that are used for specific purposes by the operating system. These groups don't appear in User Manager for Domains. Special groups are only visible in Windows NT utilities that assign permissions to network resources, such as a printer's Properties dialog box, and Windows NT Explorer. You can assign permissions to and remove permissions from special groups. You can't assign users to special groups, and you can't rename or delete these groups. Special groups are sometimes called system groups. There are five special groups: Everyone, Interactive, Network, System, and Creator Owner.

Spooler service The Windows NT Spooler service manages the entire printing process on a Windows NT computer. The Spooler service performs many of the tasks that are associated with a print server.

stand-alone server A stand-alone server is a Windows NT Server computer that is not installed as a domain controller, and that has not joined a Windows NT Server domain.

static routing Static routing is basic, no-frills IP routing. No additional software is necessary to implement static routing in multihomed Windows NT computers. Static routers are not capable of automatically building a routing table. In a static routing environment, administrators must manually configure the routing table on each individual router. If the network layout changes, the network administrator must manually update the routing tables to reflect the changes.

stripe set   A stripe set is a disk configuration consisting of two to thirty-two hard disks. In a stripe set, data is stored, a block at a time, evenly and sequentially among all of the disks in the set. Stripe sets are sometimes referred to as disk striping. Disk striping alludes to the process wherein a file is written, or striped, one block at a time, first to one disk, then to the next disk, and then to the next disk, and so on, until all of the data has been evenly distributed among all of the disks.

stripe set with parity   A stripe set with parity is similar to a stripe set, but a stripe set with parity provides a degree of fault tolerance that a stripe set cannot. In a stripe set with parity, data is not only distributed a block at a time, evenly and sequentially among all of the disks in the set, but parity information is also written across all of the disks in the set. A stripe set with parity is made up of three to thirty-two hard disks. Like stripe sets, stripe sets with parity are created from identical amounts of free space on each disk that belongs to the set. *See also* stripe set.

subfolder   A subfolder is a folder that is located within another folder. Subfolders can contain other subfolders, as well as files.

subnet mask   A subnet mask specifies which portion of an IP address represents the network ID and which portion represents the host ID. A subnet mask enables TCP/IP to correctly determine whether network traffic destined for a given IP address should be transmitted on the local subnet, or whether it should be routed to a remote subnet. A subnet mask should be the same for all computers and other network devices on a given network segment. A subnet mask is a 32-bit binary number, broken into four 8-bit sections (octets), that is normally represented in a dotted decimal format. Each 8-bit section is represented by a whole number between 0 and 255. A common subnet mask is 255.255.255.0. This particular subnet mask specifies that TCP/IP will use the first three octets of an IP address as the network ID, and use the last octet as the host ID.

synchronization   Synchronization is a process performed by the NetLogon Service. In this process, domain Directory Services database update information is periodically copied from the primary domain controller (PDC) to each backup domain controller (BDC) in the domain.

Sysdiff.exe `Sydiff.exe` is a Windows NT utility that is used to automate the installation of applications that don't support scripted installation and that would otherwise require user interaction during the installation process.

system partition The system partition is the active primary partition on the first hard disk in the computer. (This is usually the C: drive.) The system partition contains several files that are required to boot Windows NT, including: `ntldr`, `Ntdetect.com`, `Boot.ini`, and sometimes `Bootsect.dos`, and `Ntbootdd.sys`, depending on the installation type and hardware configuration. *See also* boot partition.

system policy The Windows NT system policy file is a collection of user, group, and computer policies. System policy restricts the user's ability to perform certain tasks on any Windows NT computer on the network that the user logs on to. System policy can also be used to enforce certain mandatory display settings, such as wallpaper and color scheme. You can also create a system policy file that applies to users of Windows 95 computers. System policy gives the administrator far more configurable options than a mandatory profile. Administrators can use system policy to provide a consistent environment for a large number of users, or to enforce a specified work environment for "problem users" who demand a significant amount of administrator time.

System Policy Editor System Policy Editor is a Windows NT Server tool that is used to edit Windows NT and Windows 95 system policy files. *See also* system policy.

Task Manager Windows NT Task Manager is a Windows NT administrative utility that can be used to start and stop applications; to view performance statistics, such as memory and CPU usage; and to change a process's base priority.

TCP/IP The *Transmission Control Protocol/Internet Protocol* (TCP/IP) is a widely used transport protocol that provides robust capabilities for Windows NT networking. TCP/IP is a fast, routable enterprise protocol. TCP/IP is the protocol used on the Internet. TCP/IP is supported by many other operating systems, including: Windows 95, Macintosh, UNIX, MS-DOS, and IBM mainframes. TCP/IP is typically the recommended protocol for large, heterogeneous networks.

TechNet *Microsoft TechNet* is an invaluable knowledge base and troubleshooting resource. *TechNet* is published monthly by Microsoft on multiple compact discs. *TechNet* includes a complete set of all Microsoft operating system Resource Kits (currently in a help file format), the entire Microsoft Knowledge Base, and supplemental compact discs full of patches, fixes, and drivers (so you don't have to spend time downloading them).

terabyte A terabyte is 1,024 gigabytes, or 1,099,511,627,776 bytes.

terminate-and-stay-resident (TSR) program A terminate-and-stay-resident program is an MS-DOS program that stays loaded in memory, even when it is not running.

thread A thread is the smallest unit of processing that can be scheduled by the Windows NT Schedule service. All applications require at least one thread.

trust relationship A trust relationship, or *trust*, is an agreement between two Windows NT Server domains that enables authenticated users in one domain to access resources in another domain. A trust relationship enables users from the trusted domain to access resources in the trusting domain. *See also* one-way trust, trusted domain, trusting domain, and two-way trust.

trusted domain The trusted domain is the domain that contains the user accounts of users who want to access resources in the trusting domain. The trusted domain is said to be trusted by the trusting domain. When graphically displaying a trust relationship, an arrow is used to point from the trusting domain to the trusted domain. *See also* trust relationship and trusting domain.

trusting domain The trusting domain is the domain that has resources to share with users from the trusted domain. The trusting domain is said to trust the trusted domain. When graphically displaying a trust relationship, an arrow is used to point from the trusting domain to the trusted domain. *See also* trust relationship and trusted domain.

two-way trust A two-way trust consists of two one-way trusts between two domains. *See also* one-way trust and trust relationship.

Unattend.txt *See* answer files.

UNC (universal naming convention) UNC is an accepted method of identifying individual computers and their resources on the network. A UNC name consists of a server name and a shared resource name in the following format: \\`Server_name`\`Share_name`. `Server_name` represents the name of the server that the shared folder is located on. `Share_name` represents the name of the shared folder. A UNC name in this format can be used to connect to a network share. For example, a shared folder named `Public` located on a server named Server1 would have the following UNC name: \\`Server1`\`Public`.

Uniqueness Database Files (*.UDF) Uniqueness Database Files (UDFs) are text files, similar to answer files, that make it possible for one answer file to be used for the installation of many computers that have different identifying characteristics. For example, each computer has a different computer name and user name. A UDF, used in conjunction with a network installation startup disk and an answer file, enables you to fully automate the installation of Windows NT on multiple computers on a network. The UDF is structured like an answer file, and uses the same types of entries that an answer file uses. The UDF has an additional section, named `UniqueIds`. When the appropriate command-line switch is used, selected entries in the UDF replace entries with the same name in the answer file. *See also* answer files.

UPS UPS stands for *uninterruptible power supply*. A UPS is a fault-tolerance device that enables a computer to continue operations for a short period of time after a power outage.

user account A user account is a record in the Security Accounts Manager (SAM) database that contains unique user information, such as user name, password, and logon restrictions.

user account database *See* Security Accounts Manager (SAM) database.

User Manager for Domains User Manager for Domains is a Windows NT Server administrative tool that is used to administer user accounts, group accounts, security policy, and trust relationships for the Windows NT Server domain or for an individual Windows NT Server computer.

user mode Within the Windows NT architecture, user mode is referred to as a less privileged processor mode because it does not have direct access to hardware. Applications and their subsystems run in user mode. User mode applications are limited to assigned memory address spaces and can't directly access other memory address spaces. User mode uses specific application programming interfaces (API's) to request system services from a kernel mode component. *See also* application programming interface (API) and kernel mode.

user name A user name is the name assigned to a user account in the Security Accounts Manager (SAM) database.

user policy A user policy is a collection of Registry settings that restricts a user's program and network options, and/or enforces a specified configuration of the user's work environment.

user profile A user profile is a series of Registry settings and folders in the user's profile folder that define a user's work environment. The contents of a user profile include user-specific settings for: Windows NT Explorer, Notepad, Paint, HyperTerminal, Clock, Calculator, and other built-in Windows NT applications; screen saver, background color, background pattern, wallpaper, and other display settings; applications written to run on Windows NT; network drive and printer connections;

and the Start menu, including program groups, applications, and recently accessed documents.

user rights User rights authorize users and/or groups to perform specific tasks on a Windows NT computer. User rights are not the same as permissions — user rights enable users to perform tasks; whereas permissions allow users to access objects, such as files, folders, and printers. *See also* permissions.

value A value is an individual entry in the Windows NT Registry. A value cannot contain keys or other values. *See also* key and Registry.

verbose mode Verbose mode refers to running an application in such a way that the application returns the maximum amount of information and detail to the user. The verbose mode is initiated on many applications by using the /v switch.

virtual device driver A virtual device driver is a 32-bit protected mode device driver that is used in Windows 95 and Windows for Workgroups. Virtual device drivers are not supported by Windows NT.

virtual memory Virtual memory is the physical space on a hard disk that Windows NT treats as though it were RAM. *See also* paging file.

Virtual Memory Manager Virtual Memory Manager is a Windows NT kernel mode component that manages memory in a Windows NT environment by using demand paging. *See also* demand paging and virtual memory.

volume A volume is a logical drive. *See also* logical drive.

volume set A volume set is a combination of 2 to 32 that are formatted as a single logical drive. A volume set does not use disk striping to store data on its partitions. *See also* logical drive and stripe set.

Windows NT Backup Windows NT Backup (simply called Backup in the user interface) is a Windows NT administrative tool that is used to back up and restore files, folders, and the Registry on a Windows NT computer. Windows NT Backup requires the use of a tape drive device.

Windows NT Diagnostics Windows NT Diagnostics is a Windows NT administrative tool that allows you to view detailed system configuration information and statistics. This tool can help you troubleshoot system configuration problems. Windows NT Diagnostics can also be very useful in determining service and device driver dependencies.

Windows NT Directory Services Windows NT Directory Services is a Microsoft catchall phrase that refers to the architecture, features, functionality, and benefits of Windows NT domains and trust relationships. Windows NT Directory Services (often referred to as Directory Services), as implemented in Windows NT 4.0, is not X.500 compliant. However, Microsoft plans on releasing a new version of Windows NT Directory Services, called the Active Directory, that will be X.500 compliant in a future release of Windows NT.

Windows NT file system (NTFS) NTFS is the most powerful file system supported by Windows NT. Only Windows NT supports NTFS — no other operating systems currently support this file system. Windows NT auditing and security are only supported on partitions that are formatted with NTFS.

Windows NT Server Windows NT Server is a powerful 32-bit operating system that is optimized to run on a network file, print, or applications server. Additionally, Windows NT Server is the operating system of choice for the Microsoft BackOffice products, including SQL Server, Exchange Server, and SNA Server. An NT Server computer can support several processors to provide powerful multiprocessing capability.

Windows NT Server Tools Windows NT Server Tools are a collection of Windows NT Server utilities that, when installed on a Windows 95 client computer, enable a user at the client computer to remotely manage an NT Server computer on the network. Windows NT Server Tools make remote administration of an NT Server computer practical and convenient for many administrators. Windows NT Server Tools are also referred to as Client-based Network Administration Tools. *See also* Client-based Network Administration Tools.

WINS *Windows Internet Name Service* (WINS) is a Windows NT Server service that provides NetBIOS name resolution services to client computers. A Windows NT Server computer that has WINS installed on it is called a WINS server.

workgroup A workgroup is a logical grouping of networked computers in which one or more of the computers has shared resources, such as a shared folder or a shared printer. In a workgroup environment, the security and user accounts are maintained individually on each separate computer.

Workstation service The Workstation service is a Windows NT service that enables a Windows NT computer to access shared resources on other computers across the network.

Index

D

R

Continued

my2cents.idgbooks.com

Register This Book — And Win!

Visit **http://my2cents.idgbooks.com** to register this book and we'll automatically enter you in our fantastic monthly prize giveaway. It's also your opportunity to give us feedback: let us know what you thought of this book and how you would like to see other topics covered.

Discover IDG Books Online!

The IDG Books Online Web site is your online resource for tackling technology — at home and at the office. Frequently updated, the IDG Books Online Web site features exclusive software, insider information, online books, and live events!

10 Productive & Career-Enhancing Things You Can Do at www.idgbooks.com

1. Nab source code for your own programming projects.

2. Download software.

3. Read Web exclusives: special articles and book excerpts by IDG Books Worldwide authors.

4. Take advantage of resources to help you advance your career as a Novell or Microsoft professional.

5. Buy IDG Books Worldwide titles or find a convenient bookstore that carries them.

6. Register your book and win a prize.

7. Chat live online with authors.

8. Sign up for regular e-mail updates about our latest books.

9. Suggest a book you'd like to read or write.

10. Give us your 2¢ about our books and about our Web site.

You say you're not on the Web yet? It's easy to get started with IDG Books' *Discover the Internet*, available at local retailers everywhere.